JIMI HENDRIX

Voices From Home

For Nancy,
     With appreciation for your
enthusiasm and encouragement with
The book, and your Thoughtful suggestions.
I enjoyed our visits so much, and I admire
your creative talent and approach to life!
     Affectionately, Mary

Mary Willix
10-95

Cover and book design by Carolanne Gano,
Gano Design Associates

Jacket photograph by Ann Moses, courtesy of Michael
Ochs Archives.
Back Jacket photograph by Ron Raffaelli, courtesy of
Michael Ochs Archives.

Limited Edition
ISBN 0-9645064-0-8
Published by Creative Forces Publishing,
P.O. Box 22536, San Diego, CA, 92192-2536

Contents

Dedicated to the Golden Era of

Garfield High School

where individuals appreciated individuals
    as unique expressions of the creative whole
    African Americans, Asian Americans, European
    Americans of many creeds: Baptists, Buddhists,
    Jews, Catholics, Atheists, Methodists, Episcopalians
    and more
as if tossed together by some divine plan
    we played on the moonbeams of
    our individual and collective journeys
    our eyes the windows to the inner flame
    unbound by circumstance
bonded in innocence we learned
    to reveal the infinite potential in each other
    to honor all of our brothers and sisters
    to applaud those who climbed ladders of achievement
    to pick up those who fell
    to live with good intention
    to anticipate a celebration
    and to always put on a good show
we left Garfield's womb unprepared for thundering hatred
and walls of ignorance
we reeled back in disbelief
"Oh, they don't know," our undivided cry
we mourn the dark night of judgmentalism
mourn the passing of our brothers and sisters
we return to the calm waters of our souls' bonding
    to our lakeside sanctuary
    mystical mountains
    steady rain
    birds in flight
    rhythm rhythm everywhere
    see the Great Creator in each other

The Land is Sacred

CHIEF SEALTH (1788-1866)

How can you buy or sell the land, the warmth of the sky? The idea is strange to us.

If we do not own the freshness of the air and the sparkle of the water, how can you buy them? Every part of this earth is sacred to my people.

Every shining pine needle, every sandy shore, every mist in the dark woods, every clearing and humming insect is holy in the memory and experience of my people.

The sap which courses through the trees carries the memory of the red man.

The white man's dead forget the country of their birth when they go to walk among the stars. Our dead never forget this beautiful earth, for it is the mother of the red man.

We are part of the earth and it is part of us.

The perfumed flowers are our sisters; the deer, the horse, the great eagle, these are our brothers. The rocky crests, the juices in the meadows, the body heat of the pony, and man, all belong to the same family.

So, when the Great Chief in Washington sends word that he wishes to buy our land, he asks much of us. The Great Chief sends word he will reserve us a place so that we can live comfortably to ourselves. He will be our father and we will be his children.

So we will consider your offer to buy our land. But it will not be easy. For this land is sacred to us. This shining water that moves in the streams and rivers is not just water but the blood of our ancestors.

If we sell you the land, you must remember that it is sacred, and you must teach your children that it is sacred and that each ghostly reflection in the clear water of the lakes tells of events and memories in the life of my people.

The water's murmur is the voice of my father's father.

The rivers are our brothers. They quench our thirst. The rivers carry our canoes and feed our children. If we sell you the land, you must remember, and teach your children, that the rivers are our brothers, and yours, and you must henceforth give the rivers the kindness you would give any brothers.

We know that the white man does not understand our ways. One portion of the land is the same to him as the next, for he is a stranger who comes in the night and takes from the land whatever he needs.

The earth is not his brother, but his enemy, and when he has conquered it, he moves on.

He leaves his father's grave behind, and he does not care. He kidnaps the earth from his children, and he does not care,

His father's grave and his children's birthright are forgotten. He treats his mother, the earth, and his brother, the sky, as things to be bought, plundered, sold like sheep or bright beads.

His appetite will devour the earth and leave behind only a desert.

I do not know. Our ways are different ways.

The sight of your cities pains the eyes of the red man. But perhaps it is because the red man is a savage and does not understand.

There is no quiet place in the white man's cities. No place to hear the unfurling of leaves in spring, or the rustle of an insect's wings.

But perhaps it is because I am a savage and do not understand.

The clatter only seems to insult the ears. And what is there to life if a man cannot hear the lonely cry of the whippoorwill or the arguments of the frogs around a pond at night? I am a red man and I do not understand.

The Indian prefers the soft sound of the wind darting over the face of a pond, and the smell of the wind itself, cleaned only by the midday rain, or scented with the pinon pine.

The air is precious to the red man, for all things share the same breath—the beast, the tree, the man—they all share the same breath.

The white man does not seem to notice the air he breathes. Like a man dying for many days, he is numb to the stench.

But if we sell you our land, you must remember that the air is precious to us, that the air shares its spirit with all the life it supports. The wind that gave our grandfather his first breath also receives his last sigh.

And if we sell you our land, you must keep it apart and sacred, as a place where even the white man can go to taste the wind that is sweetened by the meadow's flowers.

So we will consider your offer to buy our land. If we decide to accept, I will make one condition: The white man must treat the beasts of this land as his brothers.

I am a savage and I do not understand it any other way.

I have seen a thousand rotting buffaloes on the prairie, left by the white man who shot them from a passing train.

I am a savage and I do not understand how the smoking iron horse can be more important than the buffalo that we kill only to stay alive. What is man without the beasts? If all the beasts were gone, man would die from a great loneliness of spirit. For whatever happens to the beasts, soon happens to man. All things are connected.

You must teach your children that the ground beneath their feet is the ashes of their grandfathers. So that they will respect the land, tell your children that the earth is rich with the lives of our kin.

Teach your children what we have taught our children, that the earth is our mother. Whatever befalls the earth befalls the sons of the earth. If men spit upon the ground, they spit upon themselves.

This we know: The earth does not belong to man; man belongs to the earth. This we know.

All things are connected like the blood which unites one family. All things are connected.

Whatever befalls the earth befalls the sons of the earth. Man did not weave the web of life; he is merely a strand in it. Whatever he does to the web, he does to himself.

Even the white man, whose God walks and talks with him as friend to friend, cannot be exempt from the common destiny.

We may be brothers after all.

We shall see.

One thing we know, which the white man may one day discover—our God is the same God. You may think now that you own Him as you wish to own our land; but you cannot. He is the God of man, and His compassion is equal for the red man and the white. This earth is precious to Him, and to harm the earth is to heap contempt on its Creator.

The whites too shall pass; perhaps sooner than all other tribes. Contaminate your bed, and you will one night suffocate in your own waste.

But in perishing you will shine brightly, fired by the strength of the God who brought you to this land and for some special purpose gave you dominion over this land and over the red man.

That destiny is a mystery to us, for we do not understand when the buffalo are all slaughtered, the wild horses are tamed, the secret corners of the forest heavy with the scent of many men, and the view of the ripe hills blotted by talking wires.

Where is the thicket? Gone.

Where is the eagle? Gone.

The end of living and the beginning of survival.

Acknowledgments

*D*eepest *Appreciation* to the city of Seattle, especially the area from Montlake to Jackson Street, where I grew up assuming that the arts are a normal part of daily life, and that friends come from all different kinds of backgrounds, and to: my sons Adam, Ryan and Jason Farmer, for their vision, love, and encouragement; Janet Wolcott Flores, my best friend, for constant reminders not to get discouraged, to trust my voice, and to stay on my path; Diane Hendrix-Colley, for being like a sister to me for many years; Al Hendrix, for many conversations over the years, and for his soft laugh that comes in little waves and always seems to say that everything's okay; Jimmy Williams, for his sensitivity, his humor, and his commitment to help me with a positive and accurate rendition of Jimmy Hendrix's story; Terry Johnson, for his kind heart, humor, boundless good cheer; Diane's son Jason, my "fourth son," for his spark, intuition, affection, and for saying "play it again, Mary" with his favorite songs; the last five people collectively for mirroring aspects of Jimmy Hendrix; my father Doug Willix, my role model, for his passion for the creative

life, and for being with me in spirit these last 24 years; my mother Kathlene Wall Willix Colgrove, for her love of beauty, for teaching me to work hard and always give thanks; my grandfather J. P. Wall, for teaching me to love the woods, water, and the wild trillium, and showing me how nature can always restore us when we give it our full appreciation.

Loving thanks to people who have given direct input:
Editor Toni Thomas, Designer Carolanne Gano, Pearl Hendrix Brown, Janie Hendrix-Wright, Bob Hendrix, Bill Eisiminger, Pernell Alexander, Walter Harris, Webb Lofton, Junior Heath, Freddie Mae Gautier, Luther Rabb, Ralph Hayes, Janet Nosi Terada, Dave Lewis, George Griffin, Mike Tagawa, Barney Hilliard, Charles Woodbury, Lester Exkano, Anthony Atherton, Betty Morgan Wallace, Barbara Heath Evans, Lacy Wilbon, Theodore Murray, Robert Green, Manual Stanton, Dolores Hall, Eddie Hall, Le Anne Hendrix, James Minor, Robert Gary, Jay Hurwitz, Bob Tate, Florence Johnson, Ursie Green, Bette Dennen Luke, Steve Fletcher, Beverly Rhue, John Eng, Ken Matesich of the Purple Haze Archives, Marsha Burns, Nirvana

Reginald Gayle, Mary McClellan, Sylvia Pierson, Luis Alberto Urrea, Buddy Miles, Joey Davis Suthern, Brenda and Billy Cox, Robert Fitzpatrick, Parker Cook, Brigid Truman Stricks, Frank Hanawalt, Marylou Kaylor Brown, Norman Winton, Lynn Edwards Moxley, Allan Wyler, Nancy Yamada Jang, Beverly Bushnell Johnson, Rosemary Williamson Bushnell, Rosemary Sherwood Leiva, Mark Brenner, Katherine Kanazawa Hutchings, Richard Hutchings, Carla Reitter Greenwald, Gordon Shoji, Vernon Otani, Bob Iverson, Peter Riches, Ulvis Alberts, Dave Sygall, Jill Gibson, Joe Sia, Chris Whitney, Judy Calvo Dolnick, Fred and Eli Stahlhut, Sylvia St. James, Letealia Reid Scott, John Boitano, Dave Thomson, Robin Landholm, Eugene Tagawa, Jesse Mallinger, Ben and Gabriel Kerr, Cory Garfin, Richard Altaraz, Robert Totty, Margaret Bovingdon Pulliam, Maaike Volkersz Del Villar, the Seattle King County News Bureau, Greg Payne, Amy Markin, Sandy Blanchat Duhon, Betty Lamielle Freedman, Sally Grant Wilbon, Nancy DeMario, Linda Emery Lee Caldwell and Helene Keyssar.

Heartfelt thanks also to people who have given support from the sidelines, in big and small ways, since the project began [even when they weren't aware of it]: Michael Keller, Maura Wiegand, Rev. Harry Morgan Moses, Gladys Highly, Diane Gage, Ben Camardi, Doug and Georgette Willix, Vern Thorp, Lesley Keyes, Al Mallinger, Mary Lewis Grubbs, Eileen Herman, Dyana Crummett, Bob Scheu of the Jimi Hendrix Museum, George Farmer, Marye and Bill Harding, Glenn and Lynn Warshaw, Serena Silva, Chris and Paul Cote, Alayne Harris, Shelagh Keegan, Caterina Leu, Betty Jo Tucker, Leroy Quintana, Janny Scott, Maria del Refugio Godoy, Meritxell and David Cuspinera of Barcelona, Steve Hammond, Thomas Babeor, Patricia Traxler, Tom and Jean Wall, Joan Oppenheimer, Cesar A. Gonzalez-T., Caesar Glebbeek, Barry Hynum, Ann Harding, Patricia LeSire, Kathryn Bouldin, Janice Steinberg, Connie Rawlins, Betty Backus, Gabriela Swift, Mindy Donner, Martin Freedman, Steve Green, Mike Stang, Jeff Dennis, Kiley and Bill Flores, Jack Ofield, Betty Martin Mills, David Cornsweet, Penelope Young Andrade, Cyrila Caplan Kaplan, Shirley Lake Day, Bobby Terada, Elizabeth Aasen, Maria Caldwell, James Kelly, Bonnie ZoBell, Linda Whitney, Richard Lou, Nancy Levy Koneski, Jill Singer, Michelle Tenebruso, Linda Cohen, Elaine Hayes, Prentiss Elizabeth Thiel, Elizabeth Hamilton, Jeanne Kerr, JerriLee and Marlin Owen, Sue McCalley, Sarah Abukutsa Marshall, Yao Ronald Tamoklae Marshall, Schuyler, Lawrence Sykoff, A.J. Cervantes, Francisca Rascon, Merrilee Antrim, Richard Simkin, Mark Lamson, Jonathan Annis, Larry Luke, Debbie Pollack, Dick and Patricia Carlson, Jim Georgiev, and Beth Dugan. Deep gratitude to Paramahansa Yogananda, Ernest Holmes, Babatunde Olatunji, Rev. Michael Beckwith, Joseph Shabalala, Julia Cameron, Edith Stauffer, Insight L. A., Terry Cole Whitaker, Al Huang, Rev. Johnny Coleman, Psychosynthesis International, Rev. Barbara King, Landmark Education, and Cathy Notlhebo Parkies, for many teachings.

In these middle years of my life, I have come to know that the events of our lives are governed by human assumptions. It is not possible to experience Spirit while believing It does not

exist. I now consciously know what I intuitively understood as a child: Life is a spiritual journey, and the people we meet along our paths are there for a reason. I am grateful to Jimmy Hendrix for his friendship in childhood, and for his understanding of Spirit. Jimmy looked for Divine Love in everyone. As he invited and welcomed pure creative essence to move through him, he helped others reconnect with themselves and left a musical legacy for generations to come.

Foreword

This book is deeply rooted in my past. As a journalist's daughter, I grew up watching my dad transform observations and conversations into stories. As a small child I assumed that all fathers spent their evenings writing newspaper and magazine stories and inventing bedtime tales to be continued. Dad's study was a tiny, upstairs cubbyhole nestled under the eaves of our modest red house in Montlake in central Seattle. At night I fell asleep to the rhythmic clatter of his typewriter keys.

My father had a gift for talking with strangers as if he'd known them for a lifetime. An open-minded man from upstate New York, he was equally at ease with city officials and celebrities as he was with our friends or with somebody he had just met at a bus stop. No matter where, he'd find a conversation partner to engage in a creative exchange that might later flow across blank pages. He wrote with ease, grace and speed. For twenty-five years he authored the city news column for *The Seattle Times*. I am grateful for my father's example. I do not find it easy to write. I go through rituals before I write. I dance,

explore my dreams, listen to music, make collages, and eventually the words come.

The seed for this book was pain. Pain is a great motivator for change. When we can't stand the agony any more, we do something about it. I used to think that repressing pain was synonymous with conquering it. But it has a way of popping up when we least expect it. Jimmy Hendrix was a special childhood friend—gentle, insightful, playful, and deeply spiritual. My memories of him hold warmth and wonder; they are sacred. But why did he die so tragically? What could I do to settle the gut-wrenching feeling I had about his death? I wanted to shower the pain with enough love to heal it.

Ten years ago, as I heard Hendrix music pouring out of my son Jason's room, a yearning to take action began to stir inside me. I wanted to know why Jimmy had become a cult figure, and why he was so misunderstood. Several years passed before the yearning solidified into what felt like marching orders from the past, from the place where I grew up.

I have lived in San Diego for twenty years. But San Diego has never felt like home. I long for the Pacific Northwest—for moisture and for deep rich greens, for the taste of wild blackberries and the fragrance of roses. Like river water seeking its source, my soul longs for the mist-covered lake and rugged mountains that I knew as a child.

Often I find that attitudes here are foreign to me. I miss the attitudes we had that made our lives work together. I miss the integrated community I grew up in. When I was thirteen I fell in love with flamenco guitar and started saving my babysitting money to go to Spain. At nineteen I ran off—like Dorothy to the Emerald City—to live in Spain. My professional life, as an interpreter and teacher, has been devoted to the Spanish language. I arrived in San Diego full of love for the Mexican people. But many San Diegans don't recognize and appreciate the cultural richness of living on a border. When I met the teacher of the bilingual class my son Jason was in, she said, "It's such a pleasure having Jason. He's the only Anglo who plays with the Mexican children on the

playground." I was shocked. Years later I realized that my search to find the real story of what happened to Jimmy Hendrix had a great deal to do with attitudes.

As I sifted through the reams of material written about Jimmy, in books, magazines, and newspapers, I found inaccuracies and misconceptions. The more I learned, the more my nostalgia turned into outrage. The story of what really happened to Jimmy Hendrix was more devastating than I had ever expected. The more I found out, the more I wanted to unravel the tangled bits of misinformation. Part of me wanted to climb the highest mountain and shout "INJUSTICE!" A larger part of me wanted to run from the turmoil and silence the awful chatter. I needed time to be still, time to heal and to nurture the seed of pain. Finally it has blossomed into a community vehicle to share the Jimmy that his friends and family loved— the daydreamer, the artist, the self-taught musician, the shy, but warm, spiritual kid, the spinner of musical magic.

This collection of key Seattle stories will give you a deeper sense of Jimi's roots. As you meet his close friends from his formative years, as you hear from family members, and other people from the central Seattle community where we grew up, make your own evaluation about the connections, music, events, places, and experiences that influenced Jimi's work.

When we were students at Meany and Garfield, each experience seemed to be a springboard for the next experience. We worked like crazy to put on a show, loved every minute of the performance, and as soon as it was over, we started planning the next show. It was a constant process of inspiration, release and renewal. How we knew to maintain a vision broader than each separate goal is more than my mind can fathom. We just did it. I accept that creativity works that way. We don't need to be able to nail it down. We simply let ourselves become vehicles for creative expression. I am merely a vehicle for a vision that embraces true community and celebrates the unique creative contribution that

every individual brings to the united whole, a vision in which life is fun because recreation is constant re-creation. This book is part of the vision. It is a community book. As I anchored myself in my intention for this project, I determined that each interview section would represent the style, the tone, and the language of the person featured. Then I felt something happening. The book began to have a life of its own. I sensed a mission that reached beyond me and the contributors, and well beyond my own limited understanding. As you read these pages, I invite you to join the circle.

The Man, the Myth and Seattle Stories

Much of the mystery that surrounds the Jimi Hendrix myth stems from his friends' and family's public silence. Stunned with outrage by his victimization, and stricken with grief after Jimi's death, most of them have been unwilling to talk with those they felt were exploiting his memory. Jimi's legendary status as a rock star, and the exploitation and misinformation that went along with that status, misportrayed his true spirit. *Voices from Home* will return a sense of truth to Jimi Hendrix; it is also a collective statement about the community where he grew up.

Those of us who shared Jimi's childhood environment know that his years in central Seattle hold a key to his creative work. We find it frustrating that reverence for Jimi as a mythical folk hero, by a generation born after his death, has been based on information that is incomplete and only partially accurate. This collection of narratives interwoven with memorabilia provides a link that has been missing in Hendrix history. Here are stories about the boy behind the legend; the Seattle kid we knew

as "Jimmy," "James," or simply "Hendrix." For those of us who contributed to this book, the child is the father of the myth. Leaving that part out is like the Abe Lincoln story without the log cabin, or George Washington without the cherry tree.

I knew Jimmy Hendrix back when the only thing flashy about him was his smile. I was eleven and he was twelve when we met at Meany Jr. High School in Seattle. Most people counter with an "I don't think so" when I mention that Jimmy grew up in Seattle. Then they usually say, "Wasn't he from New York?" Most New Yorkers know Jimmy wasn't one of them. He could work crazy, long hours like any New Yorker, and his ability for conversation matched that of any Easterner, but he had a sense of playful optimism and an openness that came from somewhere else. Some fans have hastily dismissed Jimmy's origin with a shrug. Others fancifully postulate that he came from another planet. I've been thinking about that.

For years I assumed that somewhere, in another corner of another state, people had experiences

parallel to ours. Lately I have begun to wonder. Those of us who were born in Seattle's central area, and went to the neighborhood schools that fed into Garfield High School, grew up in a cocoon. We shared our daily lives, our ups and downs, our lockers and our lunch money, with individuals of different ethnicities, cultures, and classes. It's possible that our childhood experiences were unique. Certainly people across town had little understanding of what we were experiencing. The South was entirely another world to us, more foreign than World War I. In fact, when we read or heard about segregation, or shocking things like lynchings, it was like news from another century—the Stone Age maybe.

My classmates and I were rudely awakened when we left our sheltered enclave. Some of them say, "We were thirty years ahead of the times." Our reactions when running into walls of racism and xenophobia have been almost universal. We think, "Where did these people grow up? What's going on here?" or "Am I in some kind of time warp? Did the clock just zoom backwards a few hundred years?"

This book is the collective effort of many dozens of people. It is a collage of representative key people from Jimmy's Seattle circle—close friends from the decade of his formative years, family members and family friends, musicians who played with him during his junior high and high school years, classmates, and other members of the Garfield community. Nearly all of the interviews were done in multiple sessions, on the phone and in person. For me the project was an opportunity to reconnect with my home town and old friends. Though I didn't know all of the people included here before I began this project, ties connected us from earlier years; we are still a community family. An outsider might not have gained the confidence of Jimmy's Seattle circle. As we talked about the exploitation of our friend, the commitment to set the record straight, grew into a willingness to share. At times painful memories came up. Some people were more able to express their pain than others. Expressing and sharing the pain often provided an avenue for its release. Buried pain doesn't go away. We reshuffled the past, looking for

clues in the canvas of Jimmy's childhood, until a bridge emerged that connected Jimmy's early and later years.

Jimmy spent two-thirds of his twenty-seven years in Seattle. So much that happened then was later incorporated, even immortalized, in the style, the music, and the image of the Jimi Hendrix the world came to know. The ragamuffin kid with the mismatched clothes, who once built castles made of sand along the shores of Lake Washington, went on to become the flamboyant entertainer, dressed in gypsy pants and Spanish jackets and hats, wearing bright colors, ruffles, scarves, rings, boots, and headbands. The psychedelic rock poet of the sixties had his birth in the sixth-grade mural artist who listened to the blues and dreamed of flying horses and the vivid colors of Mexico.

Mexico, you ask? Our community had no Mexicans. It may seem unusual, but there were no Latin Americans at all. Some of our classmates were Sephardic Jews with Spanish ancestry, and Filipinos with Hispanic last names, but that was the extent of the Hispanic element. The Hispanic world symbolized an exotic unknown—Mexican cowboys, gypsy guitarists, Argentine gauchos—something on the wild side that was unpredictable and full of spontaneity, unbridled passion and adventure.

Perhaps adventure and creative sizzle were part of our Pacific Northwest pioneer heritage. Our parents or grandparents did not head off for that remote corner of the country looking for gold or sunshine. It was wet country, the land of fish and timber, protected salt water harbors and farmland. If they weren't loggers or farmers—with visions of the legendary lumberjack Paul Bunyan or the mythical Johnny Appleseed—they were spunky urban pioneers with a strong sense of adventure. They had come to carve out a better life, to pursue the American dream, in the city named after a local Native American, the man I consider my home town's master teacher, Chief Sealth.

Sealth was of mixed ancestry; he was a leader of the Suquamish, his father's tribe, but he preferred to speak the language of his mother's tribe, the Duwamish. The invocation for this book is taken from a speech he gave. As a boy, Jimmy and his friends played on the western shore of Lake Washington, in the heart of the sacred land Sealth talks about. Native Americans refer to Mount Rainier as Takhoma, "the mountain that is god." Nature in the Pacific Northwest comes in gigantic proportions. I think something happens to people where nature is so bold and vast. And just as our bodies hold memories, so does the land hold memory. Those who are sensitive are molded by the past, and carry the spirit of the geography deep within them.

Jimmy Hendrix loved nature deeply. Whether or not he was familiar with Sealth's speech, Jimmy's work reflects the chief's message that the land is sacred. He captured the elements of the land that birthed him in a explosive fusion of sounds, color and imagery. Jimmy Hendrix is Seattle's magical realist. The notion of magical realism—the fusion of fantasy and reality—is as old as the oldest cultures. But it was blossoming as a literary movement at the same time Jimmy began experimenting with it in music. In 1967 the first of the Latin American giants of magical realism, Miguel Angel Asturias, from Guatemala, won the Nobel Prize for literature. In 1967 Gabriel García Márquez, another Nobel Prize winner, published *One Hundred Years of Solitude*, the classic cornerstone of magical realism.

In Latin America, magical landscapes helped spawn the movement; backyards there led to dense rain forests, the majestic Andes, and thundering waterfalls. How interesting it is that Jimmy Hendrix was drawn to Latin America at the time of the birth of magical realism. Gabriel García Márquez says that he blends fantasy and reality into a greater reality. So it was with Hendrix. Known as the pioneer of the rock industry, and the finest electric guitarist of the century, he was a self-taught, left-handed guitarist, an artist and daydreamer who overcame hardship by mixing magic and reality to create a new and greater reality in the world of sound.

Voices from Home is for everyone—for those who loved and understood Jimmy, those who remained neutral, and those who judged him. Some people were put off because they disliked the hype, the stage gimmicks, or the drug scene that was a part of those times. Others thought that all he played was loud music. They missed the lyrical, soft, and bluesy songs; they missed the opportunity to appreciate the full artistry of Jimi's work.

Some fans, initially attracted by the razzle-dazzle, flash and dash, wind up hopelessly hooked by a deep jab that pierces the solar plexus with softness. Guitarist Dave Thomson says, "Jimi Hendrix literally changed my life. Nothing was the same after I heard him." A Southern California native in his late thirties who doesn't drink, smoke or take drugs, Dave adds, "I've never understood people who say he doesn't have a good voice for singing. I love his voice. It's gentle."

Ron Stevens concurs. "Jimi's voice is relaxing, not threatening. His music is mellow, not thundering.

It's very personal. It's real art," he says. "His music reflected the times. It's calm and grassrootsy. I picture him sitting in a rocking chair on a front porch somewhere, writing down his thoughts."

Jimmy has erased the color barrier and other boundaries of separation with his current audience. The new generation of listeners includes young people of all racial, socio-economic and political backgrounds. Recently I spoke with a European-American high school student who attends a southern California high school where there has been racial tension. He has friends who are African-American and friends who label themselves skinheads, and he often finds himself in the middle. A common denominator is that they are all Hendrix fans. He says, "Everyone at my school loves Jimi Hendrix." At first glance it appears ironic that young people who profess to hate others who don't look exactly the way they do, could like someone who appears so different. Yet divisiveness and xenophobia are not humankind's basic nature; those who buy into divisiveness are naturally drawn to a man who did

not believe in barriers and boundaries that separate one person from another.

Cory Garfin, a 1995 graduate of University City High School in San Diego, was deeply impacted by Hendrix's beliefs. Cory made a charcoal drawing of Hendrix that has the following caption: "Jimi has taught me through beautiful words and amazing music that I only limit myself by being a White man or a Black man, or any other type of person that can be labeled and stereotyped. We are as vast as the colors of the rainbow, and we're all bold as love."

Jimmy's friends say his early years have been wrongly portrayed. The Seattle men closest to Jimmy for a decade during his formative years are gentle, and quick witted. You will see in the interviews that they are soft-spoken and thoughtful. They grew up with a strong bond to one another, and a sense of optimisim.

Now, we stand on the edge of a critical moment. Many conversations today are a version of "What's wrong?" Turn on the television or read a newspaper.

What is society doing to the American dream for our young people? They want to dream, but many fear and lose hope. Exhaustion, pain, and loneliness appear rampant. According to Cornel West, Yale professor and lecturer, 42% of males between the ages of fourteen and twenty-four have no best friend. In these troubled times, attitudes across the nation are increasingly negative and xenophobic.

Yet, at the same time, there are strong signs of a worldwide awakening to wholistic and holistic thinking. There is a new openness to ecology, to community, to world music and art of all forms, to preventative and alternative medicine, to natural foods, mythology, and spirituality. Many of the young people who have joined this forward evolution, this pathway to higher awareness, are Hendrix fans. Fans who like to study the lyrics to Jimi's songs, and pay attention to their tone, will find a wealth of information here that offers clues for interpreting his music. Even readers who aren't looking for interpretations may find something here that will change their lives.

Jimi Hendrix is a visionary. His music expresses his desire to rekindle, expand and reshape a vision. His spiritual message of harmony, peace and creative expression has clear roots in his central Seattle upbringing and his Pacific Northwest pioneer background. His voice of spiritual love of the highest form is critically needed for the twenty-first century. *Jimi Hendrix: Voices from Home* is a modest tribute to the greatness of a friend. It celebrates Hendrix's contribution to our lives and revisits an easier, more relaxed and harmonious time in the Pacific Northwest. Sometimes a story is as important as food. I think this is one of those times.

Dear Jimmy,

For years after your tragic death, I consciously avoided reminders of you. But one day in 1983, in my son Jason's room, you emerged full blown from a poster on the wall, like some kind of genie. I had walked into the room with a pile of laundry in my arms. I stopped, frozen, when I saw you. You were clothed in fuchsia, your eyes sealed in a trance-like state, your guitar pointing to the sky. Jimi the Rock Star. Could that really be the same shy Jimmy who sat beside me in the back of the classroom, mumbling silly things to make me laugh? The same kid who shared my enthusiasm for mysterious things, like UFOs, telepathy and dreams? My friend who was my mirror for spirit? My friend, acclaimed, marketed, and now gone? A wave of loss swept over me. The pain I had shut out for so many years struck like lightning, reinvading every cell of my body. Paralyzed with emotion, I realized there was much more I needed to understand.

"Hey, Mom. Like my new poster?"

"Jason! Hi! Sorry, you startled me. Yeah, I like it lot. I guess

I'm a little spaced out. It's just so strange."

"What's strange about it?"

"Seeing such a familiar face blown up on a poster."

"Oh? You've seen Jimi Hendrix before?"

"Well, I used to know him. I thought I told you."

"No, I don't think so. Where did you meet him?"

"In Seattle."

"Really? Like at a concert or something?"

"No, at school. A really long time ago."

But you were gone, dead. Unspoken words stuck in my throat. I remember how you had approached me like a lost kitten when we first met, playful but timid, ready to dart out the door if you didn't feel safe. We were both shy. I was eleven; you were twelve. Your manner was gentle, genuine, good-humored and warmly accepting. We shared a fascination for offbeat topics, a similar sense of humor, a passion for the arts, and an understanding of spirit.

You were always there for me with words of compassion when something was bothering me. You never belittled me or laughed at me, even in those early teen years when sweet kids act rotten and rip each other apart. I could trust you with personal issues that I wouldn't tell other people. Our differences were obvious to the casual observer. What we had in common was not obvious. I was "White, middle class, an achiever at school"; you were "Black, poor, an underachiever at school." I don't like labels. They limit, restrict, and even deny the very essence of who we are. Labels carry their own karma. To me, you were "Jimmy." I was "Mary." What we had in common was far greater and more vital than any differences. A puppy looking for a playmate plays with kittens. Life energy is all the same.

Acceptance was a key to our friendship. I was younger than everybody in our class. My mother told me I'd been skipped ahead because I was too tall. She told me I wasn't very smart or very pretty. I had a too-young, too-tall, not-very-bright, ugly-duckling complex. But you accepted me as I was, an overly sensitive little creature wearing month-end-clearance clothes. Clothes meant social status. They were part of the show, and at Meany and Garfield putting on a good show mattered. I loved the stage. Performing suspended me in another dimension and allowed me to completely forget about being a "have-not." My self-doubts would vanish. Off stage, the doubts came back. And yet, a small, still voice deep inside me said I was okay, that there wasn't anything lacking in me just because I didn't have certain things that our rich classmates had. You mirrored back to me that sense of "everything's okay." Our "I'm-okay-you're-okay" friendship gave me comfort and helped me grow.

Many of our classmates say you weren't very sociable. I don't agree with people who say you were a loner. I'd say you were selective. A loner has a hard time connecting internally and with other people. You were very good at connecting—you simply chose to socialize with only a few people. With those few,

you engaged your attention instantly. You were fully present, bright, and very funny.

When I would take life too seriously, you would remind me to be playful. We laughed about silly things, and we talked about magical things. We talked about mysterious, mystical, outer-space, inner-space things—pyramid power, reincarnation, mental telepathy, precognitive dreams and exotic places. Experience has taught me that Spirit is real. As a child, I assumed everybody knew it. In my own way, I experienced the unknown at an early age, as I believe most children do. Anyone can access the greater power. Since relatives of mine talked openly about God and the healing power of the mind, I grew up feeling comfortable with and drawn to a less tangible reality.

At school, I learned quickly that I couldn't talk to most people about psychic phenomena, outer space, or spiritual things without being labeled as different. But I liked to keep testing the waters, looking for an opening. When I tested you, I felt as if I'd won the lottery. We had conversations that would knock most

people over. In three seconds we'd be in our own world. I loved our mini "what if" brainstorming sessions. What if great people, like Mozart, lived before, and that's why they know so much at an early age? What if Atlantis were real? What would you do if you were alone on a dark road at night and a UFO landed? Remember the fun we had with UFO stories? We used our childlike logic to speculate about which sitings were real and which ones were hoaxes.

When people overheard us talking about UFOs, or about tuning into a power beyond us, they'd say, "You guys don't really believe in that stuff, do you?" We weren't sure exactly what we believed, but we had an Anything's Possible Attitude. We didn't slam doors on each other. In fact, I think other people's incredulous attitude about mysterious things bonded us even more. Being with you was like being with family. I had relatives who talked about hypnosis, the workings of the mind, creativity, UFOs, and far-away places, as a normal part of daily conversation. I remember your enthusiasm about my first experiences with hypnosis, with my mom's brother,

the dentist. I loved the magic moment when I'd allow my mind to spin over, like a dial. This only happened if I chose to surrender; my subconscious would move from the bottom to the top, pushing my conscious mind to the bottom. You understood there is nothing to fear. We can say 'yes' or 'no' to a hypnotic journey. I see your music as a similar journey.

You were curious, open, and receptive. I loved your lightning-quick mind. A conversation with you was like getting on a fast train—full speed ahead. No stoppers. Your consciousness was big. Compared to someone with a closed mind and a consciousness the size of a peanut, yours was like the Goodyear Blimp. Your child's mind refused to be contaminated by the limitations of society.

It's strange, but we talked very little about music or the arts. You had friends you talked with about music. I shared the arts with my girlfriends. Dance and music were a passion and a presence in my life from the age of five. Movement and rhythm connect the body to the soul. I need to have happy feet and a dancing heart. Boys at Meany teased me about

playing the drums. Not a girl thing to do. Playing the xylophone was acceptable; I liked being called Tinkerbell. But my brother was a drummer, so I drummed too. I loved playing the snare drum in the Meany orchestra—as Leroy Hartwell's apprentice. You never made fun of my drumming. I appreciated that. Only a handful of males made me feel as comfortable as you did at that stage of my life. You had a sense of enthusiasm, play, wonder, and drama, and a gift for spontaneous, open-ended conversations that brought out the best in me. Talking with you meant spiritual validation, intellectual stimulation, and a good dose of warm acceptance.

The emotions I felt as a kid still live in my memory. At times simply being with you was healing. I'd find you alone in the back of a classroom, gazing out the window with a wistful, lost-in-daydreams look. I'd sit down beside you and say, "Hi, Jimmy!" You'd turn and look at me with such tenderness that I felt like a beautiful little bambi that you'd just spotted in a clearing. When you'd say "Mary" in

that soft, warm voice of yours, my world would be in order. Stray problems would vanish like mist in the sunshine. My head would clear and my heart would open up again.

It used to bother me when your father would tell me, "Jimmy was just an ordinary kid." I wanted to say, "No, he was extraordinary." Now I can accept the word ordinary in the Buddhist tradition; the path to self-realization is ordinary, normal and natural. Extra-ordinary is a lot more ordinary—in the enlightened sense.

You dedicated your life to an art form that allowed creativity to be expressed through you. I love your gift for noticing and appreciating beauty— beauty in people, nature, images, rhythms, words, colors and sounds. Your mission was ultimately about love, about valuing individuals and living in harmony. Some say it was about crossing the color line. I say it was about erasing it. I miss you, Jimmy. A lot of people do.

Love, *Mary*

JIMMY'S SIXTH GRADE CLASS, LESCHI GRADE SCHOOL, 1955—JIMMY: SECOND ROW, THIRD STUDENT

A Decade of Friendship

Jimmy Williams and Terry Johnson kid around, spin tales, and look for the humor in whatever's around them—something they shared with Hendrix. The three were best friends for a decade in the economically and ethnically diverse Leschi neighborhood. At school, sitting beside well-heeled classmates from rambling two and three-story Victorian homes, the boys learned that humor lightened their burden of poverty. Their passion for music bonded them.

In grade school, Terry and Jimmy Williams were the performers—not Jimmy Hendrix. Williams sang and Johnson played the piano. "Terry danced, too," says Williams. "He and his sister Anita did a wonderful tap dance in the sixth-grade talent show." "True," says Terry. "But Jimmy Williams performed more than I did. He always wore a cute little bow tie when he sang in shows. I'll never forget when he

sang, 'Wanted—someone who'll kiss me and hold me tight.' Jimmy Hendrix and I were terrible singers. All he wanted to do was play his guitar and make funny noises." "Our friend Pernell Alexander was the one who got Jimmy playing the guitar." says Williams.

The boys rode bikes, hung out at a soda fountain at 29th and Cherry—owned by the neighborhood mentor, Mr. Slaughter—and spent time by Lake Washington, a ten-minute walk down the hill. "There was something magical about the lake," says Williams. "It had a calming effect on us." At Madrona Beach and Leschi Park they swam, skipped rocks, twisted long vines to swing out over the water, ate snow cones, pretzels and potato chips, and fed the ducks. They had long conversations. "We always talked about 'big' things," recalls Williams.

Now when Williams and Johnson miss their friend Jimmy Hendrix, they dip into their treasure

KNEELING: TERRY JOHNSON, STANDING, SECOND FROM RIGHT: JIMMY HENDRIX, THIRD: JIMMY WILLIAMS

chest of remembrances. Like splashing in the magical lake, bringing back the good old days refreshes and renews them. The idyllic moments linger on.

Terry Johnson

"Jimmy loved drawing cartoons for his friends. He'd say,'Okay, Terrikins. What do you want? How about a horse?' I'd say 'sure.' At first he did mostly horse heads. Then, he started doing bodies, usually rearing up. Lots of action. But he could never get the tail right, so he just made little sweeping lines flying out the back. His favorite was a Pegasus with a flaming mane and little wings, sometimes flying down out of the clouds."

Terry Johnson was a professional musician for nearly twenty years. He and Jimmy Hendrix learned to play together by ear in grade school. In junior high they played at the Rotary Boys' Club and the Neighborhood House. In high school Terry played briefly with the Rocking Teens before he joined the Stags. Terry attended Olympic Jr. College prior to entering the Air Force. While serving as an administrative specialist in the Air Force, he played with several groups, including the Upsetters and Brief

Encounter, at NCOs and officers' clubs in Alaska, California, and overseas in Thailand and Vietnam. When he returned to McChord Air Force Base, near Seattle, in August 1970, he joined a group called Cameo. Since retiring from music, Terry has worked as a photo model, an interior decorator, and a wine steward. He and his ex-wife, Garfield graduate Linda Griffin, have a grown daughter, whose name is also Terry.

Lively, sociable, and camera-ready, Terry is a man-on-the-move. "Terry's usually booked solid," comments Williams. "But that's Terry. He's been hyper since he was a little kid." At the time of this writing, Terry and his girlfriend Donna are rebuilding the house on Lake Sammamish that he lost in a fire in early 1993. To help finance the loss, Terry works the graveyard shift as a Hostess delivery truck driver. Typical of his friendly manner, Terry calls everyone on his route by first name

as he drops off Twinkies and Ding Dongs. Sundays are devoted to family and church. "I go for the message," says Terry. "Jimmy used to go to church with me sometimes. I still go to the same church—back in the old neighborhood."

Meeting Jimmy

When I met Jimmy Hendrix, back in 1951, we liked each other instantly. He and Jimmy Williams and I were best friends for ten years. We called ourselves the Three Musketeers. We were alike in many ways—similar personalities, humor, interests, and a sense of adventure. Our main bonding interest was music. We

FLORENCE, DONNA (COUSIN) AND TERRY

lived in the same neighborhood. I lived at 29th and Lane. Jimmy lived eight blocks from me. The three of us went to school together at Leschi Elementary. Then Jimmy moved in with his aunt and uncle and went to Meany Jr. High, and Jimmy Williams and I went to Washington Jr. High. Jimmy Hendrix and I continued to play music together, and we all met up again at Garfield.

Early Memories

Jimmy Hendrix, Jimmy Williams and I spent a lot of time together, starting in third grade. I remember we liked to make funny little sounds—musical sounds. We'd all go to my house after school and talk about the latest songs—"Have you heard this one or that one?"—and what the words meant. We had nicknames for each other. Jimmy called me "Terrikins," and I called him "Jimmykins." We called James Williams "Potato Chips," for obvious reasons.

We'd sit on the red steps in front of my house and talk about songs and girls and school, and my mom would bring us lemonade, or cookies and milk. I remember we laughed a lot. We felt like the Three Musketeers.

Jimmy had only a few picked friends. With me and Jimmy Williams he talked all the time, but with other people he was withdrawn, shy. Jimmy was affectionate with people he felt really comfortable with. He'd always give me a big hug. Basically he was introverted.

Jimmy was the type of guy who would never look you straight in the eye unless he knew you really, really well. He had a sense of insecurity that made it hard for people to get to know him. They'd take him as a shy and kind of naive type of guy. Few people really knew him. He had a great sense of humor, and was very sensitive and very, very smart

and streetwise. But he did not have a good early background in relating to people.

He was very considerate of others and other peoples' feelings. He appreciated beauty, especially in music, art, women and nature. He was an excellent artist and could have pursued art, and reached the same level, but he chose music as his way of standing out in the crowd. It was a natural thing because music and performance were a part of life where we grew up.

At Leschi we had talent shows, as most elementary schools do. James Williams sang. He wore a little bow tie, and he was really great. Then I had a tap dancing team with my sister and another gentleman, named Gary Coleman. Jimmy, by the way, hated to dance. Do people know that? He really didn't like to dance. I also played the piano, and I think Jimmy played a guitar solo, but I could be

wrong about that. In junior high school we got more serious. We started a little rock 'n' roll band, and we started playing at dances, and at what they called sock hops back then. Jimmy even did some singing.

When we were kids we liked to play beside Lake Washington. We did kid things down by the lake—threw rocks, went swimming and fishing and swang on rope swings. We did what normal kids do—we'd run real fast and make a lot of noise. Sometimes we'd play little pranks and things. We'd go to the floating bridge and climb up the hill above the entrance to the floating bridge tunnel and play King Kong. We'd scoop up soft dirt and make little dirt bombs drop on cars below us and then we'd run. It was bad, but we did stuff like that.

I don't think you could ask for a better place than Seattle to grow up, as far as I'm concerned, because I love the Northwest. I'm sure Jimmy did,

too. Jimmy loved nature and beauty. Right by our house we had Lake Washington, and serene mountains, and Mount Rainier. We had all four seasons, which is great. And when you have all those things, growing up as a kid, and you have all the holidays, when the whole city is lit up, you appreciate it.

As we grew older, I became more outgoing, and Jimmy Williams became more outgoing, but Jimmy Hendrix stayed kind of shy. I don't know if it was because of his home upbringing, or because of his social environment. Jimmy wouldn't open up to just anybody. I genuinely liked Jimmy. We clicked. We had the same sense of humor. We spent so much time together that I got to know him really well. There was so much to like about him. I wish everybody could have known Jimmy as I knew him because he was one of the greatest guys in the world.

Jimmy: Part of Our Family

One of the reasons that Jimmy and I were so close is because every day after school he had nowhere to go, because, well, he didn't have a mother, actually with him at that time during his childhood. And so my mom kind of took him under her wing, as did other moms in the neighborhood. Jimmy got along with our family so well that everybody in the family accepted him. And we really felt sorry for him. But, when you're little kids, you really don't understand what's going on in the world; all you know is you just feel sorry for somebody. You don't know why. But the fact was that he didn't have a mom. Nobody really talked about it. We just understood. It was just an understood thing. So nobody talked about it and we went on just like Jimmy was part of our family and treated him as such, you know.

TERRY JOHNSON'S CHILDHOOD HOUSE

In grade school Jimmy would come over to my house, like I said, almost every night. It became a regular thing. He didn't have a key to get in his house. His father had it. His father usually wasn't home at that time. I remember times when his father was at the Mt. Baker Tavern at 25th and Jackson. There was an empty lot next door to the tavern, and we'd stand in the tall grass and look in the window to see if he was in there. Jimmy would go home with me and we'd play in the backyard. My father had hung up a large tractor tire on a cherry tree in the back yard, and all the kids in the neighborhood would come over and play on it. My house was the neighborhood hangout.

There were times when Jimmy would stay to have dinner with us and go home after dark. We became like brothers. We'd do everything together. My mom became like his mom, and she loved him almost like he was one of her own kids. She fed him and encouraged him.

Terry's Dream to See Jimmy Again

I was so hurt when Jimmy passed away. My dream was to see him again. I got back from Vietnam in August of 1970. A month later he was gone. I wanted to see him play, and to be able to come up to him and give him a hug, and just watch him melt. I knew I could have helped him put his life back together, helped him deal with the old and the new. I had the power to be that connection between him and the whole scheme of his life. I was so proud of him, and he never had that chance to say, "Look, I've made it." He was way out there, too much on his own, so far from the people from his past who meant so much to him, his family and friends. What good is all that success if you don't have the people from your past

to share it with? I wanted to be there for him, so he could share it with me, open up, and—who knows?

Our Sanctuary

In the back of our house is a room we call the playroom, where my mom has an old upright piano with a few keys missing. For me and Jimmy, it was our sanctuary when we were kids. Jimmy had a little turquoise guitar that he'd restrung. Since he was left-handed, he turned the strings around in the opposite direction. He'd tune it up, and we'd start playing. Neither one of us could sing, but we'd howl and get enough words out to make the song go along.

We played by ear, listening to 45s. And believe me, we wore out a lot of 45s on that old record player. First of all we had to figure out what key the song was in, then we'd let it play for a while, and then we'd take it off and start all over again. Jimmy

would listen to the guitar part until he had it figured out and memorized. Then I'd play the piano part. We figured out C and D, and we got better and better. Our thirst for knowledge had us going to music stores, buying the music, and figuring out the notes.

I remember us singing the latest songs at the table, and my mom would say, "No singing at the table." My mom didn't like all the noise, but she loved our enthusiasm and she encouraged us. She liked having us home instead of out there somewhere being juvenile delinquents. And she told us we were going to be great someday.

Favorite Recording Artists and Songs

As rock 'n' roll progressed, Jimmy and I started picking out our favorite recording artists. We listened to James Brown, Fats Domino, Little Anthony, and Little Richard. Little Richard was one of the best at that time. He had a lot of piano in his songs, like Jerry Lee Lewis, and a lot of guitar lines, which was the big thing in rock 'n' roll then. So some of our favorite artists were piano players with guitar backgrounds, or guitar players with piano backgrounds.

One of the songs we'd play back in those days was "What'd I Say," by Ray Charles. That was a big one. I had an electric piano then, a pink and white Wurlitzer, so we really were hot on that one. Ray Charles was one of our idols. In fact, of all the songs Jimmy and I played, that was one of our favorites, "See the girl with the red dress on." That's the one that sticks in my mom's mind, and it was her favorite tune, even though it was banned on some radio stations. Jimmy and I were getting pretty sophisticated. I used to slide up and down on the piano, eee-uur, eee-uuur, and do big da-doon doon chords. That's what drove my mother crazy, that sliding on the piano. But she put up with us because we were so enthusiastic.

Other favorites that we did were "Lucille," "Good Golly Miss Molly," "Slippin' and Slidin'," "Blueberry Hill," "Long Tall Sally," "Johnny B. Goode," "I'm Walking," "Doin' the Stroll," and "Walkin' to New Orleans" —those types of songs. We liked the Chantels and the Shirelles. We used a few Elvis Presley tunes.

Jimmy was trying, even then, to find sounds to express what he was feeling. He identified with rhythm and blues guitar players, especially Albert King, Freddie King, B.B. King, and Bobby Blue Bland. We thought Bobby Blue Bland was the greatest. He didn't play guitar, but we didn't know that then. Robert Green's parents were friends with Bobby Blue Bland and Junior Parker. I remember they traveled together.

THE BOPTONES: FLOWERS, JOHSON, SMITH AND MADAYAG

GARFIELD HIGH SCHOOL BAND—JOHNSON, THIRD ROW, SECOND FROM RIGHT

We had local idols too, especially Dave Lewis, who graduated from Garfield in '55 and played at Birdland. He taught me and Ron Holden to play the organ. He was so good on the Hammond. I ended up buying a Hammond because of him. We learned a lot from Dave just by listening. The Dave Lewis Combo was the first group in Seattle to play "Louie, Louie." When I played with the Stags, "Louie, Louie" was one of our favorite songs to play at dances, like O'Dea sock hops, along with the "Pony Walk," which Luther Rabb did, and "What'd I Say"—all that stuff. One of my idols for piano playing was Barbara Heath, Junior Heath's sister. I used to call her Tarantula Fingers. She taught me so much.

I took some clarinet lessons, but I had an old metal clarinet and everybody else had these nice wooden ones they took apart and put away in pretty cases. Well, my parents couldn't afford that fancy stuff. Anyway, I changed to alto sax and joined the band at school. Once I made the mistake of showing up at a party after a football game with my big purple uniform on—the kind with the little ropey things hanging down. My white bucks were all muddy from marching around the field in the mud. Everybody started pulling on the little ropey things and busting up. So after that I'd take the bus all the way home after the games to change and by the time I'd get to the parties, they'd be breaking up and everybody'd be saying, "Hey, that was really a good party." So I didn't last very long in the marching band.

"Let the Good Times Roll"

One of our favorite songs was "Let the Good Times Roll"—Earl King, I think—because it had a really neat guitar part in there where Jimmy could do the lead, and I could come in and do the background. We worked really hard on that one. Later on I heard that song on one of his albums ("Come On," *Electric Ladyland*), and I couldn't help but think it was like a tribute to when we were young kids playing that song. He used to sing it and sing it. We had our own version of it then though. It used to go,

"People talkin', but they just don't know.

What's in my heart and why I love you so.

I love you, baby, like a miner loves gold

Come on, baby, let the good times roll."

There was one part, one little note in there, that Jimmy loved to do. He'd always sing it. In fact, we'd sing it all the way home from school. He'd just sing that part, even when he didn't have his guitar. Then he couldn't wait to get home so he could play it on his guitar. I'd do the piano with my mouth on the way home, and he'd simulate the guitar part, until we got home and did it with our instruments.

DONNA AND TERRY

We grew stronger and stronger together and music was a solid bond that helped our friendship grow.

Jimmy's Clothes

We all had hand-me-down clothes that we wore to some degree, but Jimmy wore them out of necessity. I mean, that's all he had to wear. When we were little, we really didn't notice it. But as we got older, sometimes people made fun of Jimmy. He'd act calm and pleasant about it, and he would go along with the flow. He really was just happy to be alive. He was that kind of person. But I sensed the teasing, the criticism, made him more and more withdrawn. Kids can be cruel at that age.

Jimmy never had a chance to coordinate clothes. There was no rhyme nor reason to what he wore. He'd wear winter things in the summertime, and summer things in the wintertime. I understand now that that's all he had. I used to give him sweaters and things.

His shoes were worn out, turned over on the sides and had holes in the bottoms. He used to walk on the sides of his feet, and I don't know if that was a natural tendency or if he did that because his shoes were worn out. By sixth grade I started to notice how Jimmy was different in groups from the way he was with his friends. He was really inhibited around girls. Sometimes girls would laugh at his shoes, or the holes in his pants, or his shirts.

There were kids who wouldn't take time to notice him. And I know some of them didn't want to hang around him because of the way he dressed. They thought he looked like a flag. They were judgmental and superficial, but people can be that way.

As we got older, and music made us more noticeable, we got more popular with the girls, and girls became a more important priority in our lives. Jimmy would borrow some of my clothes, and I didn't mind giving them to him. I didn't have the best of clothes, but his were redundant because he wore them every day.

Jimmy was really shy around other people because of his background and his insecurities. He also was very shy because he had big curly hair, and sometimes he needed a haircut. This added to his insecurity, along with his clothes. So he had that shaggy-dog kind of a look, and it was stand-offish. It kind of kept people away.

In later years Jimmy turned his strange way of dressing into a marketable thing: he stood out. The more unusual he was, the more marketable he was. I think he used that to his advantage. Jimmy had great hair, nice and thick, but when he was little and couldn't afford a haircut, it would get overgrown and

THE THREE MUSKETEERS' TREEHOUSE WAS HERE

unruly. When he was a performer, he just let it grow and put a band around it. He always liked ruffles. And he loved hats. I'm sure he was deeply influenced by those early times.

Walking Girls Home

Jimmy never had enough nerve to walk a girl home after school by himself, so I'd do it with him, like a little group effort. That made it easier. So we'd walk the young ladies home together and that was good for both of us.

Art and Horses

People don't realize that if Jimmy hadn't become a musician, he could have become an artist or a cartoonist. He was a left-handed artist who had a knack for drawing almost anything. Especially cartoons. At that time cartoons were a great connection point. Jimmy would draw little cartoons

for me on my notebook. We called them "PeeChees" then. He was always making cartoons, on the boards at school, or when he'd sign his name, like on a class picture. He liked to draw little caricatures of people.

Jimmy really liked drawing horses. I remember when he first started. He drew heads, because he could never get their bodies quite right. He always said, "If you can really draw, you have to draw horses." He'd make their eyes really big, with long eyelashes. He liked to make the nostrils flared with smoke coming out of them, like the horse had been running for a long time.

Then he started doing bodies. He'd draw flaming manes, and sometimes the horses would be rearing up. He'd get the muscles and the hooves just right, but he never could get the tail right, so he made little sweeping lines flying out the back. At Christmas Jimmy progressed into reindeer. Later on he got into Woody

Woodpecker and Donald Duck, but horses were his forte. He liked to do Pegasus-like flying horses.

Sounds and Singing

Jimmy loved cartoons, and he loved making animation sounds, cartoon sound effects, like the road runner. Way back when we were little kids, sitting on the front steps of my house, we experimented with making funny little sounds, musical sounds—sometimes guitar and piano sounds. And I think he carried that over into his music, into his guitar playing, especially the way he'd use his wah-wah pedal and his facial expressions, when he'd hit high notes and play. That was all part of his upbringing.

I couldn't sing, so I joined Mr. Jones' Glee Club at Washington to learn how to sing. But all I learned to do was to harmonize and go ooo-eee-aaa and make little humming noises. I sang with a group called the Boptones. The guy who could really sing was Charles Woodbury. He was really good.

When Jimmy was a kid, he'd always suck in the side of his mouth. He'd always play the guitar and suck in the side of his mouth and make a sound, like that, all of the time. He had a lot of little noises, sound effects, that he used to like to make. But he always hated to sing in front of people. Ever notice on the videos how he tries to hurry up and finish singing so he can get back to playing his guitar?

Even though Jimmy was noted for his lyrics, and sometimes his singing—or that kind of half-talking, half-singing thing, like Bob Dylan—a lot of people didn't know that Jimmy really didn't like to sing. He would try to rush the song and he would hold his eyes down. He would never like to look at anybody when he was singing, because it would deter his confidence. So he'd hold his eyes down when he was singing. He'd look at his guitar. He'd sing, but he always wanted to get back to his guitar solo.

His guitar was his heart. He could project himself through his guitar. He could say what he wanted to say on his guitar. But he had to sing because it wasn't good to be an instrumentalist without singing back in those days. And that's how they were pushing him, marketing him, as Jimi Hendrix, the singer and the guitar player. But I look back and I know deep in his heart Jimmy really didn't like to sing, and you could tell.

Jimmy liked to write. He wrote poems. He especially liked to make words rhyme. But he didn't like to dance. In high school Jimmy never did figure out how to dance. He said it was because he didn't like to dance, but I know it was partly because he was shy.

Chewing Gum

Jimmy was always chewing gum. He was a mumbler, and chewing gum made it worse. Only then he could use it as an excuse for not talking clearly. Ever notice he was chewing gum during performances? Watch closely on those videos.

Paper Route

When I turned twelve I got a paper route with The Shopping News, an advertisement type of paper, where the local vendors would push their wares. I had to get up at three o'clock in the morning. I'd hate to do that now, but back then it was an adventure. In the summertime Jimmy would get up and go with me and we'd talk. We'd deliver papers down by the lake and talk about music. "You heard the newest songs?" All that Jimmy wanted was to belong and to have someone in his life from his peer group that he could identify with. He loved doing the paper route with me, and he helped me as well. I remember times when I was in the tenth grade when Jimmy went with me too.

Boy Scouts

We did other things together as we grew older. We became Boy Scouts together. We joined a troop that met every Wednesday night at the Garfield High School gymnasium. Other kids our age in the neighborhood joined too. Some of them we were scared of. Some of them were juvenile delinquents, and a few of them were in gangs. There was a gentleman named Mr. Slaughter, who owned the local soda fountain, who got us all together, and got us interested in Scouting. That took our minds off of juvenile delinquent-type activities that normally would be in kids' heads at that age.

So we learned that a Boy Scout is brave, clean, reverent, thrifty, courteous, and kind, and we tied little clove hitches, and different types of knots, and we'd make the Akela sign.

We also got our different badges and worked our way up through tenderfoot and so on. All the camaraderie with the guys from our neighborhood was great. So not only did we have music, but we had Boy Scouts also. And we were progressing as little young men, and my mom was proud of us.

Rotary Boys' Club and Bands

When Jimmy and I started junior high, the Rotary Boys' Club became the perfect place for us to practice. It was hard to find a place to practice rock 'n' roll in those days. We could never practice at Jimmy's house. We couldn't practice at my mom's house much any more because we were too loud. My house was the only place that had a piano, but I had five younger brothers and sisters who were trying to sleep, and doing growing-up things. Rock 'n' roll was a loud type of thing, and I think we drove my mom crazy. So the Rotary Boys' Club was perfect; it became our place.

They had an amplifier that you could check out. So Jimmy would check it out, plug in his guitar and hear what he sounded like amplified. They had a piano there. We'd get in one of the little music rooms they had and we'd refine our art, our craft, our rock 'n' roll music. It was great for us. The supervisors there talked us into forming a band. Kids from other junior high schools formed band there too, and we started the Battle of the Bands.

There were other good activities for young kids at the Rotary Club. We had classes, and played pool, and played a game called "socum" in a large gymnasium, where we threw rubber balls at each other. There were people there who cared about us. Some of the young men who worked there gave boxing lessons. We had legitimate rules and a place where we could let out our frustration.

We joined a group called the Rocking Teens, which became the Rocking Kings. Later on I joined an interracial group called the Stags. One of the members was Luther Rabb, a friend of Jimmy's who played later with Emergency Exit, Ballin' Jack, the Street Angels, and then with the well-known group War, in Los Angeles.

The Flames and the Knights

I remember back in seventh grade how sometimes we had to pay a protection fee out of our lunch money to keep from getting beat up by the bigger guys. We were innocent kids, and we didn't want to fight anyway. We wanted to play our music and get into social groups. There were gangs starting up back then, but it wasn't at all like it is today. I remember some guys wanted Jimmy to join a little gang called

the Flames. He didn't last long. There was a serious gang, called the Knights, that was out of school. These were older guys who had the cars and the chains, and they had emblems on their jackets and everything. One day the Knights showed up at Garfield looking for the Flames. So all through third and fourth periods everyone was whispering, "The Knights are looking for the Flames! There's going to be a rumble!" Just like in the movies, everybody wanted to know what a rumble was. Jimmy decided right then he wasn't a Flame any more. When school was out, the Knights were there waiting in their cars and everything, and everybody went to see what was going to happen. Well, the Flames all snuck out the back doors. Jimmy got away too, and that was the end of the gang stuff.

Tremolo, Wah Wah and Gadgets

Jimmy loved electronic stuff. He was always

experimenting with electronic things, new gadgets, wah-wahs and fuzz tones. He'd listen to all the new songs. The sounds of rock 'n' roll were changing so tremendously then. Every time a new song came out, something would be different. When Jimmy started branching out, he'd put his own little twists and turns into the music. He'd make funny faces to go along with the unconventional sounds he was getting out of his guitar. He'd say, "Hey, Terry, listen to this one."

Jimmy would fool around with amplifiers to create new sounds. In the late fifties amplifiers had two devices for altering the timbre and tempo of sounds, an echo chamber, or reverb, and a tremolo switch. A lot of groups used what they'd call tremolo back then. Jimmy liked using the reverb to get a far-away effect.

Later on Jimmy used all kinds of gimmicks. On his albums he uses all of those switches and

THE YESLER TERRACE NEIGHBORHOOD HOUSE

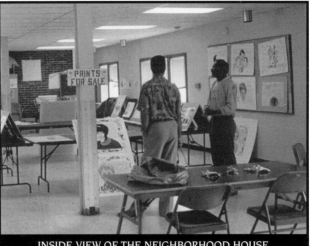
INSIDE VIEW OF THE NEIGHBORHOOD HOUSE

everything, that's why his sound is so electrifying. Electrifying Jimi Hendrix. He could make a guitar sound almost like a human. He liked to bend the strings and whine it and make it do anything. That's why the wah-wah pedal could almost make it talk.

Drugs Around Garfield

I know in one book about Jimmy, someone mentioned drugs in the area around Garfield. What little there was I didn't know about until later. There was a little deli around the corner from Garfield owned by a couple of tall, thin, good-looking Jewish brothers, and a heavy-set round guy. I'd go over there and buy these little sandwiches, salami and bologna. Turns out the guys were selling. I had no idea. I was naive about those things. Well, those guys got caught and went to jail. Now I believe their place is gone, but that could have been the place referred to in that other book about Jimmy. Stuff

like cough syrup with codeine was just coming out when I was getting out of high school. I don't know anything about Jimmy having anything to do with any kinds of drugs.

Seattle and Race Relations

Seattle was a good city. I think that Jimmy was able to get along with everybody because of his Seattle background. It made us more well rounded because we had all types of ethnic groups in our schools and in our neighborhoods. There were lots of positives. There was a lot of diversity. We were with Asians, Whites of all ethnic and religious types, Filipinos, Hawaiians and Blacks. So we had a chance to learn a little bit about everybody's background. We learned to converse with all types of people, and the diversity influenced our music. Seattle is a great city to come from as far as that's concerned, I think. The diversity made us more positive as far as getting

along with all people in the world, and it affected our music.

But the real world beyond where we grew up—down South and everything—Seattle didn't prepare us for that. There are people who are narrow minded. You're always going to have people like that. When we went out into the real world, it was a shock. But then the military throws you into that. With Jimmy's travels all around, I know he ran into it. Luckily, we had a little background from Seattle to help us, but it was a rude awakening when we got into the real world.

I ran into overt prejudice for the first time right after I was married, when I went to Amarillo, Texas for basic training in the Air Force. A friend and I decided to use our first passes to go across town to a movie. My friend was an Irish-American guy from Illinois.

After a long wait in line in front of the theater, it was finally my turn at the ticket window. The woman there looked nervous. I said, "How're you doing?" She said, "Sorry. I can't sell you a ticket." I said, "All sold out, huh?" She said, "No, it's not that." Her face turned red, so I asked, "What's wrong?" She said. "I'm sorry. But we can't allow people of your race to go in." I said, "People of my race?" She said, "That's right. It's a rule." I couldn't believe it. So I said, "But what about these Mexican guys? They're going in." She said, "Oh, they're okay. We consider them White. But—no Blacks. I'm sorry." So, I said, "Oh, I'm so sorry. I forgot I was in the South." It was a shock.

Jimmy Asks Terry to Join Him

Jimmy and I had always played together and we always dreamed about having a band together. We thought on the same wave length; we talked in the same little phrases; and we knew exactly what each other was saying.

We were such good friends, and we always thought that if one of us ever had a chance to sign a contract, it would be a natural progression for him to call me, or me to call him.

In 1966, when I was stationed in Sunnyvale, I got a letter from Jimmy asking me to join him. He said he had a trio with two gentlemen from England, and that he was making it BIG. He wanted an organ player, and he said, "Can you join us?" They were getting ready to cut an album, but he didn't have a piano player and that was the next thing he needed in his band. But I had just reenlisted for another four years, and you can't just quit the military unless you dream something up, you know, or get a dishonorable discharge, which would scar you for life.

I had no idea what he meant by "big." We used to use "really big" in such a subjective way. We'd be starving to death, but we'd say, "Hey, guys, this is the BIG time." So I didn't give Jimmy's comment a second thought. I told Jimmy I was really sorry, because I would have loved to do it. I thanked him for the offer, let him know how glad I was he was thinking of me, and wished him lots of luck. You should have seen my reaction a few months later when I saw his first album cover—the one where his hair's all kind of blown out and there's a light behind him. I was at a friend's house just browsing through his records. I couldn't believe it. That was how I found out what Jimmy meant by "big."

And so, who knows? If I had been able to be with him, maybe he'd still be alive today. Unfortunately, I was in the Air Force at that time. I was in Vietnam when Jimmy was at the peak of his

career, so we were out of touch. When I found out Jimmy was dead, I thought back to when he wrote me that letter and to when I had talked to him afterwards, and I felt so bad. My natural dream was to get out of the military and pursue that opportunity, to call him and say, "Hey, I'm out now and we can play and pursue the dream we had when we were kids."

But he died. It was so unfortunate because I noticed in his voice that he sounded kind of lonely. It's ironic that if you have a lot of money, it's no good unless you have somebody to appreciate it with. It was the same way with Jimmy. He had made it, but he had nobody there. His Seattle friends were not there, and neither was his family. He was making it, but he was lonely. He was making it, but he was in a little shell. And he was reaching out to find people to let them know, and get the applause from the people that he knew.

Jimmy was trying to find it on the road. For somebody who's running that fast, and progressing that fast, and just meeting people on the road, the anchor starts drifting. He was losing contact with the people he was raised with, the ones who represented his roots.

Tribute to Jimmy

From about the second or third grade, all the way until high school when Jimmy left, I don't think I could have had a better friend or a closer companion. I shared my life with him. He was more than a brother. We just clicked, spiritually and musically, and in so many ways. I feel fortunate that I had a chance in my life to appreciate somebody like Jimmy. Even though he's gone now, he knows, and I know, that it was a special thing. You can't buy that kind of thing. I have that in my heart, and I'm a happy individual because of that, and nobody can take that away from me.

Florence Johnson, Terry Johnson's Mother

I loved all the children, and we always had a houseful. The yard was set up so the kids could play. I was always so happy that Jimmy and Terry were doing their music. You never know what will touch a child's life, what will bring them fulfillment.

I'll never forget the time there were a lot of kids over and one of them said something unkind about Jimmy's worn-out shoes. Terry said, "Watch what you're saying. Jimmy's going to be a star some day. He's going to make a million bucks." Terry was very protective of Jimmy. I was so proud of him for saying that.

We had a picket fence, and sometimes I'd look out and see kids hanging on the picket fence outside the room where we had the piano. They'd be hanging onto that picket fence listening to the music coming from our home.

LESCHI PARK, SEATTLE

Jimmy Williams

"I remember a chalkboard mural Jimmy did in sixth grade—a Mexican village scene with a background of dusty orange and soft pink. In the foreground there was a powerful palomino carrying a rider in full Spanish regalia, charging right at the viewer. In contrast to the action, there was a man leaning up against a building, asleep, wearing an enormous, brightly colored sombrero. The contrast was startling. The mood he captured with details and colors was amazing for someone his age. One of the unique things about Jimmy was his fascination with colors."

Back in the fifties, when Jimmy Williams was singing gospel solos on Seattle's KTW radio station, Jimmy Hendrix was his biggest fan. "He used to tell me I was going to be famous," Williams recalls. "He'd come to my shows, listen to me on the radio, and say, 'Some day I'm gonna say, "Hey, that guy was my best friend." ' Funny thing is that when my voice changed, I stopped performing. I'd sing old ballads with Jimmy and Terry—the Perry Como, Dean Martin, Frank Sinatra variety—but I didn't do any more shows."

Williams wrote stories. "Great little stories," says his friend Pernell Alexander. "He used to bring them to my grandmother. We all knew he was going to be a writer. I think some kids were jealous—he was so good."

Eventually Williams joined the military, where he spent nine years in military intelligence. After a stint in Vietnam that earned him a bronze star, he was ready to reconnect with his past, especially with Jimmy Hendrix. He returned to Seattle in the summer of 1970 to learn that his friend was in Europe. Weeks later, Hendrix was dead.

Jimmy Williams studied political science for three years at Western Washington College. He has an unpublished manuscript titled *The New Feudal Order.* Reflective, soft-spoken, and verbal, Williams approaches life with a sense of commitment to humanity and a knack for global interpretations. He has worked as a grant writer and in the business machine industry. He has two daughters, Nina and Samantha, and one son, Jason. He lives in Seattle.

Jimmy's Seattle Roots

To know Jimmy, to have an accurate picture of him, you have to understand the environment we grew up in.

Seattle in the fifties was a very unique place. The original settlers were dreamers. They came here to make a better life. There was a feeling of tolerance that carried over. Our community was relatively protected from the outside world—like a safe haven—where the American dream was alive.

AL HENDRIX AND JIMMY WILLIAMS

We were raised in an integrated community in the central area, near Lake Washington. We grew up black and poor, but it wasn't the South or a big-city ghetto. We had a semi-sheltered, pastoral childhood. We had the lake and the woods, fantasy and music, good neighborhood schools, and Beaver Cleaver kid-play. And our music, of course. The music was always there.

In Seattle we knew covert prejudice, but it was after we left Seattle that we ran into the harsh realities of racism. When I joined the military, for example, and I met people from other parts of the country, I ran into real racism. As kids we hadn't figured out how we were going to overcome hardship, but we were confident we could find our place in society. Prejudice was a major issue for Jimmy. He was a genuinely compassionate, multi-faceted person, who wanted acceptance.

Ballads, Blues, Jazz, Muddy Waters

Jimmy liked the old ballads; he liked blues and jazz; he liked Ol' Muddy Waters, Louisiana-style music. He was really into that. I think mainly because Al, his father, had records that Jimmy probably heard a lot in those days. But he did take a real liking to it. When he became famous, that wasn't the music that he was famous for.

Jimmy and I basically liked the same kinds of ballads. I mean, we're talking about the middle fifties, right? Singers who were big in those days were people like Dean Martin, Perry Como, Nat King Cole, Sammy Davis, Jr., and Frank Sinatra, of course. For some reason, Jimmy always liked the songs that I did. Some of the music that we used to really like, we'd actually go out and buy the records. When he started playing guitar, and he didn't have an amplifier, he would ask me to sing a couple of Dean Martin songs

and he would play the background on it. He was literally training himself to back up a vocalist.

Meeting Jimmy

I met Jimmy in 1951, when we were third graders at Leschi Grade School. I think we were playing basketball at recess. We were just little kids. So he says, "Hey, you can dribble between your legs!" and I say, "Yeah, I learned that a while back, practicing in the backyard." That's how we became friends. Playing basketball. Basically, we had a lot of things in common, you know. We became little soul mates. We hung out together, we played marbles, and we shared little thoughts and things the way little kids did in those days. We joined the safety patrol together, and all that kind of stuff.

The Three Musketeers

Jimmy and I were really close for about ten years. I considered him my best friend. Our other closest friend was Terry Johnson. The three of us lived in the same neighborhood, a few blocks from each other, and went to school together. When we were in grade school, Jimmy, Terry, and I thought of ourselves as the Three Musketeers. We were pretty much inseparable. It was one for all and all for one. Just like in the old Gene Kelly/Van Heflin film. En garde, D'Artagnan. Meet any challenge and keep on laughing, even in the face of death itself.

We'd hang out a lot at Terry's house. His mom used to ask us how we were doing in school. I used to marvel at how pretty she was. We all appreciated the attention she gave us.

Hendrix's Support for Jimmy and Terry

In grade school, they would have talent shows every year to raise money for some little school festivals. Back then, of the three of us, Jimmy, Terry and me, Terry and I were the only ones interested in performing. But Jimmy, I don't know. He never, never showed any interest in those kinds of things in those days. He would show up at the shows, the little festival shows, and he was very supportive when Terry and I were in a show. Jimmy would show up and then he would say, "Hey, you guys were really great!" That was the kind of person he was, always supportive.

I remember when I was in a talent show at Leschi. I think I was in about the fifth grade, and I sang "Wanted," an old Perry Como ballad. I don't know if I was really that good or what, but everybody was pretty nice to me. The music teacher, Miss

Burton, said, "Oh, you're really great!" And Jimmy, when we would walk home, he'd say, "You can really sing! Why don't you sing that song? I just want to hear it again." Then he would come back again and say, "Could you sing that song for me?" "Sure, it's no problem." Until this day, Terry Johnson, who is still a good friend of mine, will call me and say, "Why don't you sing that song for me? Why don't you sing 'Wanted'?" Then I say, "Terry, grow up. We're getting old, you know."

There was a woman from Leschi named Mrs. Cooper, and I hope she's still alive because I'd love to look her up one of these days. She got me started singing on a radio program through one of the big downtown churches. I think it was the First Presbyterian. I used to sing on Sundays with a couple of other kids, throughout junior high school. I remember Jimmy coming up to me one day and he said, "You know, that was a really good show you did last night and you're going to be famous one of these days!" and he said, "Are we still going to be best friends?" "Sure, we're going to be best friends. We do everything together, don't we?" That's kind of ironic. He wanted to be completely supportive, and everything turned completely 180 degrees. He was the one with all of the talent and he became famous, and he's still my best friend. Those things are very ironic.

Pernell Alexander

Our friend Pernell was the one who inspired Jimmy to take up the guitar. Jimmy admired Pernell, and Pernell deserves credit for getting Jimmy started on the guitar. Pernell was quite a musician. We looked up to him. He was like an older brother—part of our family. It seemed like Jimmy and I were more naive. Pernell was sort of like the Fonz. If there was

anything we needed to know, we'd ask Pernell. Whatever he said carried the day. I remember thinking Pernell could talk Jimmy into doing just about anything.

Breakfast at Pernell's

There were many days when Jimmy and I would eat breakfast at Pernell Alexander's before school. Pernell's grandmother was one of the sweetest ladies I've ever known. She could always sense when we hadn't eaten. She'd say, "You boys want some breakfast?" And we'd say, "No, thanks. We're not hungry." Then she would set the table, get out the cereal and milk and tell us to come eat. It was just like a ritual. She took a real interest in us.

The Fighting Irish

When we played Little League football, all the guys on the team were Japanese or Black. Our name was

the Fighting Irish. That always made me laugh. Not an Irishman among us.

Affectionate Names

Affectionate names have different meanings in Jimmy's music. He used affectionate names from the time he was a little kid. Some were obvious; he called me Potato Chip because I used to eat potato chips when we'd hang out at Leschi Park. Other times he called me Jimmikins. His nickname for Terry was Terrikins. In his songs, when you hear the word "baby," the interpretation may not be only girlfriend, wife, or lover. It could mean friend. Or it may even have a more global meaning. It's important not to make quick assumptions because Jimmy uses a lot of symbolism.

Stories

In grade school I was inspired by little stories—like the one about the kid who gets a summer job in a doughnut factory and when he's not paying attention the doughnut machine spins out so many doughnuts that they're rolling out the door. I'd write adventure wonder stories, bind them in cardboard and make paper bag covers. Since there was a synchronism among us, Jimmy picked up on stories and wrote one called "Sabrina"—a play on Bambi—about a little deer.

Leschi Grade School and Growing up in Seattle

We had a very closely knit community. Leschi Grade School was a nicely run little neighborhood school on the western shore of Lake Washington. We went to neighborhood schools all the way through high school. Like our neighborhoods, the schools had a real dichotomy of economic and ethnic groups. It was evenly mixed, Asians, Blacks and Whites, probably a third of each.

Seattle was a very good place to grow up in many aspects. It was a quiet, family-oriented city, as opposed to other places in the country where racial issues were always very prevalent, in the forefront, you know. In Seattle the problems were there, but they were very subtle and there was a "live-and-let-live" policy. Racial issues weren't that big. Even though you could see certain things, and you felt certain things, we had an environment with multi-ethnic groups of people living in a small community. So, we were kind of sheltered and protected from other things that happened. We would get newspapers with things from down South—fighting for integration, people rioting, or some poor person getting hung—and say, "God, that's like another part of the world. It has nothing to do with Seattle." But, then, Seattle also had its own kind of subtle, de facto racist things. If you got out of the city proper, you know, you would see differences in attitude, if you were Black or of some minority group. I think those things really didn't become issues until we got further in school, like junior high school and high school.

No Money for Apples and Milk

There are some memories that are a little painful. Imagine something as simple as snack time at school. We could buy an apple for ten cents. Well, that may sound like a good thing, but if you don't have a dime, it's cruel. Kids don't understand those inequities. There was some insensitivity about poor people and poor kids in those days. Jimmy and I did discuss it a lot because a lot of the kids there were poor, but it was one of those things that you didn't talk about because it had bearing on how you got along with your peers. If you came right out and said, "God, we're so poor we can't even afford to buy snacks afterschool," or something. I mean, you just didn't talk about those things. But there were things that would bring those issues out.

I guess the benevolent apple growers here in the state had this thing about selling cheap apples to the school kids for a mid-morning snack. Everyday we had to come to school with about fifteen cents. I think it was a nickel for a little thing of milk and a dime for an apple. Someone in the class would carry a box of apples from one desk to the next. So Jimmy and I would joke about it. When the apples would reach him, he'd punch me in the back and say, "Hey,

Potato Chip! You want an apple?" So I'd say, "Not today, man, I'm saving my money for marbles."

And so we had to sit there and watch the other kids eat their apples and drink their milk. I thought that was basically kind of cruel because, if you're an adult and you can't afford something people will say, "Well, you can't afford it." But dealing with kids, I think it was a bad policy. Gosh, sometimes it was hard enough just to bring the quarter for lunch money every day. Well, those kinds of things did set you off to say, "Well, those guys must be poor, and those guys, they've got money everyday, so they must come from a higher income family or something." You don't want to be picked out and pointed out that way when you're growing up. It's very painful in a lot of ways.

Jimmy's Mom

I heard Jimmy talk about his mom only two or three times. We were careful not to ask about something that might hurt somebody's feelings. Actually, I thought Jimmy's mom was no longer living.

Jimmy the Artist

Jimmy had so much talent. If he hadn't devoted himself to music later on, he would have turned to art. Jimmy was an excellent artist. In grade school he drew a lot, little cartoons, action pictures, animals. Jimmy took a lot of satisfaction in drawing little pieces of art for people who'd say, "Can you draw me a cartoon?" And he was always very accommodating.

Jimmy had this thing about horses. He used to say, "If you want to draw, you gotta do horses first." So he drew reams of horses. I used to walk up to him and say, "Look, my little brother likes horses. Can

you draw me some of those nice horses you draw?"
He'd say, "Sure. What do you want them doing, you
know, running, or standing still, or what?" He could
draw all kinds of horses. He loved palominos. His
childhood symbol was a Pegasus.

The Mexican Mural

I remember a mural Jimmy did when we were in Mrs.
Stophenberg's sixth grade class at Leschi. It was a
full wall mural, on one of those big, wrap around
blackboards that go around the whole classroom.
He did a spectacular piece of art.

It was a Mexican village scene, really vivid and
colorful and full of details. The background was dusty
orange and soft pink. In the foreground there was a
powerful palomino carrying a rider in full Spanish
regalia. Jimmy had this thing about palomino horses.
Well, this horse seemed to be charging right at the

viewer. It was really beautiful. Then there was another person riding down the road on another palomino.

In contrast to the action, there was a man leaning up against a building, asleep, wearing an enormous, brightly colored sombrero. The contrast of the man asleep and the movement of the horses was startling. The mood that he captured with the use of details and colors was really amazing for someone his age. I mean, it was great, you know. One of the unique things about Jimmy was his fascination with colors. It was totally unique that a kid eleven or twelve years old could take something out of his imagination and draw it with such life-like presentation. And then that somebody could match and shade such hues and colors—magentas, you know—the way Jimmy could. And we're talking about chalk. We're not talking about watercolors or oils, or anything like that. He could blend colors so well. The mural scene was very powerful. I always thought that maybe he had some Mexican or Spanish heritage, because he had that knack for combining lively colors. Of course, it showed up later when he designed some of his costumes.

Jimmy's Attraction to Hispanic Culture

Jimmy's attraction to Hispanic culture was very unusual for a Black, even more so at that early age. He loved their use of vivid colors, especially the red and blue tones: magenta, violet, purple, deep rich blues. These colors were his trademark as a kid. Later he incorporated them into his wardrobe as an entertainer. They became his trademark as a performer.

I remember seeing a picture of Jimmy sitting on a stool with his guitar in this kind of Latin or Spanish regalia—the big hat with the feather sticking out of it, you know. I don't know where he got that from. It was part of his nature that he seemed to gravitate towards the Spanish culture. It could have been just a fascination with the colors, but then you also see the bandana, drapes, and the belts and the shiny tassels, and that's more of a Spanish or Latin type of dress. Of course, the hippies later on during our time wore other costumes like that. Maybe Jimmy was just a little bit ahead of his time.

Fantasy as a Protective Tool

For Jimmy there was a kind of protective, humorous fantasy. Fantasy and humor were essential tools that Jimmy used to help cope with painful aspects of life. At school, for example, we were painfully aware of economic inequities. We went to a neighborhood school, but it was an incredibly diverse

OPENING DAY BOAT PARADE: LAKE WASHINGTON, FOREGROUND PORTAGE BAY, BACKGROUND CASCADE RANGE, R. ARBORETUM & MONTLAKE DISTRICT, L. UNIV. OF WASHINGTON

neighborhood. We were poor, but less than a mile from where we lived there were incredible mansions overlooking the lake.

One of our teachers used to grill us about our diets. It was most likely a well-meant effort to stress the importance of proper eating habits, but the results were sometimes embarrassing for me and Jimmy and a few others. One morning she insisted that each kid tell what he or she had for breakfast. So we went around the room, and kids were saying things like Wheaties, scrambled eggs, and blueberry pancakes. Then she gets to Jimmy and he says, "I didn't have breakfast this morning." So she says, "Why not? Don't you know how important breakfast is, Jimmy Hendrix?" So then, really quietly, he says, "Well, all we had was eggs. And I don't like eggs."

Now I knew that wasn't true. Jimmy did like eggs. That was just his way of coming to terms with the fact that he hadn't eaten. Fantasy and humor were essential tools for him. He didn't want to feel sad, and he didn't want other people to feel sad. So he tried to protect himself and the people around him.

Fantasy at Leschi Park

It's possible that some of the little fantasies that we had when we were kids stayed with Jimmy all the way into his adult life. Most children live a portion of their world in fantasy, whether they're playing cowboys and Indians, or war games, or if they just want to block out the rest of the world when they are not coping very well with it.

As kids, Jimmy and I liked to play in Leschi Park. It's a woodsy, hilly, park with trails and dense vegetation. It's a great place for kids to play. I used to deliver papers early in the morning to the houses that were on the lake. Since we were buddies, Jimmy would often go with me. We'd pick up the papers at four or five o'clock in the morning, when it was still dark. The winding road through the woods at the park was like our own backyard, but at five in the morning you can't see what's lurking behind the bushes. It's a different ballgame. We felt like knights from the Middle Ages pitted against unknown dangers, and we had to be prepared to meet any challenge. Jimmy and I would load up our pockets with a supply of rocks in case we ran into monsters or aliens.

We'd seen all the little animals that lived in the woods, and in those days we weren't worried about real people, just space invaders and monsters. We'd seen "The Thing" and "Frankenstein." And of course there was that nagging worry about Dracula. We would imagine that these creatures were off in the woods. Sometimes we imagined we were being

LAGOON IN THE ARBORETUM

chased by space aliens, or ghouls, or mysterious ghosts.

Remember the movie about the aliens with big eyes who kidnapped people and dragged them off to caves? Well, it seemed reasonable to assume that the aliens might hide out in the woods at Leschi Park. It was quite scary down there at that hour, but the games we played got us through the early morning paper route. I was trying to make a living selling papers, you know. So there was that kind of fantasy. Then there were the things we fantasized that came from Native American Indian history.

We liked the stories about local Indians and settlers. I remember one about Chief Sealth that impressed us, about the Indian culture that lived here in Seattle, long before we got here. We'd imagine the Indians on Lake Washington, landing at Leschi Park. It's true. They really did. The story we

liked about Chief Sealth was that he and his tribe were friends of the settlers. Supposedly, there was a minor war between the settlers and another tribe of Indians. The Indians were going to come across Lake Washington in canoes and attack the settlers here at Leschi Park. Chief Sealth warned them about the raid, and saved the settlers.

Lake Washington

For both me and Jimmy, the lake was a big draw. It was a magical place. It had a calming effect on us. Even now, when I'm feeling down, a drive along Lake Washington lifts my spirits. The Leschi area where we grew up was a giving place. It has a kind of wild beauty—deep dark greens, madrona trees, scarlet berries. You go down by the lake and the ducks are there; you can hear the gentle lapping of the waves on the shore. There's a lot of history there. We

learned about it at school and somehow that made it all more magical.

Fantasy and the Right-Brain Perspective

Some people talk about Jimmy living in a sort of fantasy world. I guess people who are very sensitive tend to create worlds, or look at the world the way that they want to envision it—and maybe that's what Jimmy did. He looked at the world as being a little better place. You know that concept about the left-side-of-the-brain people and the right-side-of-the-brain people? Jimmy might have been one of those right-brained people, caught up in concepts and artistic things. In order to be creative, fantasy was the way he had to deal with the world. Whose perception is right, anyway? I mean, if you look at the world in a very physical and very practical manner, that's your perception, and that's probably real for you. But, it's just like someone saying, "Look at that sky, it's really blue," and someone else coming up and saying, "It's light blue." Your perception of the way you look at the world gets you through life.

Jimmy did have a side of him where he saw things in fantastical ways. Maybe Michael Jackson does the same thing. He likes fantasy, and he is an artist. He's a great artist, like Jimmy was. They're necessary, because we get a different perspective on the world because they paint it, or they play it, or they sing it, or they wear it. We learn from them, and that's what we use in our culture for music and fashion and literature.

Boy Scouts

Touching on a couple of lighter issues, when we were growing up, we used to hang out at a soda fountain store at 34th and Cherry Street, not too far from where we lived. It was owned by a Black guy named Mr. Slaughter, who was a real mentor for the neighborhood kids. I considered him a good friend. At his soda fountain he had a pool table and a juke box. He also had a theater at 29th and Cherry. Anyway, he asked me if I could get some of my friends together to help him put together a charter for this Boy Scout troop for the neighborhood. It sounded like fun. I think I was about eleven years old at the time.

I said, "Sure." So I went back to school and asked a few of our closest friends; Pernell Alexander, Ronelle MacGraw, Freddie Dangerfield, Terry, Jimmy, and I created a core group for this Scout troop. We brought on a few other people in the class and I remember we always had hassles getting enough people at the meetings. The meetings were on Wednesday night at seven o' clock and they had just started this new Walt Disney series, and no one wanted to miss it. So they would always say they had something else to do. We ended up changing the meeting night, just to avoid the Disney conflict. We were the initial core group, so we got the best jobs out of it. I became the patrol leader, and Jimmy was the assistant patrol leader.

I remember the day we went for our camping merit badge. Being that we were from the inner city, and we couldn't get outside of the city, I decided that we would have to do the camping badge in this little community park, not far from the school. It was a nice little park, really pretty, and full of trees. I said, "God, it would really suit our needs perfectly and we wouldn't have to walk too far, and we wouldn't have to worry about getting out of the city." So, everybody agreed, and we put our uniforms on that Saturday, and put our little backpacks on, and brought along all of the things we needed to go on a camping trip. We

THE WOODS AT LESCHI PARK

marched single file down this street until we got to this park, and we found a nice clearing, and we said, "Okay, we're going to set up here!" And we divided up the tasks. We dug a latrine, baptized it, put up a tent, and found a place for a campfire.

We had a heck of a time finding dry wood to build a fire, but Freddie finally came up with some twigs. Once we got the thing going, it was more smoke than fire. We pulled out our little cooking kits, and we started cooking our hot dogs, pork and beans. We were having a real good time. After a couple of hours we had the whole place smoked up. Then we cleaned the place up, we covered up the holes, we put out the fire, and we packed up. We were feeling good that we'd done all the merit badge requirements. What we didn't know was that one of the neighbors had seen the smoke, and called the fire department. We were marching up the hill,

when a fire truck roared by. We were saying, "God, where are they going? There must be a big fire somewhere!" We found out later that it was illegal to build fires in the park, and you surely weren't supposed to be camping there. Anyway, we got out of there just ahead of the fire chief, I guess. Somehow the Scoutmaster found out about it, and he suspended us for about a month. Anyway, those were the days of our Boy Scout troop. That was kind of fun.

Girlfriends

I'm going to date myself here by talking about girlfriends. Teenagers were a lot more naive in those days than they are now, as far as dating and hanging out with the opposite sex. Jimmy was a very shy person, and we were both probably more childlike than someone of an equivalent age right now. So it wasn't like dating or setting up dates the way kids do now. You'd go to a party or something, and you

would stand over in a corner and hope that some girl would say "Hi." And that was a real big deal in those days. That probably lasted all the way until we were sixteen or seventeen. I'm sure that he had girlfriends that he would probably meet out somewhere, or he would talk to on the phone, because that was another thing that we used to do. We would, well, if Al was gone we would get on the phone and say, "Hey, why don't we call Judy and see what she's doing!" We'd call and she'd answer the phone.

"Hello, Judy?"

"Yeah, who's this?"

"You don't know, do you?"

"No, who's this?"

"Well, you don't know, so—bye!"

And that was really, well, as corny as that sounds, that was the kind of things that you did in those days. So, that part of our life wasn't, you know, wasn't that big as far as dating and that kind of thing. We did more kid things. We played in bands. I played in a marching band; Jimmy played in a band. We hung around with the fellows; we did all kinds of fellow things like going down to the beach and throwing rocks in the water, and daring someone to jump in with their clothes, or something like that and worrying about getting in trouble later. I don't know. Dating just wasn't a real big issue in those days.

The Shroud of Turin

Jimmy was very accepting of other people's beliefs. I remember stopping for him at a relative's house, an aunt, I think, where there was a picture on the wall of the Shroud of Turin. Someone said, "That's an authentic picture of Jesus Christ." With the wisdom of my years, I said, "Now wait a minute. They didn't have cameras back then."

I don't know if I really associated the significance of that issue, but I was very skeptical and I said, "Well, obviously it's probably something that somebody either drew or faked or something." And he said no, that he believed it was a real picture and that, you know, it was real. And, I guess, the unique part of this issue is that I can't say for sure whether he believed that the Shroud was real or that the picture was real or not, except he was the kind of a person who was sensitive enough not to damage somebody else's beliefs. And so he handled it quite deftly. He just said that he believed that it might have been a true picture.

All during the time that I knew Jimmy that's the way he dealt with things; he wasn't a confrontationalist at all. He always tried to find ways to mend attitudes or grievances, and that's one of the things people should always know about him.

Jimmy Decides to Join the Army

The next-to-the-last time I saw Jimmy was at Garfield, when he came to find me in the library to say that he was quitting school to go in the Army. I thought it was kind of strange. "You've only got a year to go, what are you quitting for?" And he says, "Yeah, I just want to get out of here and go in the Army." And then I think he went to tell Terry that he was quitting school, and he might have expressed more of the reasons to Terry than he did to me. Jimmy, I guess, was having some problems either socially or with teachers in school, and you would never know this by talking to him because he never talked about problems. He would always show you this front that he was happy, and everything was fine. But, later on, I found out that there were probably things that were bothering him at that time.

Contrary to His Basic Nature

Some of the things Jimmy gained fame for were against his basic nature. You hear a lot of derogatory things, that he was heavy off into drugs and sex, or that he was one of those insensitive people who would do anything to make money. Some people saw aspects of violence about him because during a few of his shows he destroyed his guitar, but I think that was all contrived by people who were promoting him, or promoting an image. None of that was ever a part of Jimmy's nature or attitude.

Jimmy's Message

Contrary to what some fans think, Jimmy's most significant song is not "Purple Haze." To know Jimmy, you have to look at songs like "Straight Ahead." Some of his poems and his lyrics are profoundly meaningful. He writes about freedom, unity and love.

There's the line, "The best love to have is the love of life." There were times when he was leading you somewhere for fun, but the core of his philosophy is serious, and that's what needs to be looked at. There were things that troubled him socially that he commented on. A lot of his poetry and lyrics have to do with universal love and appreciation for people who are different. People gravitated to him because of his completely empathetic attitude. Jimmy was one of the most compassionate people in the world.

Jimmy's Poetry

Sometimes Jimmy saw things globally, and spoke in symbols. Some of the poetry and some of the lyrics that he wrote early on were cryptic. Most of what I read told me that there were some things troubling Jimmy socially, that he didn't like and that he

wanted to comment on. Jimmy was one of the most liberal people in the world. Look at the fact that his band members were White. But he felt rejected by American society. Those were cruel times in the United States. He had to go to England to become a star.

Most of his poems had to do with some kind of universal love, or appreciation of people who were different. The lyrics and the poetry didn't seem to have any bounds to them; it was just what he wanted to express and anyone who wanted to listen could take something from them. Some of it was serious; some of it was real serious. He saw a darker side of things. But sometimes he was quite playful, you know. Jimmy played with his lyrics, he played with his music, and that was just his nature and his character. He could do things with a very tongue-in-cheek attitude. Of all the people I know, Jimmy was probably one of the most fun-loving, humanitarian people I've ever met. It all came from this attitude. He liked to play, he loved to give people nicknames, he always saw positive things in people. I know this sounds like some kind of speech or something, but those are the things that are really unique about him.

Finding out Jimmy was Famous

I was stationed in Panama when I found out Jimmy was famous. I had just gotten off work. I worked what we called a mid-shift, from midnight to seven in the morning, and I went to the cafeteria. The PX was adjoining the cafeteria and I went in there and picked up a magazine, a *Newsweek* or a *Time*. I should have kept it because it was probably something I could write dates on and say, "God, this is when I discovered that my best friend was one of the biggest rock singers in the world." I tucked the magazine under my arm and I went back to my room and I kicked back to read some articles. Then I came to this one page and it had a picture of Jimmy standing there with this wide-brimmed hat on and with his guitar and it said, "The most exciting, new, up-and-coming rock star in the United States is Jimi Hendrix." I said, "Jimi Hendrix? I knew a guy by the name of Jimi Hendrix. He was my best friend in Seattle. But he didn't spell his name like that." So I started reading the article. It said that he went to Garfield High School, he was born in Seattle, and his dad is named Al. I said, "That's my best friend!" And I said, "Wait a minute!" and I looked at it again and I said, "Oh, wow! This is unbelievable!" I ran out of the room and I was trying to find somebody that I could wave down and say, "Hey! My best friend is in this magazine; this is the kid I grew up with." I caught a couple of people, and I said, "This is my best friend, this is Jimi Hendrix." They said, "Jimi Hendrix, that's not your best friend. Come on. You're pulling, my collar." I said, "Yeah, truthfully, that's my best friend." I guess they half-heartedly believed it because I was from Seattle.

So I made a pact with myself. I was on my way to Vietnam. I said, "Well, when I get back I'm just going to have such a great time. I'm going to look up my best friend." You know, spiritually Jimmy and I were very close for ten years. I spent my year in Vietnam kind of planning how we were going to hang out and stuff when I got back. I was so excited about it. I wrote Jimmy a letter, but I don't think he ever got it. The rest of the story is history. He died just after I got home.

BAND OF GYPSYS: BILLY COX, JIMI HENDRIX, BUDDY MILES

The Music Scene: Interviews

Pernell Alexander   Anthony Atherton

Robert Green   Luther Rabb

Lester Exkano   Walter Harris

Junior Heath   Barbara Heath Evans

Webb Lofton   Charles Woodbury

Bill Eisiminger   Donald Williams

Lacy Wilbon   Manual Stanton

Curtis Simuel

HENDRIX SEATTLE BANDS

The Velvetones	The Rocking Kings
Jimmy Hendrix	Jimmy Hendrix
Pernell Alexander	Lester Exkano
Anthony Atherton	Walter Harris
Robert Green	Junior Heath
Walter Jones	Webb Lofton
Luther Rabb	Charles Woodbury*
	Terry Johnson**
	Curtis Simuel***

*Sometimes Robert Green substituted for Charles Woodbury.

**Terry Johnson played for only a brief time with the Rocking Kings. Then he played with Luther Rabb, Bill Eisiminger, and Allan Wyler in the Stags.

***Curtis Simuel substituted for Lester Exkano, and later replaced Charles Woodbury

THE ORIGINAL DAVE LEWIS COMBO
CLUB BIRDLAND   MAY 1957

DAVE LEWIS   BARNEY HILLIARD   GEORGE GRIFFIN   J.B. ALLEN   JOHN GRAY

The Music Scene

*I*n the beginning—there was the Dave Lewis Combo. Well, not really. Dave and his musicians imitated other artists, and they had their idols. But for Hendrix and his Central District peers, who were five-to-eight years younger than Dave and his circle, the Dave Lewis Combo was the beginning of something new. They echo the same litany. "Dave Lewis was our model," says musician Luther Rabb, a childhood neighbor of Jimmy's whose group Ballin' Jack opened shows for Hendrix in 1970. "Dave's the godfather of the Seattle sound." Though I've been a sometime drummer and pianist—I am not a musicologist. Volumes could be written about the Seattle music scene. The intention of this introduction is to set the tone and the background for the interviews with the musicians who played with Jimmy Hendrix in junior high and high school.

In the fifties, a definable Seattle sound was bubbling up—and the Dave Lewis Combo was the catalyst for its creative explosion. "The Dave Lewis combo was more advanced musically than any other Seattle group," says Rabb. "They knew all about intervals and overtones and music theory. They were my first impression of what a band should be. They had the fewest guys, and they made the biggest music."

"In the forties, it was the big band sound," says Barney Hilliard, a graduate of Garfield and the University of Washington Law School, who played saxophone with Dave's group, and now plays with Carousel. "In the fifties we had small combos, three or four people. Rhythm was central to our music—a heavy back beat and shuffles. Our drummer—George Griffin—has been a legend in Seattle."

"I know I have a gift, but Dave Lewis brought it out," says Griffin. "When we were coming up, Dave was a very shy person. But Dave is a genius. He has the ability to be where Quincy Jones is or higher. For me, Dave is the essence of the Seattle sound. The Dave Lewis Combo was the transition from rhythm and blues and rock to funk. Rhythm was important in all of our music. When I was at Garfield, the first good drummer I worshipped was Ron Yoshida. We called him 'Buddy Rich' because his drum solos were like Buddy Rich, but he wouldn't ever play solos in the Battles of the Bands. Ron and I and Billy Ishida, who was a close friend of mine, played in the Garfield band together. Rhythm was a big part of our lives."

"The Seattle sound was more rhythm than anything else," says Pernell Alexander, another childhood friend of Jimmy's, who became a professional musician. "We liked a driving rhythm.

GEORGE GRIFFIN AND THE FRANTICS, SEATTLE

CAROUSEL

The rhythm sections of our bands had drums and a rhythm guitar."

Seattle physician Allan Wyler, who went to Meany and played drums with the Stags, comments, "The music scene here was dominated by Black musicians, primarily rhythm and blues groups. There was little influence by any White musicians. It was not like the Beach Boys' music in California. The Seattle sound was typified by the Dave Lewis Combo, the Playboys, and the Frantics."

"Those were the three most popular city-wide bands when we were in high school. In Tacoma it was the Wailers and the Checkers," adds Bill Eisiminger, a classmate of ours who jammed with Jimmy in Seattle basements, and was the Stags' bass player. "The Checkers had two particularly gifted players— Joe Johansen on guitar, and Mike Mandell, a blind keyboard player. In central Seattle we always looked

first to the Dave Lewis Combo. The Seattle sound basically revolved around rhythm and blues. Seattle had the duo sax—two saxophones—which gave it a different sound, some great harmonies, as well as occasional counterpoint. Both the Dave Lewis Combo and the Rocking Kings used the duo sax. Not many others did. Our band did when Anthony Atherton would play with Luther. Ron Holden's song 'Love You So' is important to Seattle music history. Ron sang with the Playboys and later recorded the song with the Thunderbirds. It was a national hit. Dave Lewis wrote some great pieces that were big hits, and he and his band made 'Louie Louie' popular. Then we all played 'Louie Louie'—everybody loved it."

"In fact," adds Bob Hendrix, Jimmy's cousin (son of Pearl and Frank Hendrix), "'Louie Louie' was so big here for so long that it was proposed as the official song for the state of Washington. In 1985 the proposal

was submitted as a House Resolution Bill, and in 1986 as a State Senate Resolution. When the second resolution was defeated, Booth Gardner, who was governor of the state of Washington at the time, made a proclamation in which 'Louie Louie' became the unofficial state rock song."

Greg Payne, the Assistant Supervisor in the Bill Room in Olympia, remembers the day. "There was a big celebration for 'Louie, Louie' Day on the Capitol steps. Seattle celebrity Ross Shafer, ex-host of 'Almost Live,' presided over the program, Paul Revere and the Raiders played on the steps, and the event was filmed by 'That's Incredible.' It was a blast. All of the staff members were dancing to 'Louie Louie' on the steps."

The December, 1957, *Washington Survey*—the Washington Junior High School newsletter—lists the Richard Berry version as #3 on the top ten. Rhythm here in Seattle was a heavy sound. We used to call it a kicking sound."

"The Seattle jungle beat made people move," says Rabb. "It was great because it could go with anything. People learned to dance to it. It's a syncopated rhythm in six- eight. If a drummer couldn't play the jungle beat, he didn't make it. Now it's the in thing—called the New Jack Swing. But it's what we were doing thirty years ago—it's the Seattle jungle beat."

"The first person I heard in Seattle doing what was called the jungle beat, was Jimmy Pipkin," says Lacy Wilbon, a Garfield graduate who occasionally practiced guitar with Hendrix. "Pipkin graduated from Garfield in '58 or '59. He had heard a rhythm in New Orleans that he liked, and he reworked it, added nuances and perfected it. The term 'jungle beat'

makes me cringe because certain people in the music media gave it a negative connotation, as if it were something to be ashamed of. But it was inspirational and rhythmically precise. It was a positive, happy sound that made me want to put on my dancing shoes."

When I asked other people to speculate about the source of the "jungle beat," someone guessed it was New York. I asked Barney Hilliard.

"What we were playing in Seattle was not a New York sound," says Hilliard. "We weren't influenced by New York. Occasionally we heard musicians who came through Seattle, but mostly we were all influenced by records. For example, we got "Louie Louie" off the original record by Richard Berry. We were doing it at Birdland back in 1958. The pioneer rhythm players here were Tommy Adams and George Griffin."

George inspired many younger drummers. When Alex Palmer, the owner of the Black and Tan nightclub, painted GEORGE GRIFFIN in 8-foot-high letters across the side of the building, George became a Seattle hero. He embodied the universal language of rhythm.

George Griffin and I sat in a Long Beach coffee shop two days after my brother told me to call Barney, who told me where to find George. This book has come together as a serendipitous odyssey. Seattle was really a small town, a handful of separate, small communities and we belonged to the central area, the Garfield community. We were a small circle then, and we're a small circle now. It is that community anchor, that connection, that has allowed this project to unfold. People leave me messages to call this person, or that person, and new material flows like a river. Or as Luther Rabb says, sometimes

THE LAGOON IN THE ARBORETUM

I tug people in. Whatever reasons people have for opening up, this project is clearly one that could go on and on. Meeting George Griffin felt like a signal for completion. For weeks I'd been immersed in memories of rhythms, rain, the mountains, the birds, the lake, and the lagoon in the Arboretum where as a child my soul felt at home. When George told me that before he goes to sleep he listens to a recording of rhythms, birds and rain, that he creates best in Seattle, and that he always liked to go down to the lagoon, I knew I was on the home stretch. In some ways, I felt as though I were listening to my own voice.

"Rhythm is earthy, haunting, and hypnotizing," says George. "My work is sacred. I always say, 'God, I give you my life.' Rhythm is my heartbeat. When I was a kid in New Orleans I heard a lot of rhythms. I liked to listen to my own heart. Rhythm releases

anxiety. It's healing. It's a universal language that everybody understands. It can put you in a trance— or make you want to move."

Across the globe, rhythm connects us, to ourselves, to God, and to each other. That connection, that link, makes us know we are not separate; we are not alone. A young man I know once thought he was dying. He lay despondent in a hospital bed. Then he heard a tapping on the wall behind his bed. It puzzled him. He heard it again. It awakened his sense of playful curiosity. He stretched his hand to the wall and tapped a rhythm with his knuckles. On the other side of the wall the rhythm was repeated. A rhythmic conversation began that woke something up inside him, reconnecting him to life beyond himself. Gypsy flamenco dancers draw life in its most passionate form out of stillness, by invoking rhythm. My "native Seattle rhythms"

resonate with the rhythms of the flamenco artists of Andalucia, the Yoruba priests of Nigeria, and the Blue Men of the Goulamine; with Native American and Asian music, and with modern groups like Azumah, Ladysmith Black Mombazo and Johnny Clegg of South Africa, Oladum and Timbalada of Bahia, Brazil, and Babatunde Olatunji's eclectic Drums of Passion. As a student at Meany and Garfield, I was relieved not to be the only irrepressible finger tapper. I learned a lot of rhythms by listening to the guys tap rhythms back and forth— with their fingers and pencils on the edges of their desks. Jimmy was a table tapper too. One of Garfield's favorite rhythms came from a Dave Lewis piece called "J. A. J."

" 'J. A. J.' was a big hit in Seattle," says Eisiminger. "It was named after Jerry Allen, Jive Ass Jerry. Everybody loved it. It had about ten more

THE JIMI HENDRIX EXPERIENCE, SEATTLE

THE JIMI HENDRIX EXPERIENCE, JIMI HENDRIX, MITCH MITCHELL AND NOEL REDDING

chords than other pieces, and a cycle of fifths that was unusual." When Bill played "J. A. J." for me on his piano, I was transported back more than thirty years and taken on an exotic global journey. "J. A. J." playfully twists and turns in and out on its own structure, using intervals that sound Middle Eastern. It is so catchy, unpredictable and light-hearted that I fall in love with it instantly every time I hear it.

Another danceable Dave Lewis piece was "David's Mood"—a take-off on "Louie, Louie," according to Dave. "It has the same duh-duh-duh, da,da, but it's heavier. It worked to get people out on the floor to dance," he says. Another popular Lewis tune was "Little Green Thing," which he recorded on a 45 with another instrumental called "Candido" on the flip side. Luther Rabb comments, "Dave's 'Little Green Thing' was a cool thing—everybody wanted to play it." Dave Lewis and his father, who gave music lessons,

are credited throughout the interviews in this section for the artistic and creative guidance they gave to Seattle musicians. "We idolized Dave," says Terry Johnson. "He was a mentor for Seattle keyboard players. Dave could play so fast. Thirty-second notes were easy for him. The timing of his presence in the music scene was crucial for those of us who played the piano back then. We always had to check out if the place where we were going to play had a piano, and if so how far we'd have to move it. If a place didn't have a piano, we felt stuck. So the fact that Dave played the Hammond B-3 organ was crucial. I remember when the Paramount Theater—owned by his brother Ulysses— had a 50-piece house band, and Dave did the arrangements. He was great at arrangements."

I met with Dave Lewis twice at his home in Seattle. A modest, soft-spoken man, Dave is reluctant to accept all the praise; he credits his father

for his knowledge of music. "He was very strict with me. He'd say things like, 'Know this by tomorrow or I won't work with you anymore.' So I'd stay up and study, because I took the threats seriously. He was not an affectionate man, but I'm grateful to him because by junior high I knew a lot about music theory and arranging."

A number of Jimmy Hendrix's friends took lessons from Dave's father. "My dad played the guitar," says Dave. "My parents worked at Boeing for many years, but music was always a part of our home life. Quincy Jones and his family were neighbors and friends of ours in Bremerton, across the Sound. Both of our families moved to Seattle when we were kids. I think I was five."

Quincy was about the same number of years older than Dave as Jimmy Hendrix was younger; both were a presence in Dave's life, but with different

DAVE LEWIS, SEATTLE, 1994

peer groups. Dave took a deep sigh as he thought about Jimmy. "You know, Jimmy Hendrix was way ahead of his time," he said. "He used to come to listen to us at the Birdland. He'd always be there in the front, listening intently. Then he'd say, 'Dave! Hey, Dave, can I sit in?' So I'd say, 'Sure.' But whenever he'd start playing something experimental, people would stop dancing. They didn't know what was going on. They weren't ready for what he was doing. They wanted to dance. So then I'd have to ask Jimmy to stop, so people could get back to dancing. It was awkward. People didn't understand. I loved Jimmy's music. When his first album came out, I played some of his songs with my group."

Mike Tagawa, a classmate who used to hang out with Jimmy at lunchtime, went with me to visit Dave one Saturday afternoon. For Mike and me, Hendrix evokes early memories that are everyday, ordinary

and comfortable, while the name Dave Lewis brings back awe. That afternoon we met with the man—and then we listened to the legend. Dave got out his portable keyboard to play us some favorite tunes. Magic came alive as his hands danced across the keys.

When he stopped playing, Dave commented on the current music scene. "It's changed so much," says Dave. "There are very few places where people can go to dance these days. It's a shame. Most people love to dance. Getting people on the dance floor was a priority of mine. And lyrics are so different today. Most of them are not inspirational. We used to write about love and things. The only song I ever recorded that I sang was 'The Tree.' You know the poem, 'I think that I shall never see, a poem as lovely as a tree.' That poem inspired me so much, I had to sing it."

In central Seattle in the fifties and early sixties, rhythm, song and movement were always there to

nurture and uplift. Even under the worst circumstances, there were artists among us who were fully committed to putting on the show. Bill Eisiminger remembers playing with George Griffin the night JFK was assassinated. "November 22, 1963. I heard the devastating news that morning on campus at Seattle University. The Stags dance scheduled for that night was canceled and I ended up going with Luther out north to the Owl Tavern on Highway 99—just south of Everett—to play with George Griffin and Ron Holden. Playing music for the large, despondent crowd of people was kind of a healing thing. They were crying away their blues. And it was good to get out of town. But in another way it was strange. I'd never played in a tavern before. It was such a contrast to the mood of the day. There was a part of me that felt like we shouldn't be playing music. Maybe silence would have been better. But I did appreciate the opportunity to play with George. At that time in Seattle he was the premiere drummer around for rock and blues."

"In the late fifties we were playing rhythm and blues and rock'n'roll," says Barney Hilliard. "Then there was a transition. There was a shift to more of a rock sound, and groups got larger. I remember when my little brother Hartzell would listen to the Supremes and I'd think how different it was."

Jimmy Hendrix left Seattle in January, 1961 to join the paratroopers. Several years later, George Griffin met up with Jimmy in New York. "I went to a club in Manhattan where Jimmy had been hanging out. I was sitting at the bar when he walked in. He spotted me right away. 'George Griffin!' he said. 'What are you doing here?' I told him I was in New York with Bobby Taylor and the Vancouvers. 'You want to play?' he said. I said, 'Yeah.' It was really

funny. We started playing and I didn't know what Jimmy was playing. I thought it was a little jazz, a little funk, a little of everything, so I started playing, and to this day I always say it was the first time fusion was ever played. People were going crazy. We were playing so many different combinations of things and people were in awe, saying, 'What is this?' That was the highlight of my life. I know somebody in that audience had a tape recorder and got a tape recording of it. That's the last time I saw Jimmy. We said goodbye, and the next thing I knew he was dead. It was devastating."

Is it possible to define the impact that Jimmy Hendrix has had? I'm not sure it is.

"It's impossible to overstate his impact," says Robert Totty, a San Diego guitarist and music teacher. "Hendrix was the first guitarist who captured the essence of the blues and brought it into the rock

genre. Stevie Ray Vaughan captured the spirit, the tone of the blues, and he is the main reason blues has become popular today. Stevie Ray Vaughan was influenced first and foremost by Hendrix. Hendrix electrified the blues. If it weren't for Hendrix, a lot of music that came later simply wouldn't be."

Hendrix and his friends listened to a lot of rhythm and blues on the radio. The Seattle giant of R & B was Bob Summerrise, a popular disc jockey, who ran a record store called Summerrise of Seattle that specialized in R & B. When Hendrix was in high school, Summerrise broadcast a rhythm and blues program from nine to twelve every night on KQDE. I asked Bob what motivated him to promote music. "Music is therapeutic," he said. "It's vital for the soul. In those days we didn't call it soul music, we called it rhythm and blues." In 1947, shortly after he moved from Los Angeles to Bremerton, Summerrise started a volunteer radio program, one night a week. Later a popular Seattle station [KRSC, which later became KAYO] recruited him. He worked for a while in Tacoma, at KMO, and then at KTAC, after getting his engineer's license. He and his wife opened the music store in 1952.

Summerrise believes in music education. "The tastes of the young people of today will govern the music of tomorrow, and if they hear enough good music, they will grow to like it. To appreciate modern jazz, a person must have a background in all kinds of music, particularly rhythm and blues. It's like a flower that must have roots before it can bloom." He goes on to say, "In the United States, we as a people are contributing so much to a world of music that has its roots in soul music. Music itself is an expression of freedom, both individually and collectively. When

we tie the ideas of freedom to music, we contribute in a very positive way."

According to his friends and family members, Jimmy also learned about "soul music" from his dad, records, the radio, friends and neighbors. One source was the father of some friends, John "Jimmy" Williams, who knew how to put his emotions into song. Jimmy and Mr. Williams would sit out on the older man's front porch together on 27th Avenue, immersed in music.

Totty knows he is one of countless people whose lives have been changed in a deeply personal way because of Hendrix. "Many beautiful relations spawned in my life because of him. That initial conversation, the spark that has bonded me with many people, not just with guitarists, has been a connection to Hendrix. Students as young as nine or ten to players in their forties and fifties come to me

to learn Hendrix licks. All of them learn the Hendrix chord—the dominant 7th sharp 9—as a valuable part of their guitar playing. I have students who come to me carrying old Hendrix albums and ask, 'What's this stuff?' I say, 'That's *the* stuff.' Hendrix has profoundly influenced them. I tell my students, 'Hendrix is a storybook of sound, a film for your ears. His guitar was an extension of his spirit'.

In terms of equipment, the use of the Marshall stack is one definable Hendrix influence on musicians and bands that have followed him. Pete Townshend of The Who invented the idea for the stack and took it to Jim Marshall, who was the technical guide. Townshend ordered eight twelve-inch speakers mounted in a cabinet. Marshall made it, but Townshend's roadies said,"This is too heavy." So they cut it in half, and put four speakers in each cabinet, stacked them one on the other, and put the amp head on top. When Hendrix decided to use that set-up, he used a straight cabinet on the bottom, and a slant cabinet on the top. That's basically how the Marshall stack, as perfected by Hendrix, has become an industry standard.

"Hendrix was also the king of the wah pedal, using it and other effects to create his signature sound," says Totty. "He and his engineer Eddie Kramer were pioneers in the studio, using multi-track recording, slowed-down voices and backward techniques."

Has anyone matched Hendrix with the guitar? "I don't think there's anyone today who can play like Jimmy," says Totty. "People get close, but no one quite gets it all. Not many people breath and live through their instruments these days. A lot of MTV is eye candy and the music is lackluster. It's synthesized and digitized, and simply not interesting. None of it

is on a par with what Hendrix was doing twenty-five years ago. With Hendrix, you don't need a video."

It feels like music is making a shift. I agree with Dave Lewis who thinks that young people need something more than grunge and rap. Something new and inspirational that draws on Hendrix and his roots is already blossoming. As Dave Lewis's wife Linda says, "We're entering the Age of Aquarius. I am very hopeful."

The eleven interviews that follow include all of the musicians who Jimmy played with in the Velvetones and the Rocking Kings—except for Walter Jones—two other musician friends, and comments from two of the musicians' mothers and one's sister. I regret not locating Jimmy's buddy Sam Johnson, who lives in Germany, or Walter Jones, who is somewhere in Seattle. "Walter was such a friendly guy," says Eisiminger. "He always had a good smile

for you." None of the people included here have granted interviews for publication before. I am deeply appreciative of their willingness to preserve their individual memories and collective stories for generations to come. When my friend Barbara Heath Evans enthusiastically exclaimed, "You did it! You've brought in the flock!" I thought, "God did it, not me. I was only here to coordinate it."

Pernell Alexander

Pernell Alexander was born in Washington, D.C., lived in Baltimore, and moved to Seattle with his grandmother on Labor Day, 1952, when he was nine years old. He met Jimmy Hendrix at Leschi Grade School. "Jimmy admired Pernell," says Jimmy Williams. "To us, Pernell was worldly. He was like an older brother. Whatever he said, we took notice."

Pernell has devoted most of his life to music. He has played with The Boss Four, Jimmy Reed, Lightning Hopkins, Big Mama Thornton, Little Richard, Bill Withers, and Billy Larkin and the Delegates.

He has six children—Charlotte Jones, Lonnie Alexander, Lammont Rose, Debra Alexander, Nicole Alexander, and Glenda Hollingsworth—and fourteen grandchildren. At the time of this writing Pernell lives in the Seattle area and works for a large merchandising chain.

Childhood

When I moved to Seattle from Baltimore, what saved me from the new-kid-on-the-block syndrome was the immediate friendships I struck up with Jimmy Hendrix, James Williams and Terry Johnson. The four of us spent a lot of time together. I met them at Leschi Grade School. I lived with my grandmother, across the street from the school. My grandmother was like Mother Goose. She always encouraged us. She used to keep Jimmy Hendrix's drawings and Jimmy Williams' little stories. Jimmy Hendrix loved football, and he would draw football pictures. He liked the Rams and the Eagles. Jimmy Williams used to write stories, and leave them for my grandmother; then he'd read them in front of the class at Leschi. It was great. I thought, he's going to grow up to be a writer.

I was the rebel in the bunch. I was bored at school because the stuff they were teaching us at Leschi I'd already had in Baltimore. I got sent to the office for being a troublemaker, but really I was bored. I remember writing book reports about Hannibal and Queen Victoria's mother, who was mulatto. My teacher didn't know about them, and she must have felt uncomfortable, or threatened, and that added to the troublemaker label they were giving me. In Maryland I had gone to a segregated school. So Seattle was a new experience—not only because of integration, but the kids were naive. It felt like some remote outback. I was in culture shock.

Then there was the fact that I felt different because of my clothes. My grandmother used to dress me in suits, and Mexican outfits from the clothing factory where she had worked in Baltimore. The Seattle kids had never seen that stuff before, so they thought I looked like Little Lord Fauntleroy, and they'd tease me. I remember being friends with two Jewish guys named Ralph and Standley, who also got picked on. Jimmy Hendrix, Jimmy Williams and Terry accepted me like brothers. They became my family. That meant a lot to me.

I didn't know until 1976 that my grandmother had kidnapped me. I loved her, but I was angry that she took me away from my mom and my family. She took me to Seattle because my father, her son, lived there and she wanted him to face up to his responsibility. I had no contact with my mom for 26 years. I finally found her through the Red Cross and

the Washington, D.C. Police Department. My dad is half White. He's whiter than Terry. My family history is like fiction.

Back in those days Jimmy Hendrix slept over with us a lot. Sometimes Jimmy slept at the Scott's, and other times at Terry Johnson's. Terry was the only one of us who lived with both parents. Terry and I both gave Jimmy clothes. We loved Jimmy and we wanted him to have what he needed.

Bikes and Hydroplanes

When we were kids, we would go bike riding every Saturday. We'd go all over the city exploring, to the Arboretum and Capitol Hill, of course, and even to West Seattle.

We loved the hydroplanes. Every kid in Seattle loved the excitement of the hydroplane races on Lake Washington. Jimmy and I used to camp out

beside the hydroplane pits on the lake. One time Joe Taggart gave us a ride across the lake and back in Slo Mo IV. One of Jimmy's albums has the sound of a hydroplane.

Jimmy's Kissing Fish Mouth

Jimmy had a habit of sucking in on his cheeks when he played. His mouth would look like a kissing fish. He did it all the time, whether he was in class, or walking down the street, or playing the guitar.

Getting Started with Music

The first guitar we played belonged to a guy name Robert McLamore—they call him Snake. His mother was a preacher. He was a hell of a dresser and a dancer. He was about three years older than us. He had a guitar that he didn't play, so we practiced on it. I wanted a drum set back in those days, and my grandmother and I had a go-around about it. She said my choices were saxophone, guitar or piano, but we couldn't afford a piano. So she bought me a guitar. Jimmy had to do a lot of chores, and cut a lot of grass, to get his.

One name no one has mentioned in the material that's been printed about Jimmy is Raleigh "Randy" Snipes. We called him Butch. The kid was amazing. He was phenomenal. He had great showmanship. He taught Jimmy the stunts. Butch was the first one here to play the guitar behind his back and with his teeth, and Jimmy learned those tricks from him. Butch taught us both a lot. He was in my life musically from 1957 until 1970. The other connection Butch and I had was that his grandmother, Birdie, and my grandmother were tight.

Jimmy and I liked to play "Honky Tonk" and "Louie Louie." We both liked Chuck Berry, Eddie Cochran, the Everly Brothers, Mickey and Sylvia—

EVELYN EZELL AND PERNELL

"Love is Strange"—and Little Richard. We both ended up playing with Little Richard. We met him down at the Eagles. We were sitting in the front row. Back in those days Jimmy was mostly into blues; I was more into jazz.

We listened to a lot of records. I had quite a collection: Red Prysock, Stil Austin, Illinois Jacquet, Count Basie, Gene Ammons, Pepper Adams, Johnny Ace, Fats Domino, the Everly Brothers, Chuck Berry, Eddie Cochran, Bill Haley and the Comets, Big Mama Thornton, Elmore James, Jimmy Reed, Lightning Hopkins, Bo Diddley, Muddy Waters, Miles Davis, John Coltrane, Nat King Cole, B.B. King, Freddie King. I liked tenor sax players. Most of the sax players whose records I had were tenors.

On my fifteenth birthday we went to the Birdland for the first time. Then I started going regularly with my next-door neighbor, Marvin Parker.

I was going to Meany then, living with my dad. Wilbur Morgan, the owner of the Birdland, lived one house over from my grandmother. He was more like a father to me than my own dad. In fact, he was the most important father figure in my life. He helped all of us with our music. The Birdland was very important to our music. The Black and Tan and the Four Ten were closed. They reopened in late '64. Jackson Street was where the gamblers and the hustlers were. There wasn't anything happening music-wise on Jackson Street in those days.

I learned a lot about music from Roy Moore. He was one of the best keyboard players in this city. After him, I credit Dave Holden, Dave Lewis's dad, and Dave Holden's dad. They helped me learn how to read music. Then there's my favorite hero, George Griffin. And Dave Holden's sax player, Gerald, Carlton Williams, Donald Mallory and Bop Daddy.

In 1960 I broadened my music base by studying jazz, classics, show tunes—especially Gershwin. In 1961 music here in Seattle was killing. I was in it up to my eyelashes. I played at the Birdland for a month, then my group, the Boss Four, made a record and we went on the road. We made four records. None of us has copies now, but I'm sure there are some out there somewhere. Anthony Atherton and I wrote all the music we recorded except for one, "Goodnight, my love."

Mr. Williams Introduces Jimmy to the Blues

Mr. Williams was the one who introduced Jimmy to the blues. Jimmy loved the blues. They used to sit out on Mr. Williams' porch on 27th Avenue, and Jimmy would listen to him play the blues. I went over there with him a few times, but frankly I wasn't as

interested in the blues as Jimmy was. It would be interesting to find his older son, Donald Williams who studied martial arts. He was a black belt.

The Velvetones

We got our little band together when we were in junior high school—the Velvetones. Walter Jones was the drummer, Robert Green played the piano, Luther Rabb played tenor and baritone sax, Anthony Atherton played alto sax, and Jimmy and I played the guitar. I think Terry Johnson played with us a couple of times. My stepmother and my dad were very supportive. So were Mr. and Mrs. Green, and Anthony Atherton's aunt and uncle. They chaperoned everything, and my dad was our manager. We played all over—at Polish Hall, Washington Hall, the Boys' Club and the YMCA. We also played at a place called The Shrine at 23rd and Madison. We always

thought it was great that all of us who were in the Velvetones, except Luther, have November birthdays. Luther's a Virgo. I was born November 9, 1942. I'm a Scorpio. Walter's is November 22, Anthony's is the 21st, Robert's is the 22nd, and Jimmy's was the 27th—all Sagittarius. We were all the same age except Anthony, who's three years younger.

The Velvetones lived in Madison Valley. The Rocking Teens lived up in the Terrace. We all knew each other. In fact, later on Jimmy joined the Rocking Teens. Anyway, we were having a North Side/South Side feud. Actually it was about girls, but the Battle of the Bands was really a serious thing. It would be the Velvetones and the Rocking Teens. It was hilarious. It was a Meany versus Washington thing. I went to both schools—back and forth from Meany to Washington, depending on whether I was at my dad's house or my grandmother's.

We didn't know about bass guitars back then. Jimmy and I would tune our guitars to low C for the bass part. I remember when we went to see Big Jay McNeilly at the YMCA on 23rd in 1957 or '58. He was one of my dad's favorites. That was the first time we'd seen a bass guitar; we were hooked. We all spent a lot of time rehearsing. And we'd fantasize about what we'd do when we made it big. The Velvetones played once for a talent show, but I don't recall the year. I know we also played at Garfield in January, 1960, out on the lawn that faces Garfield Park.

Nature—Part of Our Lives and Our Music

Nature was important to us, and to our music. The water and the mountains. We tried to get water sounds with tremolo and reverb. We liked Les Paul because

BOB SUMMERRISE

he invented those things. From his sounds, and Mary Ford, and Bo Diddly, we worked on water sounds. It was exciting. I made it a point to go to sleep with music and wake up to music. I'd go to sleep listening to jazz and wake up to Fats Domino, Chuck Berry, or Little Richard—something to get me going.

Dancing and Singing

I tried to teach Jimmy to dance by holding on to a doorknob. He was so pigeon-toed and he had big feet. But he danced with the doorknob. Jimmy tried to sing, to harmonize. We all did. The two guys who could really sing were Charles Woodbury and Robert Green.

How Distortion Started

Forget all those stories about Jimmy discovering electronic sound distortion in New York or London. The truth is he discovered it in Robert Green's

basement. One of the amplifiers blew a tube, so we were playing with distorted sound. We were too dumb to even know what had happened. We only had one amp, and we had two guitars and a mike coming out of the one amp. We had it overloaded. Then somebody—either Jimmy or Robert, but I think it was Robert because he's the get-things-done type—decided to put his hand in the back of the amp and see what was distorting the sound. A 220-volt shock hit him that sent him flying on his butt, and we rolled. He discovered electricity real fast. Butch came over later, and told us it was the tube and where to go to buy a new tube. We didn't know anything about those things. [Note: Robert later became an electrician.]

Mr. and Mrs. Bob Summerrise

Bob Summerrise was our link to the outside world. If it weren't for him, we would not have been able to

create our music. He and his wife had a music store where we bought records. They were really into music. And they were like an aunt and uncle to me. When I'd go into their store, they'd say, "Hey, we just got so-and-so's record in." They'd ask where we were playing, and then they'd come to watch us play. I had a crush on Mrs. Summerrise. I think all of us did. She was a gorgeous woman. I remember how she wore stockings with seams, and the seams were always straight. She was really something. She still is. I saw her on the news when Bill Clinton was in town recently.

Jimmy's Personality

Jimmy was very mannerable and very shy. He was very likable and very sensitive. He was gullible, too. He would let people talk him into things. The only time I saw Jimmy get angry was one day when he got frustrated with himself because he didn't do something the way he thought he was supposed to. We were at Ed Brown's house, and Jimmy was playing Ed's older brother's guitar. Ed's older brothers were tough, rough boys. Jimmy got so frustrated with himself that he threw the guitar on the floor. I decided to leave. But I guess nothing happened. Jimmy lived.

Finding Out Jimmy was Famous

When everybody went into the service, I didn't go. Maybe three of us didn't go. In 1961, I hit the road. I was on the road, traveling all over the United States, until 1968. I was living in Las Vegas, playing with Billy Larkin and the Delegates, and I was listening to the radio about 5:00 one morning when I heard the news. I woke everybody up. I said, "That's Jimmy!" I was so glad Jimmy made it.

Last Visit

The last time I saw Jimmy was when he came to Seattle for his last concert. I went out to the airport when he came in. Al and his family were there too. I hadn't seen Al in a long time. I went over to Al's with all of them, and then Jimmy came over to my house with me and met with my band. He was going to help us.

But after that visit I was never able to get through to him again. All my calls to him in New York got shortstopped by Mike Jefferey. Then my calls to England got shortstopped too. His management would not let me get through to him.

Jimmy's Passing

I found out about Jimmy's death on the radio. Right after I heard it, the phone rang. It was Buddy Miles. The timing of his call was amazing since I'd just heard the news. I'd met Buddy back in 1968. After the

funeral, he flew me to San Francisco, where he was living at the time. No one contacted me about the funeral, but I went anyway. I was not happy that Jimmy's best friends had not been asked to be his pall bearers. I don't know how that happened. That bothered me for a long time.

Final Thoughts

Jimmy has had a major impact on the music world. I knew immediately when I heard "Purple Haze" that music was going somewhere else. It was very exciting. If Jimmy were here now, being as modest as he was, he probably wouldn't understand how great he was. Like Charlie Christian, Les Paul, and Wes Montgomery, Jimmy had a style that was so different from everyone else, that it impacted not only the guitar world, but music in general.

With everything Jimmy did, he was into it completely and sincerely—his drawings, his music, his imagination. He had a lot of stuff stored up inside. He really wanted to be somebody. He wanted to prove to his family and anybody who ever said, "you're never going to amount to much" that he could make it. He did and we were all so proud of him. It breaks our hearts and makes us angry that people have exploited him and made up stories about him—stories they've made money off of—and he's not here to defend himself. Jimmy was a sweet, sensitive, likable guy. For me, he was family.

A POSITIVE PLACE FOR KIDS

THE BOYS' CLUB

Anthony Atherton

On Sunday afternoons, Anthony Lloyd Atherton plays his saxophone at Seattle coffeehouses, backing vocalist Suzanne Hewett, his girlfriend. The two have been part of the Seattle music scene for decades. In junior high Anthony played with Jimmy Hendrix in the Velvetones. Seattlite Lacy Wilbon says, "The first time I heard Anthony play, he was eleven years old. He sounded like John Coltrane. I thought, this can't be coming from an eleven-year-old. When he first started playing, folks had to lie about his age to get him jobs. Like Jimmy, Anthony was shy. I think he was the best sax player who came out of the Pacific Northwest."

Barbara Heath Evans comments, "Lloydie was very talented. I always called him 'Lloydie.' He and my brother Junior were fast friends from the time they were little kids. They banded together against the neighborhood bully. And then they played music

together. My mother's name is Lucille and she didn't like it when the guys would play 'Lucille.' "

Atherton toured with a group called the Macheen Company, traveling to Chicago, Florida, New Foundland, and Las Vegas—where they opened for Fats Domino. He also played in a group called International Love that had a management and recording contract with Quincy Jones.

"I love to play jazz and R & B," says Atherton. "My music keeps me going." In addition to playing music, Atherton worked for Boeing for 15 years. He has three children—Anthony Lloyd Atherton, Junior, Aaron Arnold Atherton and Arikia Atherton.

Early Music

I learned a lot of music at church. I played in Luther Rabb's father's church for many years. We have a gospel background. At home I started out playing

drums. My father played drums. My mother wanted me to play saxophone. She said, "Forget the drums."

I met Jimmy Hendrix in seventh grade at the Rotary Boys' Club. We used to go to the Neighborhood House a lot. It was a good place for growing. There was a man there named Mr. Lewis Wilcox who was very instrumental in the community in arts and music. His son played bass and piano. I took private lessons with Mr. Wilcox on the saxophone starting in second grade until I was about 12. Then I started playing in school bands.

Pernell Alexander and Butch Snipes were the ones who taught Jimmy how to play the guitar. I remember Jimmy's Danelectro guitar.

I played with Jimmy, Pernell, Robert Green, Luther Rabb and Walter Jones in the Velvetones. We played in the Battle of the Bands in the Yesler Terrace gym, battling the Rocking Kings. Some of the

THE BOYS' CLUB

guys were Valley People—from Madison Valley. For a while the Valley People had a group called the Disciples that I played in. Luther was in that group too. Tommy Garrett was another saxophone player who went to Meany and Garfield who could improvise really well. In my mind, Tommy Garrett was another Charlie Parker. But people saw the goodness in him and took advantage of him, and burned him out.

Pernell introduced me to jazz. His grandmother always made sure he had all the latest records. At Pernell's house some of the musicians I listened to were Cannonball Adderly, Dexter Gordon, Horace Silver, the Jazz Messengers, and John Coltrane.

We'd sneak in to see Ray Charles play at the Birdland. Buddy Catlett used to play there too. He was a bass player with Count Basie Coltrane. Quincy was too. At the Mardis Gras, across the street from Birdland, I was about fourteen and the lady would let

me go in and sit down by the stage. A couple of times me and Jimmy went in together. I remember Leon Hendrix would meet us at places and try to run around with us. He wanted to be supportive; he would try to have us meet people. Jimmy's father didn't want him playing back then. One of the people who motivated me a lot was Lester Exkano.

Pernell's Grandmother

I'll never forget that woman as long as I live—Mrs. Jones. She was an inspiration for all of us. She raised Pernell, and in a way she raised all of us—along with my mother and Pernell's father. Pernell's father encouraged us with our music. Jimmy's father really wasn't enthusiastic about it. We all went out to do landscape work for him. There was nothing wrong with that. It was good honest work, it just wasn't what we wanted to be doing. There was a lot of opportunity for music then. And music was what we

wanted. I sure appreciated Pernell's grandmother's interest in us.

Junior Heath's Mother

Junior's mother, Mrs. Heath, partially raised me, too. I'd see her at Junior's house and every Sunday at the New Hope Baptist Church. She played the piano in the Sunday School. In those days we learned about giving. Nowadays young people want to receive. They don't realize that when you give, you receive.

Seeing Jimmy in Los Angeles

Jimmy was so poor. When you have money, you have to have the mentality to deal with it. When he did have money, his family didn't help him manage it. I saw Jimmy in 1967 in Los Angeles for a few minutes before a concert. He didn't seem like himself. And his music was so loud it knocked you over. He had so many amplifiers. It wasn't a good visit. It felt like the industry had robbed his soul.

MEANY JUNIOR HIGH SCHOOL

Robert Green

Robert Green played the keyboard for many years around Seattle. In junior high school he played with Jimmy Hendrix in the Velvetones. Later he often filled in for Dave Lewis, whom he considers his mentor, with the Dave Lewis Combo. Robert is a retired journeyman electrician who still plays the piano on occasion—in spite of injuries and operations on his hands. "I suffered some injuries on the job," he says. "But I still love music and I sit in with different bands. I'm a disabled vet from the Vietnam war; lately I've been doing a lot of volunteer work." Robert and his wife Euna have four children— Rodney, Cassaundra, Derrick, and Cassandra. They live in Seattle.

Early Memories

We were all close, especially me and Jimmy and Pernell Alexander. We used to eat together and spend the night together. Many nights Jimmy sat down at my parents' table. There was a group of us that ran around together. We called each other cousins. Seattle is a great place. Being here together allowed us to come together and be creative together.

Jimmy used to be kind of shy. He was mostly in the background. You couldn't pick him out in a crowd. At a party he would mix and mingle. The ladies flocked around him. He was a nice-looking guy. But he was real skinny and pigeon-toed.

Early on I took piano lessons from a woman in the neighborhood named Miss Stevens. We were in junior high when we got our band together; we used to rehearse just about everyday in my basement. It was me, Pernell, Jimmy, Luther Rabb, Anthony Atherton and Walter Jones. We started rehearsing and rehearsing. We played for an assembly at Meany. Then we played our first gig for a womens' club event at the Polish Hall. I think the womens' club was the Rosettes. I remember we got paid $125. After that we got so many gigs we had to turn some down. Pernell's dad became our manager.

We took part of the money we made to buy Jimmy an amp. He was always plugging in with Pernell. Jimmy and Pernell were good. They had it down. They got a lot of their fingerwork by listening to Chuck Berry. Jimmy and Pernell loved Chuck Berry. We did three or four Chuck Berry numbers—like "Queenie." We also played "Lucille" by Little Richard and Fats Domino's "Blueberry Hill."

We'd play blues for the grownups and whatever was jamming at that particular time for the youngsters. We played all the pop tunes. We landed a gig at the Yesler Terrace gym and for a couple of months we played there every Friday and Saturday night for teenage dances. That's where I met my wife.

At some point the Velvetones broke up. I don't remember the timing exactly. When we started up we called ourselves the Vibertones. Then it seems like the Velvetones and the Rocking Kings merged. I played with both groups.

Being in music in Seattle allowed us to stretch. We had opportunities here. We went one time over to West Seattle to the home of a White guy we knew to make a demo tape; he had a recording studio in his basement. We learned a lot by meeting professional groups, things that once you learn you never forget. We got a lot out of it and we gave a lot back.

Dave Lewis had an enormous impact on me. He was my teacher and my mentor. I learned so much about music from him. When I was too young to get into the Birdland, they'd slip me in there so I could listen. Dave had a magnetic personality. I got to know him because he stayed next door to my parents' with his girlfriend. When I'd go listen to him play, he'd ask me to fill in for twenty or thirty minutes when he'd

take a break. In later years when Dave couldn't be there to play with the group, I'd take his place. In the early days the Dave Lewis Combo had Dave, George Griffin on drums, Barney Hilliard on sax and Jack Gray on the upright bass. Later on they had an older guy named Bud on the guitar, then Jerry Allen, who used to be called Jerry Guitar Allen, and then they added J.B. Allen on sax.

Getting Together with Jimmy in Germany

When I was in the service in Germany, I ran into Sam Johnson in the PX. Sammy and Jimmy had been good friends in Seattle, and Sammy found out Jimmy was in Germany. The three of us would get together on Saturdays and Sundays and talk about home. We would have gotten something started with music, but Jimmy didn't have much time left. I remember saying to him, "Man, you ought to go home." He said, "Man, I don't think so. I don't want to cut grass."

When friends told me Jimmy had made the big time, I was so glad. If anybody deserved it, it was Jimmy. He hadn't had a whole lot of things the rest of us had had. Hearing that did me all the good in the world.

Mrs. Ursie Green, Robert Green's Mother

All the kids came over here—Jimmy, Pernell, Luther, Anthony and Walter. They practiced in my basement. Then I'd drive them all home. They'd come over after school, usually two or three times a week. When I got so I couldn't stand the noise, I'd go visiting. But a lot of the time, I'd just listen. I love music. Robert took private lessons for a while from a lady in the neighborhood. Sometimes Pernell's father would be down there with them. He was real good for them. He acted as their manager. Those boys were all such good friends.

Luther Rabb

Luther Rabb is a musician, manager, and a creative entrepreneur. He and Jimmy Hendrix were neighbors as kids; they played music together in Seattle basements, and places like the Rotary Boys Club. Jimmy and Luther were together again in later years in New York, Los Angeles, and on tour throughout the United States when Luther's group Ballin' Jack opened for Hendrix.

"Luther is the life-of-the-party kind of guy," says Bill Eisiminger, a Garfield classmate who played with Luther in the Stags. "He's a very likable, humorous guy, with little sayings, great quips, and mannerisms of speech that make people laugh. I've never seen a bad side to him. He was always someone I could count on—a good friend."

Luther was the only one of Jimmy's Seattle friends who toured with him after his rise to fame. He was the only Seattle buddy who spent time hanging

out with Jimmy in the months before he died. Others wanted to, but their calls and letters didn't reach Hendrix. Even Luther's contact with Hendrix was discouraged by Jimmy's management. "Sometimes we'd go out at night in New York, and they'd send spies out. It was weird. One time I moved into the hotel where Jimmy was staying and they had him move out. Finally we convinced them I was an old friend from home."

Luther lives in Los Angeles where he manages artists, including Rob Mullens and Mary Katherine. At the time of this writing, he is getting a group of young musicians ready to play for a benefit for Jane Goodall, the naturalist who has worked to save the chimpanzees in Africa. "I'm a great fan of hers and the whole ecology movement," he says. "I'm also teaching these young musicians the importance of giving." Luther comes from a family of preachers—his

father, his grandfather and a cousin followed the call to the ministry. His gift for teaching the younger generation comes naturally to him. He's currently organizing a benefit in Orange County for the homeless, and managing the actors T.M.T. [Troy, Michael and Todd] who are preparing for a musical, "The Gang's New Thread," that will run for six weeks in Los Angeles. Luther has a daughter, Deja C. Rabb.

Seattle Days

Jimmy Hendrix was the nicest guy in the world. We used to hang out around the neighborhood together when we were little kids. He lived fairly close to my house. In the beginning, Jimmy didn't realize what he had. His idol was Duane Eddy. He was always kind of

STAGS: WYLER, EISIMINGER, MORRIS, RABB

different. He had a right-handed guitar that he played upside down and left handed. Jimmy always carried his guitar around. He would show up at a party and just start playing.

My father was a preacher. He also played the guitar and had some equipment. Sometimes I would sneak in and borrow his equipment. Matter of fact, one of the last times Jimmy and I talked, we were joking about how we left my father's amplifier on overnight and totally melted it. My father always joked about that.

In those days in Seattle, I was playing the saxophone. I wanted to play bass, but I didn't switch to bass until I played in the 28th Army Band at Fort Ord. By the time I came back from the Army, I played saxophone, bass, clarinet, flute and oboe. Then I went to L.A. City College and did two years of music classes. When you're in the music business in Los

Angeles, you have to know music theory and be able to read music well. You walk in for a job and get handed the music. Back in Seattle, Jimmy and I played songs that we learned by listening to the radio. We used to play in my basement—until my mother would make us stop. We were so loud. For us, it was a pretty normal situation, playing our music in the basement.

Jimmy learned a lot from Butch Snipes. Sometimes Butch would loosen his strings to play bass. He was fluid. I was amazed by his playing. And if you listened to Jimmy and then listened to Butch, you'd hear them playing each other's licks.

The Seattle Sound

We were isolated in Seattle, so Jimmy had a whole different slant on music. We were doing things that were unique, ahead of their time. There was a lot of jazz with a funky kind of rock thing with the guitar

and bass. Seattle had the dual sax, and we used the jungle beat, which was thirty years ahead of its time. It was a syncopated rhythm, a cool thing because it could go with a lot of songs and people could dance to it. Today people are calling it the New Jack Swing. The Dave Lewis Combo was the most important group musically. Ron Holden's "Love You So" was a hit. All four Holden brothers were keyboard players. The Frantics was one of the bigger groups. Then there were people like Merrilee Rush, Tiny Tony and the Statics, and the Viceroys, who were making money and playing around the state of Washington, and in Idaho and Northern California.

The Dave Lewis Combo

The musicians in the Dave Lewis Combo were our mentors. They were so advanced. I was studying music like crazy, and those guys were ahead of all of us. Dave Lewis and George Griffin and the other musicians in their combo were far better musically than any of the other groups. If Dave Lewis were playing commercially in today's market, he would be considered a virtuoso. He could play rock like Duane Eddy, blues like Lloyd Price, and jazz like Duke Ellington. He was so versatile. He could be singing "Walk, Don't Run" and switch to a concerto. I don't see that kind of dedication from musicians today.

The Dave Lewis Combo was a model for genuineness and a calm, cool, relaxed attitude. They were very real, no airs, no pretenses. Nothing ever made them rush. We'd watch the combo members calmly setting up at the Birdland. Then Dave would show up, and whoosh—everything came together. Dave was a hell of a singer and a hell of a keyboard player. I remember the way he sang "Have You Ever Had the Blues?" He could really sing it. And "I'll be loving you." He could sing independent of his

playing. He was truly bad. But he didn't get the credit he deserves.

Interracial Bands

My bands have always been interracial. The group I played with in Seattle, the Stags, was interracial. I remember an occasion when there was a Black musician who was great and I would like to have included him in the group, but he didn't want to stand beside a White musician. I said, "I'm sorry, but if you have a problem with that, that doesn't go along with our program."

Getting On the Road

My group, Ballin' Jack, was a Seattle basement band when Bill Graham heard us and got us on the road. He asked us to go to San Francisco to open for Sly Stone. Three days later we loaded all our equipment into two station wagons and took off for San

Francisco. We got there and saw Sly had two stories of equipment and a river of limos. Our stuff was dinky and ragged, and there we were with two station wagons with Washington license plates. Bill Graham tried to make us feel good; he put out a big spread in our dressing room. I remember walking into Sly's room and there were buckets and barrels of champagne and cooks standing there waiting for orders. We were blown away.

Hooking Up With Jimmy

I hooked up with Jimmy in New York, after he'd come back from London—after he'd already made an album. When I was hanging out with Jimmy, I met Paul McCartney, Ringo, Mick Jagger, all those guys— a real contrast to the early days. I told Jimmy I was going to go back and pull my band together and move to Los Angeles. After I moved to L. A., I hooked up with Jimmy again in Beverly Hills. His

management had some other guy they wanted to have back the show, but Jimmy, he said, "Hey, no, let's have Luther." Ballin' Jack's first gig here in Los Angeles was with Jimi Hendrix and Buddy Miles. We were the opening act at the Forum. About a week later we went out on tour together. We were hanging out every night, doing the warm-up show. He'd watch our set, and we'd hang out and watch his. We'd do the old rhythm and blues songs for the warm up, and everybody in the room would be singing and clapping. It was a pretty normal situation. Jimmy was always saying ours was one of the best groups that had ever toured with him.

Jimmy was the nicest guy in the world. He'd give you the shirt off his back. As a matter of fact he's done it three or four times with me. I still have a couple that he gave me. I have a coat Jimmy gave me. I gave it to my daughter. We were both skinny

guys. There's no way to get fat when you're on the road playing five or six nights a week in different cities. You know, back at the time and with the situations that everybody was faced with, the lifestyle just seemed like a pretty normal series of events. At this point, you know, it still doesn't seem noteworthy of much hoopla. Maybe it is. But it was just something we were doing, and having a hell of a lot of fun doing it. I thought nothing of going out on the road and staying for nine months.

Now when I go out on the road, it's strictly business. I'm a manager. It's something I like to do. I don't play anymore because I just don't have the taste for it, but I love what I'm doing. I always have liked the business.

Ballin' Jack

Dave Lewis's group was the model for Ballin' Jack. Ballin' Jack was one of the first groups that had a trumpet and a trombone. We had six musicians in the band most of the time. At the time we met up with Jimmy, we had an album out, and our album was doing okay. I think it did three or four hundred thousand, which at the time was not a gold record, you know. A big record then was selling two and a half or three million, so three hundred thousand wasn't any great shakes. Being from Seattle put you in a funny position with the record business because the only real record people there were consolidated distributors. Seattle hadn't grown up. It was like a two-percent market, so if you sold a million records, only two percent of them would be in Seattle. These are things I learned over the years. If you sell a million records, over twenty percent of them will be in L.A.

Jimmy had decided that he was going to produce Ballin' Jack's next record. We were going to record at Electric Ladyland. We started to formulate ideas for a Ballin' Jack album. It was getting to be pretty serious business.

Jimmy's Death

I was on my way home from San Antonio when I heard Jimmy died. I was in the airport in Sacramento and I heard he was killed. We'd just been together, the week before it happened. It was strange. It was painful, because, you know, Jimmy was a beautiful guy. He would rather give than take. His death was painful. I mean, I never talked about it to anybody. I did one radio spot about two days after Jimmy's death, and that was it. I said, "No more." For years after that people kept on calling me from all over wanting to interview me. I didn't want to be a part of it.

Jimmy Hendrix was my friend. I remember times when we'd hang out and we'd sing this song called "Further on Down the Road." He was a free spirit wanting to create music. Jimmy was all outflow. There was an aura, an electricity, a magnetism around him that was incredible. To me he was a homey—a homeboy. He was a beautiful guy.

Hendrix's The Cry of Love Concerts Supported by Ballin' Jack

April 25, 1970

Los Angeles Forum, The Cry of Love tour opens, supported by The Buddy Miles Express and Ballin' Jack

June 6, 1970

Sam Houston Coliseum, Houston, Texas. Jimi Hendrix, supported by Ballin' Jack

June 7, 1970

Assembly Center Arena, Tulsa, Oklahoma, Jimi Hendrix supported by Ballin' Jack

June 13, 1970

Baltimore Civic Center, Baltimore, Maryland, Jimi Hendrix supported by Ballin' Jack and Cactus

June 21, 1970

Ventura County Fairgrounds, Jimi Hendrix supported by Ballin' Jack and Grin

Lester Exkano

Lester Exkano played the drums with Jimmy Hendrix in the Rocking Kings. He later played with Ebony and Ivory, Frank and Connie, and spent sixteen years with the Frank Roberts Four—a group he toured with. One of his favorite tour memories is flying in by bush plane to perform in Yellow Knife, Canada. Lester also played with L.V. Parr in Seattle. Doug Bright, editor and publisher of Heritage Music Review, writes, "Lester's voice is soulful and expressive but so unassumingly natural as to make the job look easy. This is evidenced by a rendition of 'Money' that sounds as fresh and exciting as Barrett Strong's original. 'Louie Louie,' a tune that's been worn threadbare by every bad, mid-60's rock band in the world, is taken at a moderate reggae tempo and sung by the drummer with the same vitality as the other selections" (April 16, 1982). Born in New Orleans, Lester moved to Seattle when he was twelve. He works in Seattle as a security guard, and plays music on the weekends.

Memories of Jimmy and the Rocking Kings

Jimmy was very shy. Talking to him was always comfortable. We had lots of conversations. He was such an easy-going guy—never a threat to anyone. One of Jimmy Hendrix's best friends was Sam Johnson. Jimmy and Sam were always together. They were tight. All of us in the Rocking Kings connected well. We had a common bond and a good understanding of what we were doing. Sometimes Hendrix played rhythm, and sometimes he did bass by tuning his guitar low.

Webb Lofton and I were talking about when we saw him play at the Battle of the Bands—when he was playing with the Velvetones. He was amazing. Webb was reminding me about how we sort of stole him. We talked him into playing with the Rocking Kings. Jimmy didn't smoke and he didn't drink. The rest of us smoked occasionally and drank a little wine. But not Hendrix. I usually called him Hendrix.

I used to see Hendrix at the Boys Club. We'd shoot pool or play basketball. We also played a lot of Chinese checkers and Monopoly.

It seemed like Jimmy's dad didn't want him to play music. Sometimes we had to sneak Jimmy out of the house to play music. His dad wanted him to go to school and cut grass. He didn't want him to play the guitar.

I remember when we were coming back from Moses Lake, on the other side of the mountains. We'd been over there a couple of days. It was snowing really hard. Our manager, James Thomas, was tired, so I offered to drive his Studebaker. While I was driving, the car started slipping and sliding in the snow. Then it rolled over. But it turned over so smoothly—like slow motion—that there wasn't

anything to be afraid of. When it landed upside down in the ditch, we all got out, and called a tow truck.

The last time I saw Jimmy he found me under a car at the body and fender place where I was working. He and Charles Woodbury came by to see if I was interested in joining the military with them. I had dropped out of school to work. I finished my G.E.D. at the Seattle Opportunities Industrialization Center.

The Dave Lewis Combo

The Dave Lewis Combo was *the* band. They influenced all of us. I'm sure Dave was a big influence on Jimmy. George Griffin, their drummer, was my idol. When I was too young to get into the Birdland I'd sit out by the back door and listen to George. I took a few lessons from him.

There was a song by Dave Lewis called "Dave's Mood" that we played a lot. It was good for dancing;

it had a regular 4/4 downbeat. We played at the Birdland on Thursday nights for the teenagers. Charles Woodbury and I both sang. Woodbury was the clown in our group. He wrote a few songs. I only remember one he called "Naps."

Musical Favorites

My favorite musicians were Little Richard, James Brown and Ray Charles. I liked Chuck Berry, Fats Domino, and Lloyd Price too. And I loved B.B. King. Jimmy did too. Later on I liked jazz, especially George Benson. The rock songs I liked to play the most were "Lucille," "What'd I Say," "Honky Tonk," "Long Tall Sally," "Blue Monday," "Stagger Lee," "Peter Gunn," and "Louie Louie." If you couldn't do "Louie Louie," you couldn't get on the bandstand. We played "Peter Gunn" a lot because it got people dancing. It has a heavy downbeat.

We played a lot of songs with a slop beat— medium tempo with a kind of funk style. We played a lot of blues. A couple of popular ones were "Every Day I Have the Blues" and "Driving Wheel." Back then the main rhythms we played were jazz, rock 'n' roll, and blues. Sometimes we used a mambo beat that would go into a swing type of thing.

Lake Washington

I live about four blocks from the lake. It's very peaceful; it's a good place to go to collect your thoughts. Sometimes I go down there to look at the water. I look at that lake and I feel peaceful.

Jimmy's Passing

I was so shocked when I heard the news. It seemed unbelievable. It was very sad the way it happened, and so disappointing. He was young and he had a lot to offer the world. Imagine what he would have accomplished if he were still alive today.

Walter Harris

Walter Harris devoted his early years to music. "I learned to play music at church," he says. "I was a church boy." Walter played the saxophone with the Rocking Kings. When he started a family, Walter gave up the idea of a career in music. He did a nine-year stint in the military reserves; now he works in Seattle as a pipe fitter. Walter has passed his love for music on to his children, Angela, Walter, and Archie. "I taught my son how to play sax," he says. "My daughter plays flute, and my youngest kid plays cello. My twelve-year-old granddaughter is learning to play the sax. I always told my kids to get something basic, but to remember music is a way to express yourself."

I visited Walter one August afternoon at his two-story hillside home in a semirural neighborhood in south Seattle. Behind the house a Rainbird clickety-clacked, sweeping a large semicircle across the sprawling lawn. While we talked, his children and

their friends came and went in a steady stream. Walter gave his dog a pat and laughed, "Now when the kids leave, I say to my dog, 'It's just me and you, Shep.'"

Doing the Pigeon

What is it that Chuck Berry does, that little bit with his guitar? The Goose, the Duck Walk? What was that? Well, I can remember Jimmy doing it. Jimmy, he was pigeon-toed, definitely pigeon-toed. He couldn't stand straight. Jimmy would do the Pigeon, or the Duck Walk, just like Chuck Berry, across the floor. Jimmy was so pigeon-toed that one foot would actually bump into the other foot. I mean, Jimmy just actually had duck feet. But even though he had duck feet, he had feeling. The guy would just play with his toes turned in.

Blues

At that time, I didn't like blues at all. None whatsoever. But Jimmy liked a lot of blues. He idolized B. B. King, Bo Didley, Albert King, and Freddie King—all the blues players. At that time I felt only old people enjoyed the blues. Kids our age didn't know anything about blues because we never went through hardship. But Jimmy had something. The way he played blues was much different from the average young-kid blues. There was something about it. He expressed himself, the hardship, you could say; all the things it took to acquire the blues. I couldn't relate to that. Blues wasn't my bag, but it grew on me as Jimmy played it. He was so expressive. He played as if it was just there. It came naturally to him. I decided to come around a little. Other members of the group did too. So we played blues—Albert King, B. B. King style. We were influenced a lot by the blues.

WALTER AND HIS GRANDDAUGHTER

Meeting Jimmy

I met Jimmy when I was a ninth grader at Washington Junior High and he was a seventh grader at Meany. A couple of the fellows said there was a guy from Meany who always carried his guitar around. Webb Lofton and I had started a group when we were in eighth grade. Jimmy had started playing at the Rotary Boys Club, with Terry Johnson and Luther Rabb. My dad and Luther's dad played music together. Luther's dad was a preacher, but he played the sax. Luther later played with Ballin' Jack and then with War, a group out of Los Angeles. Anyway, there were a lot of connections with Jimmy before we asked him to join our group. At first we were hesitant, because he didn't have an amp, but he always managed to find someone to plug in with.

Rock 'n' Roll

The majority of the music we listened to was rock 'n' roll—Fats Domino, James Brown, Chuck Berry, and Chuck Willis. We played a lot of Chuck Willis. Let's see, we played so many—the Midnighters and Little Richard. Anything that James Brown played, we probably could play just as well. But we ad-libbed, you know; we had our own breaks. We weren't interested in playing Caucasian music, but we'd use lines from Jerry Lee Lewis or the Everly Brothers songs to joke around with each other. I was a clown. I was always ranking on Jimmy and Terry. Jimmy was a comic too. We all used lines from songs for joking around.

At dances we played "Rockin' Robin," "Do You Want to Dance?," and "Yackety Yak," but not "Charlie Brown" or "Poison Ivy." I remember once we played "Sleep Walk" at a sock hop at Blaine, because they wanted something slow. We called it slow-drag. We made up songs. I remember one called "Grandma." It was a comical thing about older people getting together to drink. Charles Woodbury's the one to ask about that.

Rocking Teens/Rocking Kings

Most of the time there were seven of us in the Rocking Teens. We started out with two sax players, a drummer, a piano player, and a guitar player. Before Jimmy, the guitar player was a Caucasian, a guy named Skinner, who played country & western. The core members of the group were Webb Lofton, Lester Exkano, Charles Woodbury, Jimmy Hendrix, Terry Johnson, and myself. Later on there were others.

Jimmy had a guitar, but no amplifiers. So later on Jimmy's friend Junior Heath came into the program with us. Junior had an amp that Jimmy could plug

WASHINGTON JUNIOR HIGH SCHOOL 1956

into. For a while Sam Johnson, who lived across the street from Hendrix, played bass guitar with us. Sam Johnson looked like Chuck Berry, straight hair, same complexion. So at that time we had three guitar players. Once upon a time we were thinking about asking Junior's sister Barbara to play with us. She plays real good piano. But that was taboo.

We played at PTA dances and teenage sock hops, after football games or basketball games, in the gym, and in 1958 we played in the Garfield Funfest. All the schools knew us. We played a lot at Birdland, in the Central District. It was open for kids with no alcohol served until 11:30, when the kids left and the adults came. During the school year we played there on Friday and Saturday nights, but during the summer it was open Wednesday through Sunday.

There were only a few of us who could actually read music, that was myself and Webb, and "T. J."— Terry Johnson, who played sax and then piano. When most of us had finished high school, we decided to rename the group from the Rocking Teens to the Rocking Kings, because we were no longer teenagers. Jimmy was still in high school then, but he was a part of the Rocking Kings.

We got a manager, back when we were the Rocking Teens. It happened one day when we were walking home from Birdland. We heard music coming from a house—it was some old guys playing. We went in and met James Thomas and the Tomcats, and James Thomas became our manager.

We were just young punks, but we were organized. We practiced together three times a week for at least four hours. Then we practiced by ourselves everyday. We knew each other's vibes and

felt it. Sometimes we'd play twenty hours a week together. We enjoyed our music. Sometimes we'd argue about what we were going to play, but we liked to be comical. I was one of the clowns in the group. The last time we played together as a group was at Lester's wedding reception, about 1963, shortly before Birdland closed.

Jimmy's Uniqueness

The most unusual thing about Jimmy is that he played his guitar upside down. The majority of musicians, you know, would just look at him, because everything was upside down. It was weird. He had this unusual technique. And he could do it so well.

Jimmy carried his guitar everywhere he went. Like B. B. King says, his guitar was his companion. It was that way with Jimmy. His guitar was there with him. I don't know. There was something unusual about Jimmy. I felt sorry for him sometimes, like during the summer when he'd be working landscaping with his dad all day and come to practice wearing the same clothes. But, as poor people, we were all in the same situation, trying to express our feelings through our music. It's just Jimmy wasn't as fortunate in some ways as the rest of us.

Jimmy was a square, like most young kids. As time went on, Jimmy began to get into the group, and into the swing of things, and he started to clown, like the rest of us. One of Jimmy's idols was Chuck Berry, because of the way he performed and clowned with the guitar. The first time I saw Jimmy clown he put his guitar behind his head and proceeded to play. And then we thought, "Wow, this kid can do it!" He could do it upside down.

Jimmy and Junior Heath

Junior was one lead guitar and Jimmy was the other. Jimmy was better than Junior, and Junior knew it. Jimmy knew Junior Heath from a previous band that he had started before he met us. They were good friends, but off stage. On stage, they were total enemies, because Jimmy could play better than Junior Heath. Plus, Hendrix was plugged into Junior's amplifier and it wasn't too kosher to plug into someone's amplifier and then show them up. Junior was good, but Jimmy put more into his playing. You could see it in his face. While Junior had a straight face, Jimmy's facial expressions showed he was enjoying himself.

Harmonizing

We grew up in the era of harmonizing. You know, shiboo, shiboo. And not only did we have a band, we also had a singing group. Every kid on the corner had a singing group. It was part of relaxation, you know. After practice, we'd walk on home and jive around, clown around. We had harmony, but we didn't know it. I mean, other people that listened to us would say, "These kids have got harmony." We were just playing around. Terry sang, but, Jimmy, he was not a singer. He was not a singer at all. I remember him trying to sing some B. B. King. But he couldn't carry a tune.

Jimmy's Radio

The first time that I went to Jimmy's house, he was living with Al in a little flophouse/hotel on East Terrace Street, between 12th and 14th. I saw he had a little radio. It turned out that Jimmy could play whatever was on the radio. Any number that came on the radio, he could play it. The same key. And he practiced a lot, because that radio was all the

THE ROCKING KINGS: EXKANO, HENDRIX, LOFTON, HARRIS, WOODBURY

company he had. He didn't have a TV. Most of us were fortunate to have a TV, but all Jimmy had was that radio.

Jimmy's Family

In our group Lester was the only one who was an only child. The rest of us had brothers and sisters, and we were always talking about them. Jimmy said he had a younger sister. He was probably talking about his cousin Diane. Leon, Jimmy's little brother, didn't live with him. I've never met Leon. All I know is that he was much younger. We knew Jimmy didn't have a mother, but we never asked about her. You don't ask about the bad things. Jimmy's dad was always working, doing his landscaping business. I still see Al Hendrix from time to time. He's always glad to see me. He's had a rough time losing his son.

Shy with Girls

Back when we were in high school, they called a girlfriend a "main squeeze," and supposedly everybody had one, and if they didn't, they pretended they did. Jimmy, well, there were girls that liked him, but Jimmy was shy. Jimmy was not aggressive. If there was a girl who liked Jimmy, he might walk her home, but probably not hand-in-hand. Knowing Jimmy, it wouldn't be the hand-in-hand caper. It would be his guitar on one shoulder and probably a foot of space in between, walking this lady home. Jimmy was a cool, lovable guy, and I think the ladies loved him, but Jimmy just didn't show any aggressive feeling. At that time, you had to be more aggressive, because of the competition. If you weren't aggressive, the competition was there, and the ladies always wanted an aggressive fellow.

Jimmy Didn't Drink or Fight

The media always has something negative to say. Some of the things that have been said about Jimmy's early life are wrong. Jimmy and I didn't drink. Jimmy didn't smoke and he didn't drink. But, sooner or later, we tried to get into the IN crowd and we participated to show that we weren't squares. Those statements that Jimmy fought or used drugs aren't true. He might have had a little wine, Thunderbird or dark port, but very little. Whatever we did, we made sure that when we got home, we were never under the influence to where we were acting crazy, like the kids are doing today. We didn't want anybody to know, especially adults, that we were under the influence.

Fighting? Jimmy was not a fighter. I mean, I never saw Jimmy fight. I saw him take verbal abuse, but I never saw Jimmy get angry or be aggressive toward anybody. Terry never got angry either. Jimmy was just a cool, non-violent, lovable guy. If Jimmy had a problem with another group member, he would tell me or Webb. He would tell me because I would express myself more so than the others in the group. I could get angry, and everybody knew when I was angry.

That bit in one book about a fight over girls in the bathroom at Birdland isn't true. Like I've said before, I never saw Jimmy get angry. There was one incident when we were playing at Birdland with a guy from down South, from Louisiana. His name was Waltz and he was a very good piano player. He could play all the Ray Charles stuff, and any religious song there was. I was probably about nineteen, and this guy was about twenty-two or twenty-three. He had been playing with us for a few months. Anyway, this guy proceeded to say that we weren't playing. So, I

grabbed Jimmy's guitar, and I was going to hit this guy with it. And all the band members were standing there watching me with this guitar and Jimmy said, "Hey, hey, uh, look. Walter, that's my guitar." You know, he never got angry, never made any aggressive move toward me. He says, "Can you just please pick up something else to hit this guy with, not my guitar?" Many times I've laughed about that. "Not with my guitar, Walter." I never saw anybody make Jimmy angry.

Military

We tried to get into the military on this buddy-buddy plan. At first we didn't want to go in the Army or the Marines. So, we tried the Navy and a couple of guys flunked. So we tried the Air Force and the same two guys flunked. And so we said, "Well, we'll just continue playing until we get drafted." When Jimmy joined the Army, I remember he went by to see

Lester, who was working at a body shop on Jackson, and Lester lent him some money.

Chipping in to Help Jimmy

Jimmy was the least fortunate of us moneywise. I remember the first time the Rocking Teens acquired a uniform. We called it a uniform, but it was a poor uniform to perform in. It was very cheap: a powder-blue summer coat that cost maybe eleven bucks, and peg-style, charcoal pants, the kind they were wearing back then, for maybe ten bucks.

We thought it was a cool uniform. It was something we had saved money for, something we could buy as a group together. We were all poor, but our parents participated or contributed to the best of their ability. But Jimmy wasn't as fortunate as the rest of us, not having a mother, and being raised by his dad, Mr. Hendrix, who worked constantly.

Jimmy never had any of the extracurricular accessories that we had. And, knowing this, every member decided to contribute a dollar apiece to help Jimmy. Jimmy would contribute his portion, and we'd buy his uniform. Jimmy, you know, he was pleased with it. Well, at first he didn't want to accept it. But, in our group we thought as one. We all helped each other.

All of us were hard up as kids. But the majority of the band members had parents that supported our interests and activities. They tried to make sure that whatever we needed, we got. Strings, at that time, for a guitar were probably less than a dollar. When Jimmy could not afford strings for his guitar, we'd all participate. Whatever the other fellow couldn't get—strings or clothing, whatever it might be—we would all get together and get it for him.

The Battle of New Orleans

We'd get into arguments about what we were going to play, and Jimmy was really comical about it. Every dude in the group would be wanting to show a particular lady his contribution to the group. We'd be back there discussing the matter, and Jimmy would walk out with the microphone and start playing Johnny Horton's "The Battle of New Orleans"—"In 1814 we took a little trip." Or he'd play some country and western music by Stonewall Jackson. All of a sudden, you know, we'd realize that Jimmy was out there playing, and the crowd was starting to clap their hands, and we'd forget our argument and crack up. We'd go out there and ad lib to the number he was playing. It was comical. Jimmy was very expressive. He'd put his whole body into it.

Making Money

We weren't interested in money, just in playing, as long as we had money for gas. Gas was nineteen cents a gallon, so we'd buy fifty cents worth, and we'd be all set.

There were a lot of adults who used us. Used us big time. Of course, we weren't playing for money. We weren't that enthused about it. We were just expressing ourselves, enjoying ourselves. It was like a hobby. It was something we wanted to do. Our manager, James Thomas, would charge us transportation fees. We were probably only making five bucks for three hours, working at Birdland. It would depend. Sometimes there was a percentage at the door. We never, never played just to make a living—we played because we enjoyed it. And whatever we had to pay to get to that point was worth it, because we enjoyed it. We probably would

YESLER TERRACE HOUSING PROJECT

have played for nothing. On several occasions we probably came out with nothing. In the end we got ripped off. But, still, no matter what we got, we enjoyed it as a group and it didn't bother us.

I just wish I had some of the pictures. I was going through a folder of photos when I was about thirty years old. I gave it to James Thomas, the manager that ripped us off, when we were little kids, for fortune and fame. It was later I found out this guy made big money off of us. We were getting paid peanuts, you know. But we didn't care back then. It was like, "This is our style. Pay us five bucks. It was nothing." We even had to chip in for gas fare, you know. Whenever James Thomas starts talking about "You young kids this, and you young kids that," I say, "Us young kids got ripped off." Then he says, "What do you mean?" And I say "You ripped us off, you know, but we're older and wiser. You'll never do that

again." But, if we had to do it again, we'd probably get ripped off again.

A Cinnamon Roll for Dinner

We'd go to practice—we lived in Yesler Terrace and Jimmy lived between thirteenth and fourteenth, near the Youth Center—we'd go walking down from the Terrace and pick Jimmy up. He'd leave a note on the table stating that, "Dad, I've had dinner." A cinnamon roll and a glass of milk. We'd get into practice and Webb used to get a little upset at me when I'd turn around and say, "Yeah, Dad, I've had dinner. A cinnamon roll and a glass of milk." Well, Webb knew what I was talking about, and Jimmy knew what I was talking about. But Webb would get defensive on Jimmy's behalf. Jimmy knew I didn't mean anything. He would even laugh himself. But Webb would just fiercely look at me, you know. And Webb and I were like brothers. For real, everybody

thought Webb and I were brothers. If anybody else had said that to Jimmy, I would probably go verbal, be more defensive. But it was like us three lived in the same neighborhood and we were good friends.

But it was sad, you know. Today I think about how Jimmy had no one to cook dinner for him. Whatever there was at the time, that's what he would have for dinner. If I had to do it again, I wouldn't make those statements. I'm more understanding now, and I know that, hey, it's rough out there, out there as kids. And kids even have it rougher now with all the drugs. I think the only reason a lot of kids today are relying on drugs is because there's nobody there to support them, to help them out and be understanding. I believe they rely on drugs because there's nobody out there.

Seattle Radio

There were only two Black radio stations in Seattle. KZAM was our favorite. Bob Summerrise was the disc jockey we listened to on KFKF, then KZAM. He was the only Black disc jockey who played R & B and Soul. He had his own record shop. His kids are DJs now.

Talent in Seattle

In Seattle, if you didn't have connections, you didn't make it. Dave Lewis never got to where he should have. We followed him because he had great showmanship. Dave could have been in the same league as Quincy Jones. But he never left Seattle. Dave was younger than Quincy, but older than us. We were playing at Birdland at the same time Dave and Quincy were playing at Mardi Gras.

We had chances to really make it in music. We wanted to make a record. One of the ladies who wanted to sponsor us was Bonnie Guitar of Seattle. I think she sponsored a Tacoma group back in the fifties, either the Wailers or the Ventures. I just felt, and the other band members felt, that we couldn't take a chance. At that time in Seattle it was hit or miss. You actually had to know somebody to acquire fame.

We have talented musicians right here in Seattle, but, if you notice, all the really talented musicians have had to leave Seattle to actually make it— Quincy Jones, Ballin' Jack, which is Luther Rabb, and the latest kid here, Kenny G, the guy from Franklin.

Jimmy Wants Walter and Webb to Join Him

In 1962, shortly before I got married, I got this phone call. Webb called me up and said, "Hey, Jimmy's got an outstanding group he's playing with." I think it was Little Richard. It might have been Little Willie John. It was a group that was really popular, cutting records ninety miles an hour, and Jimmy was performing with them. I don't know how he got tied up with them, but he called Webb and says, "Hey, come on down. I can bring you guys in. Get Walter and, you know, we can get it, have it made. I can pull you guys into the group." I had begun a steady job and I had just begun to cut music loose, and I said, "Hey, I can't make it in music." Webb had just gotten married and he was starting a family. He had acquired a job with the county and we didn't feel that we could sacrifice our jobs for hit or miss on music.

Jimmy's Friends

I get bent out of shape about guys saying they were Jimmy's friends when they weren't. Jimmy had very few friends. There were half a dozen of us, maybe a

few more, who saw him a lot, and supported him as a friend. It really tees me off that guys came around after he died and said they were his close friends, because when he was younger, and needed their friendship, they never helped him out. But because Jimmy made fame, people who had never acknowledged him wanted to participate in his funeral. Some of the guys who were his pall bearers hardly knew him. I regret that I didn't go, that I wasn't there for Jimmy's last moments. But I just couldn't do it. Knowing there were pall bearers who weren't close friends of Jimmy's, I just couldn't go. To this day, I haven't been able to speak to those people.

Jimmy's Fame

I felt Jimmy was probably the utmost musician in Seattle, but nobody recognized him. When he made fame, then everybody wanted to be linked with him.

For me, he was always my friend, not a star. He was my friend before he made fame, and he was my friend in fame. Even though I disliked some of the things that he did to his body, he was still my friend, and I know the other band members feel the same, you know.

I wonder about myself, being Walter, a working man, if I acquired fame overnight, could I really accept it? Would I take it in stride and act the same? Act nonchalant? Or could I, could I really accept it? Jimmy, being poor, wanted to be somebody, and all he had for comfort was his guitar and gaining that fame—saying, "I did it." I think this kid had to do something to relieve himself of all the pressure. Jimmy was not a bad kid. I think that with publicity, and the people on his back constantly—he had to do something. I mean, you can be sane and you can wind up insane by being taunted and watched, if

with every step you make somebody's watching you. Jimmy was not that type of fellow. He was an average American kid wanting to be somebody. He became the utmost musician in Seattle, and he finally made it big, expressing himself through his music, and I'm glad for him. It's only one in a million that makes it.

Jimmy

Jimmy is idolized by so many young people today for what he left behind. He's a legend. Even though I can hear him sometimes speaking, it's his guitar that speaks louder than words. And it will continue to speak louder than words.

Our band members, the guys who played with Jimmy, we grew up with him through the end. We were one body as a group. If everyone felt that way today, I feel that this world would be a better place.

Junior Heath
1945-1992

Junior Heath, a Seattle musician for thirty years, attended Washington Junior High, Garfield High School and studied music at Cornish College of the Arts. A professional guitarist and keyboard player, Junior last played with a rhythm and blues group called Sweet Talking Jones.

In November, 1992, Junior put his belongings in storage and prepared documents for a professional engagement in Asia. A delay in confirmation of the departure date led Junior to suspect something was wrong. When he called, he learned the group had gone without him.

Barbara Heath Evans, his sister, explains "Junior intended to move on to Plan B. He had a demo to do, and an engagement in Atlanta. He had faith that he was going to succeed in a big way some day, and he knew he could count on the family for support. I saw him the day before Thanksgiving, and he assured me

he was okay. Clearly he covered up his devastation about the group leaving without him. When Junior didn't show up for Thanksgiving dinner, we knew something was very wrong."

Junior Heath was found dead the day after Thanksgiving, on November 27, 1992. The cause of his death was a bullet wound. It was Jimmy Hendrix's birthday. He is survived by two sons, Andrew and Charles.

A Tribute to Junior Heath
by Barbara Heath Evans (sister)

Junior lived and breathed music. He practiced an amazing number of hours in a solitary way, absolutely consumed by music. He was constantly honing his technique. He seemed to always believe in his ultimate success. That's why his suicide was so out of character. I look around here at all of Junior's things, and I keep thinking he's going to come back.

Duane Eddy and Other Musical Influences

When we were younger, we had more of a hard edge to the blues. Then my sound sometimes leaned towards a jazzy sound. But Jimmy always liked a real hard edge on his sound. He was an innovator. He kind of went across the track and took the country sound and mixed it with a country rock sound and rhythm and blues. He was really into the Duane Eddy sound. That's why Jimmy's playing was always different from any of the rest of us. It was that Duane Eddy influence. Jimmy got the fusion idea, of combining country rock, R & B, and the rock 'n' roll of that era. There were very few Blacks, if any, doing that then. Was anybody doing it? I'm not sure.

For years White musicians crossed the color line to hang out with the brothers. Then they crossed back over and made a killing. That's what Jimmy did. He took that Duane Eddy sound and took it back across the line. He was one of the first ones.

We listened to people like Little Richard, Johnny Otis, and James Brown, of course. Then there was Hank Ballard, and Bobby Bland, and the guitar player who played with Bobby Bland. I finally met the guy about six months ago. Bo Diddley was another big influence, especially on me. Jimmy liked to listen to Richie Valens and the Big Bopper. Well, we all did. And Jimmy and I both liked B.B. King a lot.

Music was Our Magic

Not many people knew the Jimmy Hendrix of the times when we were kids. Jimmy and I spent a lot of time together. I met Jimmy when I was going to Washington Jr. High. We used to practice together in my parents' basement. I remember on nice summer days we'd be down in the basement playing the guitar. "La Bamba" was our favorite. Two other favorites were "Lucille" and "Rockin' Pneumonia." Music allowed us magic. It made us feel happy, and we could be somebody in our little sphere.

A Song for a Ride

I remember me and Jimmy bought Sears guitars for $49.95. We couldn't afford cases, so we used straps to carry our guitars. One time we were walking down 23rd and a car slowed down and a guy said, "Hey can you play those guitars?" We said, "Sure." He said,

"Play me a song, and I'll give you a ride, wherever you want to go." A song for a ride.

Battle of the Bands and the Rocking Kings

Jimmy and I played together for a few years, back in 1958, '59, '60. We used to play a lot of sock hops, Rotary Boys' Clubs, dances, at the Birdland, and at the Neighborhood House. Terry Johnson was always around. We used to have our Battles of the Bands, with other local bands, at the Rotary Boys' Club.

Then Jimmy and I played with a band called the Rocking Kings. With two guitar players, one had to tune his guitar down like a bass, while the other played lead. We'd take turns, going back and forth. And Jimmy was always a performer. He like to play his guitar between his legs, and behind his back, and with his teeth.

Around here Jimmy, Pernell Alexander, Raleigh "Butch" Snipes and I were the Teenage Bad Asses of the Guitar World. I knew Pernell before I met Jimmy. Jimmy also played with Robert Green. They had a group called the Velvetones. Walter Jones and Anthony Atherton played with them. They were Valley People. That's what we called the people who lived off Madison Street.

Pernell's Grandmother

Pernell's grandmother was a tough old bird. When she said "Jump!" you said "How high?" She was somebody you could not con. She was the type of person we felt respect for right from the first time we met her.

A Cinnamon Roll for Dinner

I never will forget one time we went by Jimmy's house, and for his dinner, there was nothing there but a cinnamon roll on the table. When I found out that it was the Jimmy Hendrix I'd grown up with who had come into fame and fortune, that's the first thing that came to my mind, going to Jimmy's house and seeing that cinnamon roll on the table for his dinner, and I was really glad in my heart that Jimmy made it.

Whenever I think about Jimmy making it big, that is the first image that comes to my mind, him sitting there eating that roll. That made such a strong impression on me. It was like not even eating.

His family wasn't as well off as the rest of us, and it made me feel fortunate that I'd had what I did. He and his dad lived in a small sparsely furnished apartment. It had one bedroom and the other room was a living room/dining room/kitchen combination. I think the reason Jimmy went into the service was that he was tired of the life he had there. By contrast to the rest of us, he was much poorer, and didn't have

the support we had. My parents were always encouraging me with things like taking lessons. They didn't want me to make a career out of music though.

Seattle Musical Influences

The art and music scene in Seattle has been bustling since way back in the forties. There have been a lot of good players that came out of Seattle, and nobody knows they're from Seattle. A lot of heavy guys. Even today, in 1990, there's a big pool of excellent players in the Seattle area still scuffling, trying to get the brass ring—just like me, trying to get the brass ring.

Back in the old days, Jimmy and I were influenced not only by national acts, but by a lot of good players in the Seattle area. Of course there was Dave Lewis and his trio. Another band was the Wailers. They were hot. There was Little Bill and the

Blue Notes, and the Dynamics. Back then Larry Coryell was with the Dynamics, and he was one of my idols. Jimmy listened to him too. When we were playing low-paid jobs in the ghetto, those were the people we looked up to. They inspired us. They were like gods to us. A lot of those people are still out on the music scene. I wish Jimmy was.

Ray Charles, who lived in Seattle, was also an influence on us. One tune by Ray Charles, "What'd I Say," influenced everybody on the music scene. Every hot band in Seattle was playing it. A lot of talented people have come from Seattle. And there are still a lot of talented people here. There was always music in the Central District.

They Cleaned House on Us

Road stories. I think everybody who's been in the business for a while has road stories. When we were kids, and the older generation around town that was scuffling found out that we were talented, they started taking us all over the countryside, playing gigs, and making money off of us. We were just so glad to be playing music, and making a little money, that we never did pressure anybody or question anybody. But I'm sure that we lost thousands due to shady booking agents and shady older gentlemen who were our so-called friends. They cleaned house on us.

More Recordings Out There Somewhere

You know a lot of people think they know all about Jimmy, and all of his recordings, but there's more. Somewhere out there, there are recordings from the days when we were kids that nobody knows about, but I don't know where they are.

Final Tribute to Jimmy

You know it's such a shame that such a talented guy as Jimmy had to die so young, at that point when he had just started to live. But I'll never forget him. It was just a shock, you know. It's a hard feeling to explain. It was a shock. I hadn't seen Jimmy in so many years, and then to find out that he had become famous, I really applauded him for making it. Then, just as fast, it seemed like, his life was over. Just like that. There was no time to enjoy the riches. They worked him so hard. There was no time for him to lay back and enjoy the roses. And now it's too late. He's gone.

Barbara Heath Evans

In junior high and high school, Barbara Heath was known for her ability to play the piano. "Barbara is the one who really taught me to play," says Terry Johnson. "I used to call her Tarantula Fingers. I give her a lot of credit."

"We wanted to invite her to join the Rocking Kings," says Walter Harris, "but in those days it was a taboo to have a woman in a band. Barbara is an excellent pianist." Barbara also sang with Washington Junior High's Choraleers, and with a harmony group called The Shalimars that performed at assemblies, talent shows, holiday programs and dances. A dance program lists the members as Barbara Heath, Lynn Edwards, Patricia Jackson, Kenny Wakazura, and Webb Lofton. Barbara lives in Seattle, where she works for the city.

Memories of Early Days

Jimmy Hendrix used to come over with the hordes my brother brought home. I saw him as a pesky little kid running around the house getting in my way. He'd be playing the guitar and plinking away on the piano, making lots of racket. Jimmy was fun; they were all fun. Music was always being played in our house, in one form or another. My dad was pretty good on the guitar. He used to play a piece that I really loved—a Spanish fandango. He played it on request fairly often. It was by far my favorite piece. I don't know if Jimmy Hendrix ever heard it, but I know he would have appreciated it if he did. Junior was always fascinated with dad's playing. Junior first learned to play on an acoustic guitar. He had a habit of playing quietly in his room.

I started playing the piano at my grandmother's house, and when I showed an interest in it, my parents arranged for me to take lessons with Mr. Wilcox. He was an important figure in the music community. He had a marching band. All of his children played four or five instruments. He taught me to play the tenor sax too. I wanted to play the B-flat baritone, but that was out of the question. I spent hours on the piano, whether I was happpy, or sad, or mad. I'd use any excuse to play. What I played for entertainment was mostly rock 'n' roll and rhythm and blues.

Thinking of Junior, Lloydie [Anthony Atherton], and Jimmy, I remember coming home one day, rounding the corner onto the Charles Street hill, and

TERRY JOHNSON, DONNA (COUSIN) AND BARBARA

they had an amplifier on the front porch that you could hear a mile away. It was so loud I thought someone would call the police. On the Charles Street hill every little noise echoes, so this was really awesome. My mother was not impressed. She still talks about it to this day. The Charles Street hill echo was so pronounced that you could yell to the hill and hear your voice. With the amplifier incident, the echo took on a whole new meaning.

Music was such an important part of our lives. I was surrounded by music away from home, as well as at home. We had so much fun in those days. I have fond memories of the weekly teeny bopper dances we had at the East Cherry YWCA, at 29th and East Cherry. We danced and socialized, and had a really good time. We had so many positive activities to keep us out of trouble when we were young.

George Griffin's Drum Duo

One of the most exciting theatrical performances I've ever seen, was an extremely innovative drum duo by George Griffin and another drummer. They had the drums in front of the other musicians, in center stage. The lights were turned down low, and the focus was on their hands. They wore white gloves. The imagery was incredibly unique and beautiful. The drummers played off each other, back and forth. Their drumming was central; everything else was incidental. It was dynamic visually and rhythmically. It was so unique. I still think about it.

Webb Lofton

Webb Lofton remembers when Jimmy called him from New York to ask him to come and play with him. "I was married and working for the county. I'd decided that since I was going to have a family, I had to give up my music. Sometimes I wish I were still playing. I listen to a lot of music, especially on the oldies stations. That brings back a lot of good memories." Webb has been with King County for thirty-three years now, and has been back with his first love, Dollie Star, for sixteen years. They enjoy trips together across the mountains to the eastern part of the state of Washington to go fishing. Webb has two children, Larnel Webb Lofton and VeLillian "Peaches" Lofton Campbell, and one grandson, Rowell.

The Rocking Teens

I met Jimmy at the Rotary Boys' Club. He was playing with another group then, and we invited him to join the Rocking Teens, a group Walter Harris, Charles Woodbury, Lester Exkano and I started. I was in the ninth grade then. We would practice in the club room at the Neighborhood House at Yesler Terrace. I lived in the project, Yesler Terrace. Sometimes we practiced in Robert Green's basement, when he became part of our group. We thought there was nothing greater than our little world.

James Thomas was our manager, more or less. I remember one trip we made to Moses Lake in the winter, and coming home over Snoqualmie Pass we hit black ice and turned the car over. We had an offer to play in Alaska, but we turned it down because we were all in school. When I think back on those years, I remember how our group lived for music.

Walter and I were the only ones in the group who had formal training in music. I started in the seventh grade. At Garfield I was in the marching band that played at athletic events, when "Peter Gunn" was our theme song. I took some summer classes. Anyway, it was always Jimmy who would take the lead as far as making up songs, and we'd follow along. Jimmy loved music. Back then he was one hundred percent Chuck Berry. Chuck Berry was his idol.

We played once a week on Thursday nights at Birdland. Dave Lewis played on the weekends. We were drawing such good crowds, I think Dave Lewis was jealous. After Charles and Walter graduated, we kept the group together. At one point we were going to ask Bill Stull, a White guitarist, to join our group. We went to his house in Broadmoor. But he only played Ricky Nelson style.

We went on some camping trips together. I remember one time we were staying in a two-story bunk house north of Seattle, playing a gig at Fort

Warden, in Port Townsend. Lester and Charles were the pranksters in the group, and they tried to tie Jimmy to a bed. Jimmy was screaming. He was easy to pick on, if you wanted to have fun.

Jimmy and Junior Heath

We all knew Jimmy was good. He played behind his back and between his legs. Jimmy had a used guitar when he joined our group, but no amp. Eventually the group bought an amp, but we didn't have one then. When Junior Heath joined the group, he had an amp, so Jimmy could plug his guitar into Junior's amp. Now that wasn't always so easy. I remember times Walter and I had to bribe Junior to get him to let Jimmy plug in with him. Junior was very good on the guitar, but Jimmy was better, and you know, he probably didn't like Jimmy showing him up.

Jimmy's First Guitar

Walter and I wanted to help Jimmy get a new guitar. This story's never been told before. I think about it every time I hear a story about Jimmy's first new guitar. My uncle helped us with the down payment and co-signed the deal at Meyers Music, where we bought the guitar. But when Jimmy took the guitar home, Al told him to take it back. So he didn't have it very long, but that's the story of Jimmy's first new guitar.

Memories of Jimmy

Jimmy was a nature lover, a daydreamer. I was a softy for people like Jimmy. I called him James. He was different. Some people would tease him about his worn-out shoes and his clothes. He acted as if it didn't bother him, but I think it probably did bother him deep inside. I gave him clothes. We all helped

dress him up. We all chipped in to help buy his uniform.

Jimmy was a bashful person. I don't know if he had girlfriends. I remember Betty Jean Morgan. She was maybe a couple of years younger and I think she went to Pacific. There were probably a lot of girls who liked Jimmy.

Jimmy was a real obedient kid. His dad had a good rein on him. If Al told Jimmy he had to be home at ten, he'd do it. Al always gave Jimmy a curfew, so we didn't participate in after-hours things. We played at adult dances, like at the Masonic Hall. Jimmy would go with us, but Al would meet him outside afterwards. Jimmy didn't drink and he didn't do drugs. If we got a bottle of wine, we had to twist his arm to get him to take a drink. One time we got some wine and Jimmy did not want to drink, but we insisted. He got drunk and threw his guitar down and said, "I don't need you guys!" I know he didn't want alcohol or drugs. Sometimes we'd hang out at the Burger King at 23rd and Jefferson, or at Keith's at 15th and Madison, or at Hills Brothers Barbecue.

One of Jimmy's best friends was Sam Johnson. Sam lived on 14th off Jefferson. When Sam went in the service, he was stationed in Germany. As far as I know, he stayed there. He'd be a good person to talk to about Jimmy, but I don't know how you'd find him.

When Jimmy died, the funeral was an invitational event. You had to be invited to go. Most of the guys who had been really close to him didn't get invitations. We couldn't figure it out, you know. We were hurt about it. But we didn't want to bother Jimmy's dad. He was going through a lot. My sister was upset about it and she decided to do something about it. So she called Al Hendrix and got invitations for me and Walter. There were other guys who were good friends of Jimmy's who would like to have been invited and weren't.

I haven't wanted to get involved with all the Hendrix publicity stuff that's been going on. Jimmy Hendrix was my friend. I guess my picture and my name's in all the books, so a lot of people want to talk to me. But I have preferred to stay quiet.

JIMMY HENDRIX AND WEBB LOFTON

Charles Woodbury

Charles Woodbury was known by his classmates for his ability to sing and play the piano. "I have a vivid memory," says Eugene Tagawa, "of walking into Mr. Jones' music classroom at Washington Junior High and Charles Woodbury was in there playing an old R & B doowap piece on the piano called 'Night Owl.' He was singing away, 'Here comes the night owl—hoo, hoo,' in a great falsetto voice." Charles played with Jimmy Hendrix in the Rocking Kings. Charles lives in Seattle, where he is an assistant foreman and a welder for a large firm.

The Rocking Kings and Jimmy

I was a pianist and vocalist for the Rocking Kings. Jimmy was our lead guitar player. As a matter of fact, for a while he was our only guitar player. I remember the dude as being kind of a quiet type of guy, you know. He wanted to be successful and he wanted to learn everything he could about a guitar. I remember when I first met him, he came to a practice and he had borrowed a bass guitar from his cousin Sam. And he could really play. I mean, he could play the things that we were doing at that time by Fats Domino, Little Richard, Johnny Taylor, and he could really play the blues. I mean, the dude could really play the blues.

Jimmy was a fanatic when it came to the guitar. He was fascinated with B.B. King and Albert King and Kenny Burrell. Jimmy was into the blues and would try to figure out how to get that sound. The sound he came up with was a mixture of the two Kings.

When we formed our group we had two sax players, a drummer, me, and Jimmy on guitar. Before Jimmy we had a White guy whose last name was Skinner playing guitar. That was the way it started out. Before we got Jimmy we were just a little, mediocre group, but after we got Jimmy, I mean, we started to kind of blossom. We started getting a lot of gigs around town and we really started to go.

I remember we were playing a gig one night at one of the halls and Jimmy was playing the blues. And I mean he had these people really going, and after he finished the song these people started throwing money! They really started throwing money up there. So we all stopped playing because we were only making like five dollars apiece for this gig. So we stopped playing, and started going to get the money. So the only person left up there playing was Jimmy.

The members of the Rocking Kings were Webb Lofton, Walter Harris, Lester Exkano, Jimmy Hendrix, Junior Heath, me and Terry Johnson. I remember in 1959, when we played for the Garfield Funfest, the band members were mad at me because the act was called Charles Woodbury's Band in *The Arrow*, the yearbook. [See page 105]

Jimmy was left handed, which meant that he had to take a standard right-handed person's guitar and play it backwards. Turn the thing backwards. I mean, it was weird that he could do this and I guess that maybe this is why he could play the thing so good and behind his head and stuff.

I kind of grew up with Jimmy. He lived about a block from where I lived, which was at 25th and Washington. He lived on 26th, at the corner of Washington. Jimmy and my nephew were friends. At the time, from my association with Jimmy, I couldn't believe that he became what he was. I mean, he just seemed like he changed personalities overnight. I remember Jimmy just being a real quiet type of dude.

James Thomas

One night we were coming home from a gig we did at Birdland. During those times we didn't even have any cars, so we would usually just pack our stuff on the bus or however we could get there. That's the way we carried our instruments. But we had finished this gig at Birdland and we were walking home, you know, singing like we do, rapping and singing. We passed by this house and we heard these dudes in there— they were playing. So, we decided to check it out.

So we just walked up to the house. We knocked and someone said, "Come on in." We had our instruments and they wanted us to play. So we set up and we started playing. This is how we met James Thomas, who eventually became our manager. As a matter of fact, I think James Thomas bought Jimmy his first guitar. And, I believe that he might have been a major influence in developing Jimmy. A lot of his showmanship reminded me of James Thomas. Some of his moves. James Thomas got us a lot of jobs. And he took our money.

Girls

The dude was kind of bashful. I can't ever remember Jimmy having a girlfriend. A lot of girls liked him because he could play the guitar and they could see some of the things that we couldn't see, that he might be somebody.

Songs We Wrote

We wrote a few songs. We didn't do anything with them, but Jimmy had a major influence in writing these things. Many of the songs were ones Lester Exkano and I wrote. There was one called "Naps," one called "Closer to You," and another called "Tee-Bone." Jimmy wrote one called "Jimmy's Blues." Most were in the key of C. We'd change the tempo. There was another one called "Grandma" written by an older gentleman named Mr. Williams, who had a son named Donald who was a senior at Garfield. Mr. Williams was good with harmony, and helped us harmonize.

Bill Eisiminger

Bill Eisiminger graduated from Garfield High School in 1961. He began his musical career playing the piano, and switched to electric bass with the Stags, a group he played with for five years. Bill was a teacher and a vice principal for five years in Seattle, and a principal in Kirkland for eight years. He lives in Seattle, where he works in real estate investment and property management.

Music Days

Music was big at Garfield long before we got there. There were many young people who were actively involved in music and the arts, both at school and outside of school. Both the performing and visual arts were well supported by our community. St. Peter Claver Church, for example, at 17th and Jefferson, had talent shows, and other events and activities for young people.

I knew Jimmy Hendrix because we were in Mr. Steele-Shaw's English class together. Jimmy was kind of shy, but he always had a friendly smile. We would talk about music, records, brands of guitars and basses—and different musicians. At that time I was playing in a band called the Stags with Luther Rabb, Terry Johnson, Bill Stull, and Rick Morey. Later Al Wyler replaced Rick on drums.

I met Luther, Bill, and Rick at a young musicians' workshop at St. Theresa's Church in Madrona. The event was organized by Mr. Wilcox, a music teacher, to bring musicians together so bands could be formed, and it was that event that was the catalyst for the Stags. I was the piano player for a time. Luther brought Terry to a practice once, and since Terry played the piano better than I did, he became the piano player, and I switched to electric bass. At that

point I began lessons with Floyd Standifer, who is somewhat of a legend in Seattle music history.

Sometimes I'd see Jimmy Hendrix at Terry Johnson's on Sunday afternoons, when we'd have jam sessions in Terry's basement. Terry's mom and dad were very supportive. They let us have both regular band practices and jam sessions in the basement, even with a full drum set and all the amplifiers. When we jammed, it was mostly guitar players who were there—Jimmy, Pernell, and Junior Heath. They were all great soulful players. Anthony Atherton would come over too. Randy Snipes was also a tremendous guitar and bass player. Sometimes we called him Randy, and other times we called him Butch. He played with amazing speed. I used to go to his house, up in the hills in north Renton. Sometimes I'd go with Luther.

EISIMINGER AND RABB

We were playing music when rock 'n' roll was just beginning. It was an exciting time. Bill Haley's "Rock Around the Clock" had come out in 1955 or 1956. Some of our favorite musicians were Little Richard, Fats Domino, Chuck Berry, James Brown and Hank Ballard. We started mixing rock 'n' roll with rhythm and blues.

We liked to play Earl King's "Come On" |Let the Good Times Roll|. It was a kicking tune with a syncopated rhythm. Then there was Johnny Otis. Everybody knew "Handjive." Even at school people would play around with the rhythm and that great line, "doing that crazy handjive." It was fun. We also liked Hank Ballard and the Midnighters. Some of my favorites were Hank Ballard's "Finger Poppin' Time," and Lloyd Price's "Personality" |Over and over|, and "Have You Ever Had the Blues?"—which Terry really sang well. He was really pumped up by that song. He's

the one who brought it to our group, and we all loved the way he sang it. When we played "Louie Louie," we all took turns singing and playing the drums.

We liked the blues and rhythm and blues. Normally what we called the blues were slower tempo songs with a lot of guitar licks, like ones by Muddy Waters and B.B. King. The blues were something people could slow-dance to. I remember times when dance chaperones would tell us to speed it up, to break up the clutches on the dance floor. Rhythm and blues tunes were sometimes slow too, but more often they were uptempo, like Hank Ballard's "There's a Thrill Upon the Hill."

We played at a lot of dances around town. Our band name, the Stags, had a double meaning. Stag refers to a male deer, but in those days, tickets for dances were usually sold as "stag" or "drag." "Stag" meant single, and "drag" meant couples. Usually

there was a price break for couples—$.75 for stag and $1.25 for drag.

We also had Battles of the Bands at the Roycroft Theater on 19th, and at the Masonic Temple, at Harvard and Pine. We played at the Birdland, sometimes during regular hours, and other times we'd play there after hours. Wilbur Morgan, the owner of the Birdland, was very important in the music scene in the central area. He helped a lot of young musicians, and provided a place where adults and teenagers could go to dance and socialize. Bands would get a chance for exposure. Another person who supported the rhythm and blues music scene, and Seattle bands, was Bob Summerrise, the disc jockey. When we'd go into his record shop on Jackson—between 12th and 14th—to check out the records, he always expressed an interest in what we were doing.

I used to work at the Burger King, at 23rd and Jefferson, across from Garfield. Jimmy Hendrix would stop by to say hello when he was walking down 23rd Avenue. He always had his Danelectro guitar slung over his shoulder. I never saw it in a case. Later I worked at Keith's, at 15th and Madison, and I'd see Jimmy and his friends there too—guys like Webb Lofton, Charles Woodbury, and other people from Garfield. Ron Holden, who wrote that great song "Love You So," worked there too.

The Dave Lewis Combo

I remember first seeing the Dave Lewis Combo at the Knights of Columbus Hall, at Harvard and Union, at a Friday night CYO [Catholic Youth Organization] dance. I was in the eighth grade. After hearing Dave play there, I wanted to see him more, so I'd go to see him at the Encore Ballroom, at 13th and Pike, and at the Birdland. Dave did so many things that we hadn't heard, and we were interested in learning from him. He was an inspiration to all of the musicians in Seattle.

Jimmy's Portland Concert

In September, 1968, I took some of my former junior high school students who had a band that I managed—Midnight Sun—to Portland to see the Jimi Hendrix /Vanilla Fudge concert. We had backstage passes, and we sat on the stairs leading to the stage—not more than eight or ten feet from where Jimmy was standing. It was fantastic. After the concert, we had a chance to talk to Jimmy. For my students, it was the thrill of their lives. Jimmy had a major impact on young people then, and that impact has not diminished in any way over twenty-five years.

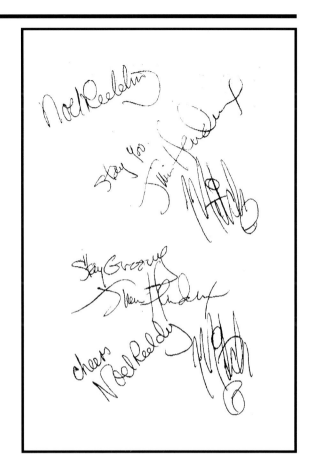

Don Williams

Donald Williams was born in Florida and moved to Seattle when he was fourteen. "In Florida, I was a varsity football player, but when I got to Seattle and saw that the guys playing football looked like lumberjacks, I turned to music," he says. He sang with a group called the Songcrafters, and played percussion instruments at home and in jam sessions around town. Donald studied the martial arts under grand master Yochi Nakachi, an opponent of Bruce Lee. In 1965, he opened the Seattle Karate Dojo. Donald has six children.

My Dad, Jimmy and Music

I think Jimmy started visiting our house because he liked my sister Harriett. Jimmy always had his little blue guitar. I never saw him without it. My dad took an interest in Jimmy's music. Dad actively supported neighborhood kids who were interested in music. He tried to help them get ahead by promoting their ambitions. He even used family funds to rent instruments. I remember the arguments that ensued when my mom got upset about it. Dad was a baritone bass. He sang with a male quartet and at churches.

My dad was a homespun musician who sang what he felt. He fancied himself a songwriter, but I wouldn't call him a songwriter. He had a way of expressing his emotions through music. I suppose it could be classified as the blues, but it wasn't called the blues then. The title came later. At the time of origin, specific kinds of music don't have names. But this kind of music has been passed on for centuries. Very few things are totally new. They're recreations of things from the past.

My dad started a neighborhood band. I remember that Webb, Walter, Lester, and Terry used to come over with Jimmy. Sometimes my dad worked one on one with Jimmy. At first when Dad was with him, I was standoffish. As I matured, that all changed. I could set my jealousy and ignorance aside as the necessity arose, and make contributions. When Dad let me know that if I wanted to contribute I could, I got involved with the kids. I spent time practicing with them, helping them with their music. When I graduated from high school, I took over the management for a while. What I provided for them was an adaptation of things from my past, which was rooted in the rich culture of the Bahamas, on my mother's side, and in Creole and Native American culture on my father's side.

My father was of mixed ethnicities–some of which I'm not exactly certain about. His father was a Native American of mixed ancestry, a very tall, very light-skinned man who had a handlebar moustache. He must have been Creole, and as far as we can determine, Cherokee. My father's mother was Black. My father's name was John, but everyone called him

Jimmy. He was an ambitious man with brilliant ideas who made a contribution to music in our community.

You know, the music of Africa is very much alive in Caribbean music. African music has permeated today's music; they can't be separated. African rhythms are soul rhythms. Drums were based on the heartbeat, and music was for dancing. When I got together with the neighborhood kids for music sessions, rhythm was central to everything we were doing.

At Garfield, the two best dance drummers were Ron Yoshida and George Griffin. We called Ron "Mamo"—that was his Japanese name. There was a Japanese girl from Garfield who was an extraordinary vocalist—Pat Suzuki. I think she was the first Garfield musician to become popular. In my class the two most popular dance bands were the ones Ron and George played with, the Skyliners and the Dave Lewis Combo.

Ron was a mathematical technician with his drumming; it was technically perfect. George was a soul drummer.

Bahamian Influences

I was born and raised in Florida, where the Bahamian influence of my mother's relatives was strong. We moved to Seattle when I was fourteen. I graduated from Garfield in 1956. My Bahamian ancestry has influenced me musically. One of my fondest memories of my years in Florida is a popular dance that's of Bahamian origin called the Curry. People beat on goatskin drums and knock on tambourines, and they dance from sunset until sunrise. They use homemade instruments, like the woodsaw. A woodsaw sounds like gourd rattles, and the tone could be changed by bending the blade. The woodsaw is always used in the Curry. I think the Curry has impacted many musicians. For example, a lot of reggae is an upgrade of the Curry.

"Tukukuru" and "Purple Haze"

There were many times when Jimmy and his friends and I would sit around the living room, working out rhythms and tunes. There was a tune that Jimmy, Lester Exkano and I worked out that I believe was the source of "Purple Haze." We liked to create acoustical tunes, using sticks. I had a set of three sticks that I made out of tool handles. I'd hold one stick between my knees, and I'd strike it with the other two sticks. It worked very well for tone and rhythm. We'd use Lester's drum sticks to tap out rhythms on the floor. I had the most musical background, but all of us contributed. We worked some basic themes into a piece we called "Tukukuru." That was a word we made up that we thought sounded a bit Latin, and was appropriate for this piece which was way out, in a fantastic sort of way. Jimmy tended to reflect on that one. He'd come back to it again and again. We'd tape it on an old wire recorder, then sit back and listen to it.

Lacy Wilbon

Lacy Wilbon knew Jimmy Hendrix in the early days. By chance, Lacy and Jimmy bought guitars on the same day at the Meyers Music Store. Wilbon played saxophone with Sounds East and the Lady Rose Quartet. He served twenty years in the Air Force, and is currently a financial services representative with a firm in the Seattle area, where he lives with his wife Sally. He has twin daughters, Tanya and Sanya Hall, and a stepson, Arthur Easterwood.

Early Days

I met Jimmy one day when I was over at my aunt's house at 27th and Howell. I looked out the window of my house and saw two little kids about to have a fight. I went out to see what it was all about and to make them stop. I said, "You don't want to do that. You can talk it out." One of them was my cousin Gerald, and the other one was Jimmy's cousin Bobby.

Jimmy had come out to see what was going on too, so that's how we met. In a matter of minutes, Bobby and Gerald were playing with each other again, and Jimmy and I struck up a friendship.

I was from "the valley." The guys from "the valley" had a friendly rivalry with the guys who lived farther south. The rivalry was really about girls, but sometimes we formed our musical groups with guys in our immediate neighborhood. I played in a group with Tommy Garrett, Freddie Dangerfield, and Sam Johnson. Jimmy and Sam were inseparable friends. Later I had a group called the Lady Rose Quartet with Lady Rose, Melvin Harding and Fred Rollins. Fred played with Jimmy sometimes, and later went on to be a sideman with groups like Big Mama Thornton.

I met Pernell Alexander through his cousin Durwood Moore, who was a friend of mine. Pernell had a record collection that wouldn't quit.

Sometimes I'd go over and listen to his records. Then I found out he played guitar, so I'd bring my guitar over and we'd pick a bit and compare notes musically. We learned a lot together. Pernell had the good fortune to go on tour and record with Billy Larkin and the Delegates. Pernell was the guitarist on the recording the Delegates made. I lived across the street from Robert Green. Jimmy played with Robert and Pernell and other guys over there, so I'd see him there sometimes.

Playing the Guitar One on One with Jimmy

When I played with Jimmy, it was one on one, strictly instructional. We never played a gig together. It was by chance that the day I went to the Meyers Music Store to buy a guitar—in August 1958—Jimmy was there buying a guitar. Jimmy was really into the blues in those days. He was way ahead of the rest of us as far as dexterity goes. He was so good at sixteen and seventeen. He was phenomenal. I used to sit in awe. He used his single-note technique. He wasn't proficient in chord building. I suggested he get some books and teach himself. I said, "If you do that, you'll be unstoppable." He said, "It would take too much time." So I taught him six chords—and six inversions.

Musical Influences

The Dave Lewis Combo had a major impact on all of us. They were my heroes. Musically they were the ones everybody looked up to. I'm sure they had a big influence on Jimmy Hendrix. They came up with a unique sound. I remember when Dick Clark credited them on American Bandstand after "Little Green Thing" was recorded. Dick Clark said, "There's a new sound coming out of Seattle. It's a big, fat, rich sound and the man behind it is Dave Lewis."

I started playing instruments when I was three years old—piano and sax. When I bought my guitar, lessons came with it, but it was country western, not what I wanted. Someone recommended Dave Lewis's father, so I took lessons from him. Later I played with Dave's brother Eulysses in a group we called Sounds East, with Larry Smith and Jimmy Hannah. We called it "east" because we played almost exclusively in minor keys. It was that eastern or oriental influence. Ulysses was drawn to minor chords. At that time Horace Silver had an album out called "Tokyo Blues," and we were awestruck by it.

Is This Our Jimmy Hendrix?

When I came back home from overseas, I went with a friend to see Pernell. He showed me The Experience album. I said, "Is this our Jimmy Hendrix?" He said, "Yeah, listen to it." It was phenomenal.

The Press

I've been so devastated by how the press has made Jimmy out to be. A lot of things get perpetuated by ill-founded rumors. The sickening part of it is that the system allows it to happen. Anything can be printed. There's a responsibility to verify the facts.

The press said things that made Jimmy seem ghoulish. People do change, but even if half of what has been said about him were true, he would have had to have made a 180-degree change. People don't usually change that much. When you know someone intimately in their formative years, you know essentially what the person will be like as an adult.

So much of what the press said about Jimmy was not in line with his basic nature. Labeling him a party animal was a contradiction. The stage persona, yes. I understand the P. R. A psychedelic image was created

for that first album so it would be eye-catching and
ear-grabbing.

Musically Jimmy was a genius. He was a pioneer.
He created a genre all his own. He was very bright,
very articulate. But he was very shy. You wouldn't
think someone that talented would be that way,
but he was. One on one, Jimmy was reserved, shy.
He wasn't brash. He didn't brag. One time after a
performance he told me, "It was a nice deal." He
always downplayed his talent.

I Cried

I was stationed in England with the Air Force from
June, 1969 until October,1971—at R.A.F. Chicksand.
The day Jimmy died, I was going to London to look
him up when I heard the news on the radio. I parked
my car and I sat there and cried. I do not believe
Jimmy had any intention of killing himself. Jimmy
loved life. He was not a quitter.

Manual Stanton

Manual Stanton graduated from Garfield in 1963. He attended Leschi Grade School and Washington Junior High. He was a bass player with the Black and White Affair and a professional dancer with Little Richard. He lives in Seattle.

Jimmy's First Guitar: Green Silvertone from Sears Roebuck

I was with Jimmy when he bought his first guitar at Sears and Roebuck on First Avenue South. He may have bought a guitar later at Meyers Music, but the first one came from Sears. It was a green Silvertone. We called it a Chiang Kai Chek guitar, because it was made in China. He used to paint it different colors. It seemed like every week he'd paint it a new color— red, purple, then back to green, only uglier than the original color. It had a tinny sound. He earned the money to buy it by picking beans. We used to go pick beans together. We'd get the bus in front of Sears.

Other Memories

His best buddy was Sam Johnson. Sam played the bass part on the guitar by loosening his strings. Sam stayed at 15th and Spruce. I stayed at 22nd and Spruce. Jimmy stayed at 13th and Spruce—before he and his dad moved to 26th and Yesler. I always called Jimmy "James." One day I said to James, "Hey, James, why don't you string your guitar upside down?" He did. Then he tuned it the Ike and Tina Turner way. It was an unorthodox way of tuning it, and anybody who picked it up couldn't play it. James played with a cold, funky rhythm. We called it "raw" and "in the cut." I remember he played at Garfield at an assembly just before he went into the service.

James was always practicing. All the time. He didn't ever sit around. He worked at it all the time. He did not chase girls. Except Betty. And he was not streetwise. We all admired the way James could play. He played even if his strings were broken and he didn't have money to buy more strings. He'd play with two strings, or he'd tie two strings together. He could make his guitar say anything he wanted it to say. He was a gift from God.

Curtis Simuel

Did He Drop Out of the Sky?

I usually don't tell people any more that I knew Jimmy Hendrix. Most of the time people don't believe me. They say, "Oh, yeah. Right." What do they think? That nobody knew him? Did he drop out of the sky already grown up? It's upsetting that people don't want to know his history. Jimmy was a kid with feelings, with ups and downs like everybody else.

Imitating the Way People Danced

Jimmy and I were great friends. We met in the seventh grade. One of my fondest memories is walking home with Jimmy after we had played at a dance. Neither one of us had money, so we walked. Dances usually got over at eleven o'clock, so we'd be walking along 23rd Avenue between eleven and twelve o'clock, laughing all the way home. That was

when Jimmy lived at 14th and Terrace and I was living in Yesler Terrace. Sometimes we'd laugh just to be laughing. We loved to imitate how people walked, and how they ran, and how they danced. The funniest part was how we'd imitate the way people had been dancing on the dance floor where we'd just played a gig. Back then people danced the Bop and the Slow Drag. Jimmy was good at imitating the way people danced. He didn't have a dance style of his own. In fact I never saw him ask a girl to dance.

The Rocking Kings

Sometimes I played with the Rocking Kings. I'd fill in for Lester Exkano on the drums. Lester was older than us, and he worked and had a set of drums. I didn't have a drum set, but Lester would let me play his. I'd sit in for him when he couldn't do a gig. I used to pray that he'd have to work, so I could fill in for him. When Charles Woodbury graduated and joined

the Playboys, I was the keyboard player for the Rocking Kings for a while.

One of Jimmy's favorite tunes was "Ramrod," by Duane Eddy. He lit up when he'd play it. He also liked Chuck Berry, especially "Johnny B. Goode." We liked playing "Louie Louie." We listened to the Richard Barry version. I remember playing "Louie Louie" at the Neighborhood House and at the Yesler Terrace gym. Back then we didn't have a bass player; we used two guitars and one played the bass part. Jimmy could play both parts. We used to practice at the Neighborhood House every Tuesday. I also remember going over to James Thomas' house— at 918 24th Street, I think.

GARFIELD FUNFEST: ROCKING KINGS

Jimmy's House at 26th and Yesler

One time Jimmy borrowed my only pair of black slacks for a gig. We were both poor. These were my Sunday slacks and band slacks. Well, he didn't give them back. So I had to go over to his house and get them. He and his dad had moved to a little house at 26th and Yesler. I was glad to see Jimmy living in a house. It was tiny, but it was kind of cute.

Tribute

Jimmy changed the way people play the guitar. After all those years apart, I thought we'd finally be together again. His death was very upsetting. There's not a day that goes by that I don't think about him, and I still feel that part of him that we had together. I really feel good about that.

The Music Scene continued . . .

HENDRIX AND THE ISLEY BROTHERS

THE KING KASUALS: HENDRIX, BILLY & LEONARD MOSES

The Family: Interviews

Al Hendrix

Pearl Hendrix Brown

Diane Hendrix-Colley

Janie Hendrix-Wright

Leon Hendrix

Dolores Jeeter Hall

Eddie Hall

James Allen "Al" Hendrix

THE FOLLOWING IS A SERIES OF INTERVIEWS
CONDUCTED IN 1988, 1989, AND 1991,
BY MARY WILLIX.

You told me once that the public had the wrong idea about Jimmy. What was that public image that didn't represent who he really was?

Al–The public Jimi was flamboyant, but the private Jimmy was withdrawn and shy. Flamboyancy was just a stage act. He couldn't be shy and drab up there on stage, playing the kind of music he was playing. In reality, Jimmy was quiet, even though with his friends he would jive and carry on. They'd do a lot of bull-corning around.

What doesn't the public know that they should know?

Al–That's hard to say. Everybody would like to know everybody else's business. People like to know the way, deep-down secrets.

Maybe there's a way without invading privacy to straighten out an image that's been tampered with.

Al–Well, they should know that he was one who just liked to play his music, and to express himself with his music. He was against a lot of the corruption that was going on.

In the music world, you mean?

Al–All around. In Vietnam, and other places. And he was against the drug scene, too.

Did he talk to you about those things?

Al–Oh yeah.

Did you have long phone conversations?

Al–Usually we didn't talk much on the phone. But he came home on tour, and we talked about a lot of the different things going on.

What were Jimmy's early years like?

Al–Well, I tell people all the time that he was just like an ordinary kid. There was nothing spectacular. A lot of people expect he had some sort of halo or special glow about him. But Jimmy didn't look at himself as being special.

Was he quiet as a toddler, or was it later that he became shy?

Al–He was three years old when I met him, but he seemed like an ordinary kid to me. Going into the service brought about a big change in Jimmy. He met a lot of people. He met Billy Cox, for one. He met a lot of other musicians. I can't recall their names. When he'd go on a weekend pass to whatever towns were close by, he'd take his guitar to see if he could play in jam sessions. That's how he met a lot of other musicians.

How might that have changed his outlook on life?

Al– He decided to become a musician. That was his thing in life. He enjoyed the guitar.

Do you know how he made that decision? Was it gradual?

Al–He talked about it before he went into the service. He had tried to get a job elsewhere, but he couldn't. He worked with me in the landscape business. He was a good worker. He enjoyed it. But he used to tell me that he was going to become a big musician.

So, becoming a professional musician was pretty settled in his mind back in 1960?

Al–He wanted to make a name for himself and for the Hendrix family.

How well do you think he coped with fame?

Al–He seemed to handle it okay. He told me he was going to buy me a home. At that time I was buying a home, so I told him, "Just keep your nose clean, and take care of yourself. Keep on wailing and doing what you're doing." He called me from London and told me they were building a group around him, and they were auditioning for a bass player and a drummer. That was where Mitch Mitchell and Noel Redding came into the picture.

He didn't let fame go to his head. I told him, "Don't ever get a big head." And he didn't.

He was still just Jimmy?

Al–Oh yeah.

LUCILLE JEETER HENDRIX

Was Jimmy one to pick up the phone and call every once in a while?

Al–Occasionally, though when he was stateside he sent postcards. But he was traveling so much, I wouldn't answer. He played with a lot of different groups then. Wherever he sent the cards from, he wouldn't be there for a return, for an answer. He was living the life of a Gypsy.

And when he was living in London?

Al–He only called a couple of times from London. It wasn't long after that that he came back to the states. He kept in contact, by writing or something like that. He always said he was busy. I said, "I know you're pretty busy. There's no use in trying to write. I understand how that goes." Otherwise, I would read about how he was doing in magazines and so on.

What was it like when he came home? Did he seem like the same Jimmy?

AI–Yeah. Yeah. It had been five years since he had been home, and he kept repeating that. He'd say, "Dad, you know it's been five years since I've been home?"

He was so excited being here. The time went so fast. They were all checked in down there at the hotel, and there was a lot of picture taking out there at the airport, and a lot of excitement. Yeah, he was really overjoyed about being home. That must have been in about 1967 or 1968.

So he hadn't been home since 1962 or 1963?

AI–Yeah, something like that. He'd been home when he was in the service on furlough. You know he

injured his back in a parachute jump and got a medical discharge. Well, he had met a lot of musicians, and he decided that where he'd been there was more of a chance in the music line, like back East.

He played around with different people in New York, and Chicago. Like I said, I'd get postcards from him. There were a lot of ups and downs. He ran into financial troubles, and I sent him money.

Jimmy got so run-down and skinny. He looked like he needed a good meal. He wanted me to travel with him, but I said no. I wanted to, but I had just gotten married. So I couldn't. But Jimmy, he understood.

Then there was the time when he was playing with a group in a nightclub, I think in Virginia. There was segregation, and Blacks weren't allowed to sit in

JAMES MARSHALL HENDRIX, 1943

the theater in the front row, or they'd be put in jail. Jimmy and his group sat in the front row and got put in jail, so the club owner had to get them out of jail so they could play in his club. He said to me, "Dad, I know you would have done the same thing." During that time there was also a lot of fighting going on in Africa. Jimmy told me about pictures that he'd seen in *Life* magazine. He was against all that turmoil.

He was in a lot of the civil rights marches. He gave money to Martin Luther King. He knew that I took part in demonstrations and parades here. Jimmy wrote me about the sit-ins in the theater. I forget which city it was in.

He was following in your footsteps, hm? I know how strongly you feel about civil rights, and how you raised Jimmy to be tolerant.

Al–I was brought up that way, to be accepting of everyone, no matter what race or religion. That's the only way I knew. And that's the way Jimmy was raised. There were no prejudices in our family. That was the way he was brought up, and he was that way all the way.

I was born and raised in Vancouver, Canada, the youngest of four kids. My sister's name was Patricia, and my brothers were Leon Marshall, who died young, and Frank, who married Pearl and had a son and a daughter.

In Vancouver they didn't have prejudice the way they did in the South. All the schools were open to all races. I was one of very few Blacks. A lot of times, I was the only Black in the class. Every once in a while somebody would call me a name, or sometimes a teacher would be a little prejudiced. And I remember one kid who didn't like Blacks. (Laughs) And there was a swimming pool where they didn't allow anyone with dark skin.

A private club?

Al–No, a public pool. The Crystal Pool, in Vancouver. The White kids I ran around with didn't go there because they didn't allow Blacks or Japanese.

Then there were certain jobs, especially government jobs, that weren't open to everybody. That changed a lot after the Second World War. Then I came here to Seattle. There were more Blacks here, and jobs were more open. At least to me they seemed to be. But still there was that segregated feeling, in certain hotels, for example.

"GRANDMA" NORA HENDRIX

Have you spent time in any other part of the country?

Al–Oh, yeah, when I was in the service I went down to Fort Sill, Oklahoma. (Laughs) Naturally, it's prejudiced. I never did go to town the whole time I was in the service, stateside, because I was always in the South. They always give you weekend passes so you can go into town Friday evening and stay in town until Sunday evening. I always felt, here I am wearing the same uniform as the White soldiers, but on the buses that go into town Blacks had to stand back until all the Whites got on.

AL AND HIS GOLF BUDDIES

Is that right? I've never seen anything like that.

Al—Well, I didn't go. I said, if I get into town I might get into trouble. (Laughs) This is the South. In the North it's different. From Oklahoma I went to Georgia. It was the same there, and from there I went to Alabama.

That's where I was when Jimmy was born. I tried to get a furlough to get home when he was born. But I lived too far away. I was the only one who lived in the state of Washington. There were some Californians. Most of the guys lived right around there in the area.

In the Articles of War, they tell you that for death, sickness or birth, you're supposed to get a furlough. Anyway, I went to see the commanding officer and he told me, "Hendrix, they're giving ten-day furloughs to the guys, " he said. "But if you get a furlough, it would take too long for you to get home. The trains are traveling slow because of the war effort, and by

the time you'd get home, you'd have to turn around and come back." So I just saluted him, and headed toward the door. Then he hailed me back. (Laughs) He said, "Hendrix, now don't you get any ideas of going over the hill." And I said, "No, sir." Not long after that they put me in the stockade, and I don't even know what for.

Oh, no.

Al—They never did tell me what for. But I figured that they thought I was going to go over the hill. But, shoot, I was too doggone far away from home.

I don't understand. They would do that without giving you a reason?

Al—They're not supposed to hold you for over 48 hours, or something like that, without charging you with something. But I was never charged with anything. I had just gotten a telegram that Jimmy

had been born. Eight pounds, eleven ounces. (Chuckle) My sister-in-law sent it to me. I still have the original telegram.

You do?

Al—Yes, I saved it. It said his name was Johnny Allen Hendrix, born November 27, 1942. We renamed him Jimmy, James Marshall.

How long were you in the stockade?

Al—About two months.

You're kidding.

Al—No. And I didn't lose any pay either. My outfit was getting ready to go overseas. The M.P.'s came down one day and got me and took me back to the barracks to my regular outfit. I got all my gear together, and that evening I went back down and spent the night in the stockade. The next morning the M.P.'s released me to my outfit, and I got on the

train with the rest of them. We went out to San Francisco and embarked for overseas.

When I got overseas, I'd missed three pay checks. I hadn't been paid for two months. When you're put in the stockade, they usually fine you for the time you're in there. But I didn't lose any money, and it's not on my record.

So, it's essentially as if you were never in there.

Al—It's not on my record. When we got to the Fiji Islands, I got paid. I had three months pay coming, and nothing was deducted. There was no fine. I asked the sergeant why I was in the stockade, and he said, "Just general principles."

How did you meet Lucille?

Al—I met her where I was staying. A girl there brought her by. Fats Waller was in town and I invited her to go. I didn't know she was so young, only seventeen,

or I wouldn't have asked her to go. After that she started coming by where I was working at the foundry. Then I had an operation, and she came by to see me at Harborview Hospital. She lived with her parents a block from Garfield on 23rd. I used to go by there.

Can you tell me about your family background? There's so much information in print that is incorrect.

Al—My mother's grandmother was a full-blooded Cherokee. My mother's grandfather was English or Irish. She remembered him always singing Irish ditties. My mother's mother's name was Sammie. Of course, she was part Cherokee. She married a Black fellow, but I don't know his name,

I don't know much about my dad's folks. He was born in Urbana, Ohio. He was quite a bit older than my mother. There are quite a number of Hendrixes down there in Ohio where he came from. I've never

been there myself. My mother was never there either. I remember meeting a fellow in the Army who said he'd been to Urbana and he said it was a small town with a bunch of Hendrixes. My mother was born in Tennessee and raised in Georgia. I have her birth certificate and things of that sort. And I have a little something on my father, but it's not the sort of document they have now. It's more like a doctor's or a midwife's report.

My dad traveled a good deal. At one time he was a policeman in Chicago. That would have been in the late 1800s. After they moved to Vancouver, he worked as a steward at a private golf club. We kids had dual citizenship. My mother didn't work outside the home after she had children. In those days people used to do a lot of entertaining when visitors would come by. Mother enjoyed making her own wine—grape, dandelion and other kinds. In those

JIMMY AND AL LIVED HERE FOR A WHILE

days we had a coal stove. She used to keep her wine behind a small, hot water heater.

My brother Leon was very talented. My father gave him violin lessons. He had piano lessons, too, and got very good. We got a piano. I picked up the piano by ear. My mother and my sister played too. I wanted lessons, but since Leon was the firstborn and he was Dad's favorite, he got the music lessons. I remember my friend Buddy Hamilton complaining on the way home from school about having to go to piano lessons. I thought, doggone, I wish I could take lessons. I wanted to learn guitar too, but my fingers were too big, and we didn't have a guitar.

My parents were both in show business. My mom was a chorus girl and my dad was a stage hand. That's how they met, at a show out here. My mom taught me and Leon tap. And we took tap dancing. We'd put on shows and she'd pay us. When visitors would come by, we'd dance for the company. It was kind of like a family thing.

Like a recital?

Al–Yeah, nearly all the time we'd do that. It was fun. Then the guests would give us a nickel, or a dime, or whatever. It was nice.

Did you have some kind of routine to perform, or did you make it up on the spot?

Al–We always had songs to sing. I used to hear my mother singing around the house. We'd all chime in. It was a way for us to entertain each other. That was our home entertainment. We didn't have a radio, and, of course, no TV.

Did you learn to harmonize?

Al–Oh, sure. Especially when we'd have house parties. I remember how much I enjoyed them because my brother and I would get in there and sing. People would make up their own rhythms. It was really enjoyable.

Sounds like a living-room jam session. And everyone knew how it worked?

Al–Yeah. Someone would start singing something, and another one would come in with baritone, or whatever, and it would go all around the house. It was a lot of fun. I used to get a kick out of listening to the grownups sing. They were good.

Did your dad sing too?

Al–Not too much. He sang in one choir. He went along with the singing, but he didn't do any dancing. My mother, she did all the dancing. I guess I got the dancing from my mother. She showed me a lot of different steps.

Do you remember any of them?

Al–Sure. I still do a little hoofing. I used to tap dance and do what they called "Falling off the Log." And there was another one called "Possum on the Log."

That's great! Do you remember how to do it?

Al–Yeah. People used to laugh at that one. Most people make up their dances. Here we had the Possum on the Log. I remember how my Jitterbug partner, Dorothy, used to laugh about that.

Did you do dances like that when you had company over?

Al–Sure. And I used to do the Charleston for them. And the Alexander Hop. That's one my brother taught me. It seemed to be something the neighbors and visitors would look for. They'd ask us to dance or sing. My brothers and sisters and I didn't rehearse. We'd just get out there and perform. Later I signed up with an agent and did weekend gigs. I'd be like

an intermission entertainer. I enjoyed it. I planned on being an entertainer. It's in my blood. I liked Bill 'Bo Jangles' Robinson. I'd watch and pick up steps and improvise. I got my kicks, and people loved it. Jimmy loved entertaining too. I equate Jimmy's playing to my dancing. I remember how I'd get tickled thinking these people are going to pay for something I love to do.

Do you remember any of the songs your family did?

Al–Off hand, I don't remember anything specific. But we did some of the spirituals, and the modern songs of that era. But mostly they'd be spirituals, like the one about the chariots. It was a kind of family thing. Practically all of the black families I knew did it. Somebody would start a tune, and somebody else would pick up on it and harmonize. Then, I remember later on when I was grown, and I'd be shooting pool at the pool hall, and the guys there

would do it. Usually it would be songs that everybody knew, but if they didn't know the words, they'd at least hum along.

So pretty soon everybody would be harmonizing?

Al–Uh, huh. Everybody would get a little piece in there. Yeah, I'd get a kick out of it. We'd all laugh, and I'd say, "Man, we gotta get on stage."

That would have been great. Did you sing around Jimmy?

Al–Oh, yeah. When I'd be doing different things, I'd be singing. But he was three years old when I first saw him, so I didn't have a chance to rock-a-bye him. But I used to do a lot of singing around the house.

Spirituals?

Al–Spirituals or blues or whatever popped into my mind.

Are there any favorite pieces that you remember?

Al–Not right off. I remember one time I was singing and my wife, Lucille, was on the phone, and whoever she was talking to said, "Have you got your radio on?" So she said, "That's Al." And the other person said, "Oh, no it isn't." I had to laugh about that. Sometimes I used to think, "I'm in the wrong business if I sound that good on the phone."

Were the songs you sang ones you learned at home?

Al–Before we got a radio, back when I was a kid, we had a gramophone. I used to play it constantly and I learned a whole lot of blues. My older brother Leon used to listen, too.

Do you remember Jimmy singing spirituals?

Al–I know he did. He used to go to Sunday school. But Jimmy didn't have much of a voice. No voice for singing, anyhow. He took after his mother. She didn't

have a voice either. She couldn't hold a tune. Jimmy knew he couldn't hold a tune. He used to say sometimes, "Dad, those guys are just hollering anyhow. Especially those rock stars, you know. You can't understand what they're saying half the time."

What did the family think about Jimmy's singing?

Al–Oh, |laughs| Jimmy's singing ability was not too fine. I used to tease him about it. |Laughs| But, he told me one day—before he became "The Experience"—he either wrote to me, or called me, and said, "Dad, all the other people are singing, and they can't sing worth a doggone." (Laughs) He said, "I'm going to try it too. I'm just going to be out there shouting all over the place; my music's going to be the same," which it was. He said, "You know I can't carry a tune in a bag." I said, "I agree with you there." |Laughs| But he went on and did his thing. He wasn't

noted for his singing. He was noted for his guitar playing.

What kind of music did Jimmy listen to at home?

Al–He got a lot of music from the records I had—B.B. King, Muddy Waters, and different artists of that sort. When he was learning to play the guitar, he would accompany the records. I always told him, "When you get into music, you do your own thing, whatever it is. Everybody likes something original." And he really did that, of course.

When you got out of the service, when Jimmy was three years old, you picked him up in Berkeley and brought him back to Seattle, right?

Al–That's right. A lot of people wonder how he happened to be there in Berkeley, California. That's a long story. Jimmy got bounced around from pillow to post when he was a baby. He was three years old, and

he didn't know me. But, still, I thought a great deal of him during the time I was in the service. A lot of the time I was just thinking about my son. I had a son out there, and that's what I wanted to get home to.

What was Jimmy interested in, other than music, when he was growing up?

Al–A lot of people ask me about his interests. "Did he like sports?" they ask. I say, "Oh, yeah. He liked sports." He belonged to a football team. He played two years in Little League, with the Fighting Irish. He enjoyed that. He liked to play baseball. Also, he was kind of ambidextrous. Well, he batted left handed and he pitched right handed, so that's where he got a little mixed up. But, he was just an ordinary youngster.

I always told him, keep up the way you just do your own thing and do the best you can. I felt he was

going to become, oh, popular, though he became a bigger star than what I had thought. I figured that maybe he'd be playing around on a circuit, like playing in cabarets, clubs, things of that sort. But then he became nationwide and I saw it. Well, that really floored me though. I used to pinch myself to think that here was my son doing this. It really made me feel good. I told him, "Don't get swell-headed. Don't ever get too big for your britches." Which he didn't. I mean, he was just still ordinary Jimmy. Still kind of shy. The way he carried on on-stage was flamboyant. Sometimes he might be a little nervous, and he'd be trying to fight with the crowd, so then he'd come off real strong. And I used do that myself, when I used to dance sometimes. That's the way it went with him in that respect.

Let's talk about Jimmy's artwork. When he was at Meany he was considering becoming a commercial artist.

Al–Yeah, he always worked well with his hands. He always spoke of becoming a commercial artist, and he did a lot of drawings, really good drawings. He had his own ideas on different things, and he'd do all kinds of space things, most anything—cars, battle scenes, or football games or whatever. Well, all kinds of things.

Jimmy had extra large hands, extra long fingers. They came in real handy playing the guitar. He reminded me of my oldest brother, Leon. Leon had delicate fingers. He was a great pianist and dancer, also. Jimmy didn't do any dancing, but he was good in the entertainment line.

AL HENDRIX, JIMMY'S DAD

BOB HENDRIX AND DIANE HENDRIX-COLLEY, JIMMY'S COUSINS

"WITH SLEEVES ROLLED UP, WE'D PUT ON OUR WILD ONE HATS & PRETEND OUR BIKES WERE MOTORCYCLES" JIMMY & BOB HENDRIX

FRANK AND PEARL HENDRIX

Pearl Proctor Hendrix Brown

Blinded by diabetes, a disease that nearly took her life more than fifteen years ago, Pearl turned to Christian Science and began singing again. She lives in Vancouver, where she gives regular concerts. She has been a guest artist several times on "Let's Sing Again," a television program that is broadcast across Canada. She has three children—Bob Hendrix, an executive for a large corporation in Seattle, Diane Hendrix-Colley, a budget analyst for a firm in Manhattan, and Henry Brown, a Vancouver-based musician.

Personal Background

My husband Frank was a dreamer. Frank Hendrix was very bright, and quite an artist. He could have done very well, but he never had faith in himself. Once he drew plans for someone's house, but he never got paid. Frank and Allen, Jimmy's dad, were brothers. So Jimmy was my nephew.

Before we moved to Seattle in 1952, I had always lived in Canada. I was born and raised in Edmonton, Alberta. There were very few Blacks in Canada, and they lived in different areas. My family had gone to Athabasca, Alberta, a farming area. My father's people were from Ohio. My mother was from Oklahoma. In school I wasn't around other Black children until I was 14. There was only one other Black family with children in the same school I went to.

When Jimmy Lived with Us

As a young child, Jimmy would come to Vancouver with Pat, Frank and Al's sister, for a couple of weeks during the summers. But to my knowledge, he never lived in Vancouver, as some of the biographies say. It was during those summer visits that he'd see his Grandma Hendrix. When he'd come to stay with me

in the summer, he came in rags. I'd buy him new underwear and get him clean clothes.

Jimmy came to live with us in Seattle in 1955, near the end of his sixth-grade year. We were on Cherry Street, then we moved to the corner of 22nd and East John, a few blocks from Meany Junior High School. I can't remember dates too well, but I think Jimmy was with me during grades six, seven and eight. Most of those three years.

Junior high is a time when kids need special love, and I was hoping to be of some help to Jimmy during that period. I thought he really needed it. I loved Jimmy so much, but I guess he couldn't feel it. We all loved Jimmy, but he wouldn't let anyone get close to him except for my daughter Diane. He and Diane got along so well. Jimmy could be warm and wonderful. Diane was no threat to him. But he didn't do as well with my son Bobby.

"MOM HENDRIX"

JIMMY, WHILE AT MEANY, LIVED WITH UNCLE FRANK & AUNT PEARL

We always had lots of kids around, streaming in and out. I was always on the run, working the early shift, and then hurrying home to take care of everybody. I don't remember the names of Jimmy's friends. I called them all Sweetheart. I'd come home blurry-eyed and do the routine things, make dinner and all. I worked all the time and I worked long hours, and it was very important that certain things had to be done. Jimmy always showed me extreme consideration and love. He needed to get what he wanted from me, and there was nothing that he couldn't have received or achieved in that way. I did the very best I could, but I didn't have the time I would like to have given to Jimmy with all of the demands on my time.

Jimmy's Art

When he was at Meany, Jimmy took art classes. He drew beautifully. He made me some scenery pictures because he knew I loved water, mountains and trees. He did other kinds of art, but that was the part I liked best. His artistic ability came naturally from the family background.

Grandma Hendrix

Nora Hendrix, Frank and Al's mother, came to live with me in 1971, and was with me until she died in July of 1985. I called her Mom—Mom Hendrix. She moved to Vancouver in 1911, shortly after she was married. I've got a picture of her and her husband, a nice one, that was taken in 1911.

Mom Hendrix had been an entertainer. She danced until she was in her nineties. Well into her nineties she used to say, "When I was young, when I was seventy-some, I could dance all night. If only I were 75 again. I used to dance and work and do everything! Those were the good old days." She was a very special lady. I loved that woman. She had so much to offer. Jimmy had entertaining in his blood from her. He loved his grandmother. He loved her dearly.

Mom Hendrix and I didn't like the fanfare of being recognized in public as Jimmy's relatives. But she did enjoy getting a card from the Queen of England on her 99th birthday. She lived to be 100. We have a video of her 99th birthday party.

There was a pioneer study done, and several Blacks were featured in a book called Heritage. Our part was on the heritage of the east side of Vancouver, where the Chinese and Blacks lived. Mom Hendrix has a page and a half, with a picture of her.

Blacks and Whites in Seattle

I found my first two years in Seattle fascinating. The Black population there had grown tremendously

before and after the war. It went from something like 2300 to 23,000. I had never seen so many Black people in my life. A lot of the Blacks I met were from the South. I don't know what I'd be like if I had been raised there.

For two years I was PTA president at Harrison school, where the Whites wanted to enlarge the school boundaries to equalize the races. I acted as the liaison between the White community and the Black community. It was fascinating because the Blacks were after me and the Whites were after me. I befriended the Whites and the Blacks got angry, because I didn't feel like they did.

I'd say, "Look. I wasn't brought up like you. I didn't grow up knowing all the innuendos that you know. Sure, there's prejudice in Canada. Don't get me wrong. But it wasn't the kind you lived through. So when you tell me you don't trust them with a ten-foot

pole, I say, 'Whoa. Wait a minute here. What is this tunnel vision?' The Blacks gave me far more trouble than the Whites. But I offered what I thought was the right way to handle certain things, and I smoothed things out. And in those two years there was far more communication between the two sides than there had ever been before.

Jimmy's Concerts

Allen and I and Grandma always wore earplugs at Jimmy's concerts. And even doing that, I couldn't stand the physical vibrations that would plummet my body from the noise. Did you ever think about the guys on stage behind the amps?

Jimmy's Loneliness

Diane was very angry that they never let Jimmy have a vacation. He wanted to visit her in Vancouver. Jimmy also wanted to spend time in Seattle when

he came for concerts. The management wouldn't allow it. Jimmy insisted on sleeping one night at his dad's and one of the management people slept right there too to keep an eye on him.

I see a lot of loneliness and despair in Jimmy's music. In later years he was so lonely. He was so young and vulnerable. He suffered from a lack of mothering in grade school. It's the music of a young man who was trapped and asking for freedom. He couldn't defend himself. There was so much exploitation.

We can't bring him back, but we can set the record straight. Drugs? I think he took them to survive. Uppers to go on stage and downers to go to sleep. Jimmy was a wonderful person, but he had problems he wasn't able to cope with.

Diane Hendrix-Colley

Diane Hendrix-Colley spent her early years in Vancouver, Seattle and Spokane. Her father Frank Hendrix and Jimmy's father, Al, were brothers. Diane studied business, and has worked as a model and in various business capacities. She lives in New York with her husband Ed, an actor, and her son Jason. She works as a budget analyst for a large corporation in Manhattan.

Jimmy's Poetry and Dreams

Jimmy would read his poetry to me. Sometimes I'd have to ask him to reread a line, or maybe an entire poem. He poured his heart into those poems. They were deeply philosophical. I had to concentrate so totally to understand them. And then sometimes I still didn't understand. Some of the things he would read to me were pretty far out.

I knew he was reaching out to me. I felt his anguish. I understood on some level, but I didn't know what to do. Jimmy was nine years older than me. I was too young, and too involved with my own life. I didn't realize how urgent the situation was. I thought there was time.

Jimmy would tell me about his dreams. His dreams were like science fiction. His mind was way out there. I was reading a lot of science fiction then, and I had vivid, pretty wild dreams, so we related well. We could share these ideas. Jimmy's dreams and thoughts were like a slice of science fiction. We would talk about people and things that might exist on other planets. Maybe that's why he communicated with me, because I understood to some degree that level of thinking, dealing with science. Jimmy's mind was brilliant in that sense. But the difference was that I had balance and love—the balance of a stable home life which he hadn't had.

Phone Calls

Jimmy and I had long conversations on the phone. When I called him I called collect, because he never wanted to hang up. My attitude was, "I'm sorry, Jimmy. I love you dearly, but I can't afford to call and talk for two or three hours." I was scraping by on a tiny budget. But having him pay the phone bill all the time bothered me, so if we talked for more than an hour and a half, I always thought of some reason to hang up. I'd start worrying about the phone bill.

Most of the time I was at a pay phone. Our conversations were always heavy. I would call from a pay phone so I wouldn't be disturbed. So you have to visualize me there, standing outside at a public phone beside a country store in rural Vancouver,

groping with this heavy stuff my favorite cousin wanted me to understand.

He was living in New York then, with a woman—apparently his girlfriend. When I'd call collect, the operator would say, "Diane Hendrix is calling collect. Will you pay?" At Jimmy's funeral, the woman who had been living with him asked my mom, "Who is Diane Hendrix?" My mother told me his girlfriend thought I was Jimmy's wife! See, when I'd call, Jimmy would be very secretive. He'd take the phone in the other room and lock the door. He didn't tell anyone who I was. This woman didn't have a clue. I was a secret.

Probably the girlfriend knew nothing of Jimmy's family. Maybe he purposely kept his family a secret as a source of strength, and of stability. Being secretive about family in Vancouver was also important because he was planning a vacation in Vancouver.

Entertainment and Art in the Family

Everyone in my family, except my father, has been involved in the entertainment business. My mother sings. She still gives concerts. She and her sisters did radio. They sang and did plays. My grandmother was very musical. Grandma loved to dance. My Uncle Al had musical ability. His older brother Leon was apparently a musical genius. Unfortunately he died at eighteen, before he had time to develop his talents. If he had lived, I have envisioned that he would have worked with Duke Ellington. My father, Frank Hendrix, was a very fine artist. The Hendrix family is very artistic.

Jimmy's Years with Us

Jimmy lived with us when I was a child. We were living in Seattle on East John, and Jimmy was going to Meany Jr. High School. I felt very close to Jimmy, even as a child. He was my favorite cousin. I don't know

the reason for the attraction, but I know he took good care of me. I was his little cousin. He was like an older brother, very attentive. I felt very close to both my brother Bobby and Jimmy.

They used to get mad at me, just the way brothers do. I thought I was so grown up. I was five, six, seven, but I didn't feel like a little kid. I thought I should be with them all the time, but sometimes they didn't want me around all the time. Jimmy taught me to play cards. We'd sit around the dining-room table and play a game called Tonk.

I loved the way Jimmy laughed. He put his whole self into it. I don't know if that's a Hendrix trait or not, but I love to laugh too. I've always related to people who can laugh. I remember when Jimmy laughed, it was a hearty laugh. We laughed and laughed. Jimmy was lots of fun. And he was very witty.

DIANE AND HER HUSBAND ED

I remember one afternoon Jimmy yelled at me and Bobby to come upstairs. He said, "Major's having kittens on the bed." We thought Major was a boy, you know, a big old tomcat. So that was the day I learned all about the birds and the bees from Jimmy and Bobby, watching Major have kittens.

Jimmy was a very giving person, but he was private. Our personalities were very different in that way. I'm an open book. I don't hide my emotions. Jimmy wasn't open about his feelings. With me he was very caring. We developed a special bond. I didn't threaten him in any way. But with other people he was cautious. He'd had a tough life, and the scars were apparent.

"You Ain't Nothin' But a Hound-dog"

Elvis Presley was really hot when Jimmy was living with us. We liked him. "You ain't nothin' but a hound-dog"—that stuff. Bobby and Jimmy used to practice

to Elvis's records, using brooms as guitars. I loved watching them. They would put on a show for me. I loved to be entertained, and they loved to entertain me. They sang and played those brooms.

It's funny, even though I was only about six years old, I remember being socially conscious. I had bought an Elvis record for Bobby and Jimmy. Then I heard a statement that turned me off right there. I was told Elvis made a statement about Black people—that all they can do is shine shoes. I heard that statement and I never appreciated the man after that. Even if it wasn't true, if he hadn't said it, it put me off as a child. I stopped loving Elvis. It was a heavy thing for me.

Philosophy and Emotions

Jimmy didn't express his emotions very well. To tell you the truth, I don't know if anyone knew him very well. He talked heavy philosophy, but that's different.

You can talk all the philosophy in the world, but expressing your innermost emotions is another story. He was never that way as a child. He couldn't open himself up. I think there were strong signs of trouble. My mom saw the signs. But there was only so much she could do. I think Uncle Al didn't realize how bad things were. He had a son who was so heavy, and he did the best he could.

Jimmy had so much anguish to vent, and he let it out through his music. He reached out to very few people. And the recording industry could care less, as long as he was making that dollar. Now there were people in the arts who cared a lot about Jimmy. They admired and liked him. He was such a nice, nice person. But did anyone have in-depth conversations with him? Or did he just party with people and stay distant?

When Jimmy would call and tell me his dreams, and read to me, he wanted to know how I felt. He would tell me I was the one person he could relate to. I was too young to understand, or to know what he wanted from me. As I got older I started to understand what had been going on, and how much pain he had been going through. It's very bad at that age when you don't know, when you can't do anything about it.

My mom genuinely loved Jimmy. I know Jimmy really appreciated the years he lived with us. But there was only so much my mom could do. Jimmy was about twelve when he came to live with us.

I think Jimmy felt a void in his life. If there was closeness with his mother, it was very brief. I believe strongly that every boy needs a mother's love. Men who haven't had that seem lost. I believe there's something biochemical about these needs. As

women we carry a certain amount of maternal instinct within us. Boys need to receive that motherly love. I've been told that Jimmy's mother had a drinking problem. I know very little about her. I never met her. The women Jimmy picked were not motherly, but who's to say they weren't like his mother?

New York

New York is a very difficult place, especially for Blacks. I never really knew prejudice before I came to New York. There's a negative attitude toward minorities here in New York that disturbs me. Jimmy and I both came here from the Pacific Northwest. So I know what it was like for him.

The Pacific Northwest is so uniquely clean and awesome. But you don't realize how spectacular it is until you leave, until you come to a place like New York. I love New York. It has the best of everything—shows, entertainment, never a dull moment. But

there's a very negative side. It's an intense city; there are a lot of workaholics here. New York is a city that never sleeps. It can eat you alive. You pay the price, if you choose to live here.

The pace here is extremely fast. People don't have time for each other. At home in Vancouver my friends and I make time for each other. I've had a great foundation in life, so while I'm a different person now because of the awareness I got in New York, I haven't become hung up in it. But let's think about Jimmy. Who did he have to turn to? I don't think he had healthy people to go to.

I think New York was definitely the wrong place for him. He would have been more laid-back than New Yorkers. New York is such a hyper, uptight city. How can you be physically and mentally healthy if you don't give yourself a break?

DIANE AND HER SON JASON

It's interesting that Jimmy wasn't accepted here initially by the Black community or the White community. He had to go to Europe to get recognition and love.

Rejection and Love

Jimmy had been rejected by his own country, and that's sad. He must have felt a kind of bitterness. He had given so much of himself, and he wasn't getting enough back. His music was so far out there that most people didn't understand him. Today there's a much greater awareness, but back then people weren't ready for change. And Jimmy's music was change.

Of course, after he proved his genius, after he made it big in Europe, attitudes changed. Then a lot of White people here loved him. And that was during the Civil Rights movements. And you have to remember he was Black, but young White people loved him.

Trapped

Jimmy had become trapped. People need guidelines, especially when it comes to money, so they don't overstep their bounds. You can't let people take over. There are too many greedy people. Jimmy wanted to make it so badly, and he didn't know the price he'd have to pay by relying on other people. He became trapped by contracts, and by people who had so much money wrapped up in his career, they wouldn't let him go. I wish I'd known enough then to help him. He needed someone from his family, from his past, to help him.

There were times when Jimmy was performing all the time. What was his management thinking? During the sixties young artists were used and abused. Nowadays musicians are smarter, and they are not being taken advantage of the way they were then. Recording artists have more control over their finances. Money was not Jimmy's main concern. He was really into his music. During that time it was very difficult for a Black man to get into recording anyway.

The day Jimmy died was one of those days when you feel something's very wrong. I had a terrible nightmare. I dreamed I was walking down a street, on my way to work. I was about to go up some steps, when I noticed a parked van, off to my side. Two men got out of the van, pointed guns at me, and shot me in the chest. I remember falling back, then to the ground. I was trying to fight, trying to fight death. But, all of a sudden—if you've ever had anybody just come at you, and grab your eyelids and just shut them—that's what it felt like. Like death. I thought I was dead.

RENTON, WASHINGTON

RENTON, WASHINGTON

I woke up in a cold sweat. I was working in Vancouver then, and I had to be at work at six in the morning. When I got to work, someone told me I had just missed a call from San Francisco. I didn't know anyone in San Francisco. They said it was very important. I don't even know who it was to this day. Later that morning another call came. I found out Jimmy had died. It blew me away. I don't know if there was a connection, but if he was trying to contact me, boy, it was not very pretty. I was in shock.

But that dream, I'll never forget that dream as long as I live. I'll remember, at least—if that's what death is all about—that it was very, very scary. Just to go that way. It wasn't a peaceful death, it was violent. It was a very violent dream and I've never had violence in that manner in my life, not even in my dreams. It was something that I never want to go through again.

Jimmy's Plan to Visit Diane in Vancouver

Jimmy had been planning to come out and visit me. He was going to spend two weeks with me in Vancouver at the end of the summer of 1970. He had been feeling terrible, going through all kinds of mental anguish. Apparently no one he worked with knew about me or his plan. I wonder if he was planning to run away, to break some sort of contract and hide in Vancouver. If he had stayed with me, no one would have found him.

My mom told me later that he wanted out of the contract, and they wouldn't let him out. I wanted him to visit me. I knew something was wrong, very wrong. He needed a vacation. He was completely drained. He said he wanted to come to my place to rest. He needed help with his business desperately. They were using him and he was exhausted, physically and emotionally. But I didn't realize how bad it was. I think he was reaching out to me because I was an empathetic connection with the past, someone nonjudgmental. He needed someone to listen. He was totally burned out.

His Guitar

I think the basis for a good life is love. When love was missing from Jimmy's life, he found it in his instrument. I think his guitar was his real love, and he loved his guitar more than he loved any woman. His guitar would never disappoint him. It would do everything he wanted it to do. And, remember, Jimmy was a very shy person who didn't relate easily to people. His guitar gave him a way to relate to others. His guitar was his voice.

Janie Hendrix Wright

JANIE AND JIMMY

Janie Hendrix Wright is a dedicated spokesperson for the Hendrix family. Born March 1, 1961, Janie was adopted by Al Hendrix after her mother and Al were married on June 23, 1965. Janie has a B.A. in Education from Central Washington University. She and her husband Troy E. Wright have four sons (Austin, Quinntin, Claytin and Langstin). They live in Kent, Washington.

Memories of Jimmy

*J*immy called us from London to say that he had made it, and that he had changed the spelling on his name, and that he was calling his group the Jimi Hendrix Experience. He came to Seattle in 1968. My sisters and I made him a big banner that said "Welcome Home Jimi. Love, your sisters." There was a picture of Jimmy that Linda had drawn. The second time he came, he had this big cape, and after the concert he chased me down the hall, in the hotel. He

knew that I loved Batman. Batman was a favorite of mine. So he chased me down the hall, and he was singing the Batman theme song. Then he scooped me up in the cape, and hugged me, and tickled me. That was a lot of fun. Then we visited him in his hotel room, and in his ashtray there was a little agate heart on a chain. I asked him what it was. And he said, "Oh that's for you. I got that for you." So he put it on me. And he drew a little picture of him on my hand. After that concert we went up to Canada. He performed up in Canada. We rode in the car that he bought for my parents the first time he visited. He was so excited to ride in the car with us. The first time he visited the house, we had a family forum and we all sat in a circle and everybody asked him questions. He was talking about what it was like. He was so shy. He closed himself in, and talked with his hand over his mouth. He told us about different

situations on the road. One time he was in the kitchen and I was playing with his hair. I used to love his hair. I was combing through it.

Another time we had went to his hotel, and he had his leg over this balcony. I said, "Jimmy, you shouldn't do that because you might fall, and I don't want anything to happen to you. I don't want you to die." He told me that God would always be taking care of him. And there's one picture that did bring that out. We used it for our tribute. It's a picture of me and Jimmy looking at each other. We were backstage. He said that I would never have to worry about anything, that he would always take care of me. That I was his baby sister. That no matter what anybody said, that I was his sister. You know, people used to make comments like, he's your stepbrother, or you're his stepsister. And I asked him what that meant. Step sounded like somebody that you step on. And he said, "No you are my sister. You will always be my sister. You are my only sister." That was real special. And then after that, he held my hand, and we walked through the Coliseum to get to the limo, and all these people were trying to get his autograph. But not at any time did he let go of my hand. He just held my hand the whole time until we got into the limo.

And then at his last concert, at the Sicks Stadium in Seattle, he was singing "Purple Haze." I always loved the song "Purple Haze" when I was a kid. I was on the side of the stage and it was pouring down rain, and they were all trying to keep the rain off his head, and I was fearful that he was going to get electrocuted. In the middle of the song, he turned around, and he said, "That girl put a spell on me," and he was pointing at me, and all the audience was trying to look to see who he was pointing at. Then he did this little smile, and he scrunched his nose, and did this little thing with his tongue, and the crowd went crazy. The people beside me said, "He was pointing at you." I said, "I know."

You know the interview he had with Dick Cavette on the Dick Cavette Show? It was the epitome of Jimmy. You could be talking to him, and he could turn the conversation around. He started interviewing Dick Cavette before he knew what was going on. I love that interview.

The Space Ship's Missing Door: Janie's Dream of Jimmy

I used to dream about Jimmy when he was alive. The last dream that I had before the space ship dream, was when my mom told me that they were sending for Jimmy's body. So as a nine-year-old, I envisioned that a casket would be sitting on our porch. I had a dream about it, and that was my last dream of Jimmy until recently.

When we started the court case, there were so many papers—all the documents that I had to deal with. It was really kind of strange. I woke up very early one morning, and I thought, well, I'm going to try to get a little more sleep. So I went back to sleep, and I had a dream that my dad and I were in a field. The field was a very overgrown, grassy field, and the grass was almost as high as I was. In the distance we saw Jimmy, and there was a space ship beside him. It was missing a door. He was looking around like he had lost something. And I said, "Jimmy, what are you doing?" He said, "I'm looking for my door in order for me to go to heaven and finish my mission. In order

for me to finish my mission, I need to find my door." I said, "Well, I'll help you look for the door. I really need to talk to you about some things." I couldn't possibly tell you what we talked about. I asked him some questions, about people in his life, his managers, trying to find out some information that would be helpful. It was really like he was there. He was talking to me in his same voice. He said, "Well, Janie, that's something you have to do, because I need to find my door. That's my mission." After that, I woke up, though I wanted to stay there talking to him. Shortly after that, I called my attorney. He asked me what I thought the dream meant. I said, "When everything is over, we will have found the door, and Jimmy can rest in peace. When we find the door, it answers all the questions." That was the conclusion. In a newspaper article where this dream was described, it said, "When we find the door, then

we'll find Jimmy." And that wasn't right. The door is the answer to everything we're looking for. The interesting part about it being a space ship was that Jimmy used to talk a lot about space ships. People don't usually dream about space ships. And then Diane told me she dreams about space ships all the time. She says it's a Hendrix thing.

Spirituality

First of all, what people don't realize is Jimmy was raised in church. He was raised in a Baptist church. My dad has always taught us not to say God's name in vain, to pray before you eat, and to pray before you go to bed. And although my dad wasn't an avid church goer, he gave us the basics. And I know Grandma took Jimmy to church when he was little, to the Goodwill Baptist Church. And the thing about Jimmy is, he was a firm believer in God, not all these other entities that people talk about, but God, the

Creator. In the lyrics to some of his songs, it shows. For instance, "Purple Haze." I've known this for years, but now, more and more, we're finding things out.

In *Cherokee Mist*, there's a piece of paper in there where he had wrote, "Purple Haze, Jesus Saves." That was the original title to that song. It was a twenty-minute-long song, in the original version. But the manager said that was too long. So it was cut, and that's what we know today. But the original was "Purple Haze, Jesus Saves."

The other thing is Jimmy was very concerned about sin, and how it looks in God's eyes. That's another thing that disturbs me, when people say that he committed suicide. Because he spoke in depth about suicide, and how he knew that it was a sin in God's eyes that if you committed suicide, then you wouldn't go to heaven because you've

JANIE AND HER SON LANGSTIN

LANGSTIN, JANIE, AL AND AUSTIN

committed the ultimate sin. So knowing that, I know he didn't commit suicide.

The song, "The Wind Cries Mary," was written about Mary, the mother of Jesus. The other thing is, with regard to harmony of races, Jimmy was very ahead of his time. In the sixties, there was heated racism. Civil rights was just getting underway. He could see far into the future to where people would all get along, when people wouldn't look at each other as a color, but as a person. You know he used to get quite offended because people would say, "You have mainly a White audience. How come you don't cater to the people of your color?" They didn't realize when he played in Harlem, the people didn't want to hear him. And that hurt him. He wanted all the people of all races, of all colors, to love him, and to enjoy his music.

And I think my main point—and I stressed this at the tribute, and in every interview that I've given—is that I wish that people would not concentrate on Jimmy's death and how short of a life that he lived, but on his music that he produced during his lifetime, and on his words that he was trying to teach us in his songs. They should concentrate on that. If they really want to know him, then they need to dig into his music, and learn. Because he had a lot to say, that we all still learn from. Most people don't accomplish in a lifetime what he accomplished in a short time.

My Dad, Al Hendrix

My dad is the best father anyone could have. He has been, and is still, my best friend. I was fortunate to have more leisure time with him than Jimmy did. We went swimming together, ran around the track together, and had many long talks. He turned 75 on June 10th, 1994.

Uncle Frank, Dad's Brother

Uncle Frank would come over about once a week to visit. Diane [Frank's daughter] looks just like him. I think Diane looks like Frank, and Bobby looks like Pearl. I used to like it when Uncle Frank would come over. He was a character. He was an Adonis, such a good-looking man. Women loved him. I don't remember if he had three or four wives after Pearl, but there were at least three. He was something.

Hendrix Family Benefits for Children

Jimmy loved children. They are our future. The benefit we had in New York on June 12, 1994, was for children. The family is planning more benefits to fund scholarships for children. I am working as a spokesperson for the family, doing things for the family, in Jimmy's name. We have exciting plans for the future.

Dolores Jeeter Hall and son, Eddie Hall

Dolores:

I took care of Jimmy for the first four years of his life. His mother, my sister Lucille, was only sixteen when she married Al, and then Al went into the service right away. Jimmy was born at the home of our friend Dorothy Harding. She is still one of my closest friends. The story about Jimmy going to California while Al was in the service needs to be clarified. A church woman friend of ours took Jimmy to California with her on a vacation. Nobody took him away. Then when Al got out of the service, they all stayed with me for a year. Later on I'd see Jimmy at birthday parties. I wish my sister Nancy were alive to tell about Jimmy. The last time we saw Jimmy was at his last concert here in Seattle. We went to the concert, then we went over to Al's house afterwards.

Eddie:

My cousin Jimmy was eleven years older than me, so I didn't know him well when I was growing up. In spite of the age difference, Jimmy has been very important to me—as a person and as a musician. I play the guitar, and Jimmy's music influenced me in many ways. His lyrics are powerful. He spoke a lot about freedom. It was heavy. He wanted to let us know about so many things. There's a lot left to be told about Jimmy.

I saw Jimmy when he was in Seattle for the last time. He was so stressed out before that concert. I think he was burned out and frustrated. Before the concert he was sitting in the house, at his dad's, looking out the window. There was a limo out there waiting to take him to Sick's Stadium. He didn't want to ride in a limo, and that's what he told his manager. Then June and I drove him. After the concert, he

listened to me play. It was the first time I'd played for him. He said, "I'll be back in a month. Then I want you to come to New York and record."

The night Jimmy died, the dogs howled and howled. I think they felt something was wrong. London is nine hours ahead of our time, and the timing of their howling coincided with Jimmy's death.

After Jimmy's death, Mike Jefferey wanted me to go to New York with him, but my parents wouldn't let me go. That was a good decision, actually. I understand so much more now. Several of Jimmy's girlfriends have stayed in touch with us over the years. There's a lot more to Jimmy's story yet to be told.

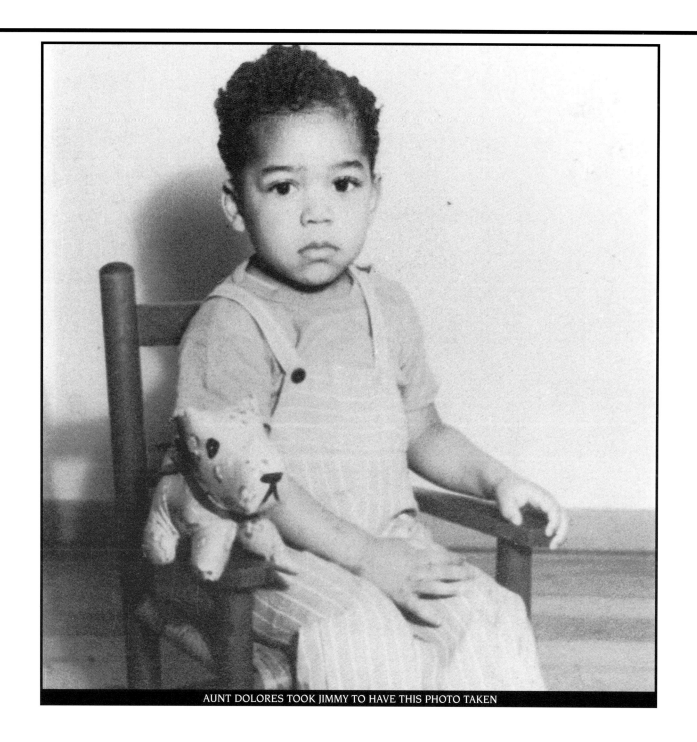

AUNT DOLORES TOOK JIMMY TO HAVE THIS PHOTO TAKEN

Leon Hendrix

"My dad loved Jimmy so much. He was truly inspired by him. A lot of my dad's art work deals with freedom, the unity theme, and symbols of mystical concepts—like butterflies, fairies and the Pegasus. Back in the mid-eighties he became a homespun preacher. He used to have us get together for Bible study every Tuesday. He talked to me often about spiritual things. He still does. He talks to me and my friends about God. I'm proud of my dad. He's very talented. There's still a part of Jimmy alive inside of him." LeAnne Hendrix, daughter of Leon Hendrix

Leon Hendrix has six children: Leontine, LeAnne, Alex, Jason, Jimi and Jonelle. He lives in Seattle.

Hendrix Friends: Interviews

FRIENDS, SCHOOL AND CENTRAL SEATTLE

Freddie Mae Gautier

Beverly Rhue

Theodore Murray

Ralph Hayes

Betty Morgan Wallace

Janet Nosi Terada

John Eng

James Minor

Steve Fletcher

Mike Tagawa

Garfield High School and memorabilia

Meany Junior High (memorabilia only)

Washington Junior High (memorabilia only)

Life at Garfield

Postscript

Quotes for Life

Freddie Mae Gautier

"I remember when Jimmy was little, he would sit by himself like he was meditating. I think that in every generation the Lord gives us someone—we might not appreciate them—but, they're about something within their soul, and that's what Jimmy was about. He talked about spirituals and the gospels—the depth of them—and the singing, and how much it meant. Sometimes he'd just sneak into churches. He said, 'I just go in and sit and listen to the choir and get an inspiration, and then I go on.'"

Born and raised in Seattle, Freddie Mae Gautier is a vibrant woman with unshakable faith in turning negatives into positives. "Take lemons and make lemonade," she says. "I believe in maintaining a positive attitude. My grandmother—who was an ex-slave, had 17 children and lived to be 109—was my role model for family values and positive living."

Mrs. Gautier worked actively with Dr. Martin Luther King for many years. "I remember when Rev. Jesse Jackson first came to the board and I jokingly said to Dr. King, 'Assign him to me. I'll work with him.' Well, he did, and Rev. Jackson and his family have become like family to me."

Mrs. Gautier is the Customer Service Manager for the municipal court for the city of Seattle. She has two grown children, a daughter who lives in Georgia, and a son who lives with her. Her son finished his college degree after he was paralyzed from the chest down in a swimming accident. "I taught my children to always have faith, and to continue making a contribution. My son is in a wheelchair, but he finished college after the accident, he drives, and he works for an organization that helps handicapped people."

Mrs. Gautier is still active in community service projects and she volunteers her time with organizations that support young people. "My current project is a health and nutrition program founded by Dr. Constance Rice, wife of Seattle Mayor Norman Rice. The program is being piloted in eight schools, where families are fed on Friday nights while they are taught about nutrition, health and how to buy food. It is proving to be a very successful family-unit program."

Mrs. Gautier is a friend of the Hendrix family. She helped with the arrangements for Jimmy's funeral, where she read his poem, "Angels."

Baby Jimmy is Taken in by the Gautiers

My first experience with Jimmy Hendrix was when he was one or two weeks old. His grandmother, his mother's mother, Mrs. Jeeter, worked in our home. My mother needed help with maintenance because my parents had a business, a bakery. So she hired Mrs. Jeeter because she was a good friend of my grandmother's and my mother. Mrs. Jeeter came at least once or twice a week, and sometimes every day.

One cold winter day, towards the end of November or first part of December, Mrs. Jeeter came to our house with a bundle with little baby feet sticking out. It was fascinating to me because my mother kept foster children. I was an adopted child. So my mother said to her, "What in the world are you doing with that little baby like that, as cold as it is? Look at his little feet. They're so cold they've almost turned blue." So she said, "Oh, this is Lucille's baby." So my mother said, "Well, where in the world is Lucille?"

Mrs. Jeeter said she had not seen Lucille since she came home from the hospital, so she had the

baby. Then my mother said, "Give me this baby and let me warm him up." Well, poor Jimmy was so cold. He had turned blue; his little legs were blue. The diapers were sopping wet. In fact, it was so cold that the diapers were stiff. So my mother took him and bathed him. I remember getting a pan of warm water and putting it on the table for his bath. Jimmy was tiny, you know, just tiny. Then my mother put her elbow in the water to test it.

Then my mother asked again, "Now where IS Lucille?" And Mrs. Jeeter said again that she had not seen Lucille since she came home from the hospital. When Mrs. Jeeter was getting ready to leave, my mother said to her, "You can't take this baby home. Who's feeding him?" Well, Mrs. Jeeter was kind of noncommittal, because I don't think she knew what was going on with Lucille. So my mother kept Jimmy there. My mother said, "Tell Lucille that she'll need

to come over here and get this baby because I need to talk to Lucille, and see why she left the baby with you." So, for the next few years, off and on, we kept Jimmy in our home, with the other foster children that we had. I helped take care of him, babysat him. You know, it was a common occurrence for us to have extra children in our home, so we didn't think anything about having Jimmy there. When babies would leave to be placed, we'd cry. So it wasn't unusual having Jimmy there, except with Jimmy we knew his family, the Hendrixes and the Jeeters. During that period of time, Jimmy sometimes stayed with his Aunt Dolores, on the maternal side, and his dad's brother's wife, Pearl, who lived in Canada. During the first few years of Jimmy's life my mother had a lot of input. She was disgusted with Lucille for leaving the baby.

When Jimmy got older he'd come over and visit. He'd come by to see us at the house, or he'd stop by the bakery.

A Secret with Mrs. Jeeter

Lucille's mother, I guess, was a wonderful lady, but she was not too swift about some things. We all loved her to death. She worked for us off and on for about fifteen years. I remember the first secret I ever had with anybody was with Mrs. Jeeter. One day my mother wasn't home and Mrs. Jeeter washed the mop she had washed the floor with in the kitchen sink. She was supposed to use a bucket. I wasn't supposed to tell. I'd never had a secret with anybody before. That was our secret. So I never did tell. As long as my mother lived, I never told. That was something that I wasn't supposed to tell. So Mrs. Jeeter was special to me because we had a secret. I was twelve or thirteen years old.

Jimmy's Legacy from His Grandmother Nora

We knew his dad's family up in Canada. We knew his father's mother, Nora Hendrix. Jimmy came from a family background that had a lot of theatrical talent in it. His grandmother Nora Hendrix, was really a kick. She kept me in stitches all the time. In her nineties, one time, Al gave her a trip to Hawaii with one of his sisters-in-law and I said, "Now, Mama Hendrix, when you go over there, we've got to get discovered, so see if you can find one of those beach boys for me." "For you?!" she said. "I'm going over there to find one for myself!" We laughed because she was always very humorous. She always used to sit around and tell stories about, you know, when they were on the stage singing and dancing. So Jimmy had that in his blood, that theatrical ability.

Mrs. Hendrix was a very precious lady, a joy to be around. I believe she lived to be a hundred. Jimmy did spend time with her up in Canada. As I said, she was very special. Some of that bloodline came through in Jimmy. It was in his presence. Jimmy was a very pleasant person—warm, low-key, not loud and boisterous. That was the Jimmy that I knew.

Civil Rights

Jimmy and I talked a lot about the Civil Rights movement, because he knew that I was on the board of the Southern Christian Leadership Conference. Jimmy had made sizable donations to the Southern Christian Leadership Conference and the NAACP, and he was very fascinated with Dr. King, and how this man gave of himself. We talked about the idea of giving back. Since I knew Dr. King personally, Jimmy wanted me to tell him more about him and his work.

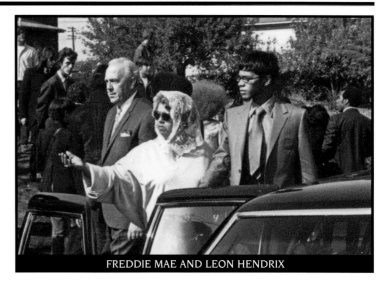

FREDDIE MAE AND LEON HENDRIX

Freddie Mae's Last Visit with Jimmy, 1970

The last time I saw Jimmy was the last trip he made to Seattle for a musical engagement, I think at Sicks' Stadium. I don't remember exactly. You see those things weren't a big deal for me to remember. When you know people who are celebrities I guess it isn't the same as for people who don't know them, and make on over them. Jimmy came on over to the house. This was the same year he died.

It was after midnight when Jimmy got there, and he had never really done that before, so I felt something was bothering Jimmy. I didn't know what it was. But he just wanted to talk, and I listened. Jimmy's traveling manager—I can't remember his name now—called a lot of times during the morning.

It was a real funny feeling sitting there talking to him. You know how you get eerie feelings. What's

going on? What's going to happen? At least I do, when you get that deep and involved in a moody kind of conversation. His road manager kept calling and saying, "When's he coming home? What's going on?" So I finally said, "Quit calling over here. Leave him alone." Because Jimmy kept saying, "I don't want to talk to him."

He was very nervous about it. Of course, later on I found out what the nervousness was about. After Jimmy died I learned how they wanted to control him.

Race Relations in Seattle

Seattle, of course, was like the far West. It had to grow and we are growing, even in race relations. Even though in Seattle there were laws against segregation, sometimes it was unspoken. When my dad came to Seattle in 1914, there were some things that were unspoken. There weren't too many Blacks

here, and we used to say that to see a Black you had to go down to the railroad station to see a pullman porter. My dad came here from Arkansas to work for one of the big bakeries. They brought him here. He was the first Black baker in the state of Washington, the first one who actually did baking, and not washing pots and pans.

Seattle has a reputation as a "rainbow city." And we are, in reality, because this is a port city. We're now part of the Pacific Rim. We get all different nationalities. Seattle was built by people coming from all over. We do have a melting pot. Certainly we do better than the South, and maybe the East. We've still got a lot of growing to do, but it's individual growing, not en masse. You cannot legislate morality and rightness. It has to come from people's hearts. So we keep working on it. We've got to work together to make it a reality.

MILES DAVIS

Jimmy's Will

We had a long talk and I asked, "Are you taking care of your business? Have you got a will?" He said, "Yeah, but it's not signed." I said, "I know this is like old folks talking that crazy talk." He said, "I'm leaving everything to my dad." I said, "Well, you've got to sign the will." So he showed it to me. He had a little pouch or something, whatever it was that he kept everything in.

His Mom

Jimmy was very interested in knowing more about his mother, Lucille, more than what his mother's sister had told him. I really couldn't tell him too much. I didn't want to because she was his mother, win, lose, or draw. And I'm a firm believer that when the Bible says, "Honor thy father and thy mother" that, whether parents are right or wrong, they are to be honored.

I'm a mother, too. I told him, things happen in life, and some times people don't get along.

Come Work and Travel with Me

He said, "Freddie Mae, why don't you come and work and travel with me?" And I said, "Honey, I've got a family. I wouldn't be bothered with those people who surround you because they're users. As soon as you're no longer at the top, they're going to be through with you." I see that happen all the time.

Having a Family

I talked to Jimmy about personal relationships with a young lady. I said, "Jimmy, you're getting older. What about having a family? What about getting married?" He said, "Oh, yeah, yeah. I don't have time for that. If I have a child, I'd want to have good surroundings and spend time with him."

Al was a hard worker. He spent a lot of time trying to do the best he could for both Jimmy and Leon. He wasn't a perfect father. None of us are, as parents, all the time. We make mistakes. But all in all, Al was a good father. Jimmy appreciated him. He remembered.

Money

I talked to Jimmy about him saving money. Well, money wasn't important to him. He just wanted to be sure his family was taken care of. That was his utmost concern. He worried about his dad doing that gardening work. He said, "He's getting old. He doesn't need to be doing that." I asked him where his money was. Well, he didn't really know, but they had it in different banks, and he thought some of it was in the Bahamas. He didn't know where all of it was.

Music in the Central District

We had good music in Seattle, like Bumps Blackwell's Band, where Quincy Jones started out in the junior band. Many Black musicians came here to the Palomar Theater and to the Orpheum and after hours they congregated at the Washington Social Club, Sike Roses' Club at 23rd and East Madison, the Rocking Chair, or the Black and Tan to have jam sessions. If those buildings could talk today, they'd have some stories to tell. I think the Black and Tan is still standing today, at 1200 Jackson, and the Washington Social Club at 23rd and Madison. People came from all over to hear them. It was a fun thing, and people got into the rhythm of the music. Ray Charles was doing his thing, and it ended up like a big party. People from all over the city of Seattle came. You know, it was like they were sneaking from Ballard and Greenwood to hear the Black musicians.

Jimmy and Quincy

Quincy did meet Jimmy here in Seattle and then later they crossed paths in their musical careers. When Jimmy died Quincy was one of the first ones to call his father to give his condolences, "Anything I can do to help?" Two different types of music, but Quincy and Jimmy were of the same spirit.

A Prophet Has No Honor in His Own Land

When people here decided to do a really nice memorial to Jimmy, it turned out to be in the safari gardens at the Woodland Park Zoo. I asked, "Why are you putting Jimmy in the zoo?" Did people think that Jimmy played zoo music or something? People resist something new, or music that is different. I think Jimmy was disappointed. When I think of people who have grown up in Seattle, I think of the Biblical phrase, "A prophet has no honor in his own land."

I think of Jimmy, Quincy, Diane Schuur, and Ray Charles. They all had to go away away to be recognized. Then as soon as they're recognized, everybody wants to claim them. Oh, they're not from Seattle, they're from thus and so. But Seattle's their home. And for those musicians who have made it, it's important for their families and friends and home town to praise them. Everybody in Seattle is clamoring about Quincy Jones, and he's feeling good about it. He had talent way back then, but he had to leave here to be recognized.

Jimmy's Death, Drugs and Control

I do not believe that Jimmy died of an overdose of drugs, based on his conversation with me, and the fact that he was definitely trying to get off of it. Now, when our young people are doing drugs. Their minds are being controlled. It's terrible when peoples' lives go the wrong direction because of drugs, or being

MILES DAVIS, HENDRIX'S FUNERAL

with the wrong people. Jimmy said to me, "You know, it's important that young people and our kids not let drugs and things control them, because that's what it's all about. Controlling them."

For some reason, I feel very strongly that at the time of his death Jimmy wasn't on drugs. Perhaps he had a cold and was taking cold medicine. He could have very well suffocated or had spasms and couldn't get his breath. But, it was interesting, the outcome of it all. Even with the manager, Michael Jefferey. I say this because he was very nervous when he came here. He was interested to see if there was anything that I wanted, "You know, whatever you need, Freddie Mae, you know, you let me know." I don't know what report the road manager gave him regarding the time when Jimmy had come to my house, and we had the long talk. He did not know what Jimmy had said to me, and he was

nervous about what was said. He asked, "What did Jimmy say?" I said, "Oh, I don't know, you know, we just talked."

Jimmy's Funeral

I spent a lot of time with Mr. Hendrix, helping him with the preparations for the funeral, the program itself. I'd kind of been there all along, since I was a little girl, with the Hendrix family.

After Jimmy had passed, there was a time before his body was brought back from England. His dad went to New York to talk to the attorneys and to get some things from Jimmy's apartment. By the time he got there, the place had been ransacked. Mr. Hendrix went to Jimmy's Electric Ladyland and brought some of his things back. I looked through them. That's when I found the angel poem that I used in the service.

Everybody was calling. Little Richard wanted to come by. Why doesn't Aretha Franklin come? I said, "Well, now, this is a funeral. This is not a circus or a show, and out of respect to his father, let's not make it one." Some people who came were not coming out of anything for Jimmy, but just to see other people. I felt a funeral must be respectful. The Bible does say rejoice when a person dies, so technically it's a joyful time, but it should not be a circus or a sideshow.

We felt we wanted to keep the funeral to local talent, you know, not bring in anybody, though we certainly appreciated these people offering to come. So I selected a young lady and I asked her to sing the song "Angels Watching Over Me." I read the poem of Jimmy's about angels. Reading the poem was very important to me, to let people know what Jimmy was really about, what his inner soul was. They saw what his managers knew would sell and would make

FREDDIE MAE AND LEON HENDRIX AT THE FUNERAL

money. But, I wanted people to see Jimmy's spiritual side. And "Angels" was a very moving and deep poem.

The funeral was held at Dunlap Baptist Church, where Janie Hendrix attended Sunday School. The service was done in good taste and it let Jimmy have some quietness. The mayor at that time was Wes Uhlman and he attended, representing the city of Seattle. People came from all over, and the place was packed and crowded. Everything was done with dignity and in very good taste; Jimmy would have liked it very much.

Spiritual Things

Most of our last talk centered around spiritual and deep things and about being right with one another. We talked about what he wanted out of life, like children, and a different lifestyle.

People did not understand what was really in his soul and what Jimmy was about. He tried to portray that in his message, what his ideas and thoughts were. He believed in a Supreme Being, a higher power. He recalled when he was little and going to church with his grandmother. His grandmother attended the Church of Christ, the Pentecostal. And of course when he was with us my parents took him to our church, the Seventh-Day Adventist Church. And somebody else he stayed with had taken him to church. He talked about those experiences, and the music—the spirituals and the gospels—the depth of them, and how much it all meant to him. Sometimes he'd just sneak into churches. He said, "I just go in and sit and listen to the choir and get an inspiration, and then I go on."

I remember when Jimmy was little, and how he thought a lot. He would sit by himself like he was meditating. I think that in every generation the Lord gives us someone like Jimmy. We might not appreciate them—but, they're about something within their soul and that's what Jimmy was about.

The New Hendrix Museum

I think the new Hendrix museum is a positive, wonderful move. It will allow young people to see what Jimmy was about. He was beyond his time, you know. Jimmy left a very positive message. People in Europe have honored him far more than people in our country have. The museum will be very fitting for him. Paul Allen and his family have the right idea, and I'm happy about it.

DIANE HENDRIX-COLLEY AND BEVERLY RHUE

Beverly Rhue

Beverly Rhue has had a lifelong friendship with Pearl Proctor Hendrix Brown—since the two women were seven years old. "I admire Pearl's optimistic attitude and her ability to overcome adversity," says Beverly. The Proctor family is very talented. Pearl's sister Ruby was an award-winning concert pianist and she was the Vancouver representative for the Japanese Suzuki Music Program. Ruby's daughters were musicians—one graduated from Juilliard in piano, and the other one is a concert violinist. Pearl's sister Eleanor was called the Lena Horne of Canada. Pearl let Eleanor have the limelight, and when Eleanor retired, Pearl began giving concerts."

Beverly Rhue was an administrator for the departments of Physiology and Biophysics at the University of Southern California's School of Medicine for twenty-seven years. She has two children, Dr. Sylvia F. Rhue and Dr. Thomas A. Rhue. She lives in Los Angeles.

Vancouver and the Hendrix Family

I grew up in Vancouver, Canada with the Hendrixes. There were only a few Black families there at the time. Where I lived, we were the only Black family at our school and at our church. I met the Hendrixes through a club called the Douglass Forum, which was started by an elderly gentleman named Mr. Wallace, who wanted Canadian Blacks to know their history and to meet one another. The Forum was named after Frederick Douglass, who was a Black activist in the States earlier in the century.

About every two months the Douglass Forum rented the Ukrainian Hall for a big party. We brought lots of food and all of the young people who were taking music lessons would perform. We met new people there and danced to the music of a local band. Older people gave readings about how they got to Canada, who their parents were and what our background was. The Douglass Forum parties became the biggest event in our lives.

Oral history has been an important part of our culture. My grandmother used to tell us about growing up in Blair House in Washington, D.C. She was half Black and half White. Her mother, who was a slave, was the cook and her father was the man of the house. At the turn of the century when Canada began the land grant, there was no color line. A network of Black families migrated there between 1900 and 1910. My family, the Ramseys, initially went to Alberta.

Another important meeting place in British Columbia was a small church on Jackson Avenue in Vancouver called the Colored Church. There was so much talent in our church. My mother was the organist and pianist, and we all sang in the choir. I knew Allen, Frank and Pat Hendrix at church. I was younger than them. Nora Hendrix, their mother, was by far the strongest figure in the family. She was a marvelous, intelligent, high-class, well-dressed woman. She had gorgeous clothes. She wore felt hats, beautiful dresses, and a cashmere coat. We all admired Jimmy's grandmother Nora.

BRITISH COLUMBIA, CANADA

Ted Murray

Ted Murray and Jimmy Hendrix were neighbors in the Leschi district in their elementary school days. Ted attended Washington Junior High and Garfield High School. He lives in Seattle where he works for King County.

Mixing Marbles and Music

Back in the early days, Jimmy mixed his marbles with his music. Playing marbles was a way for us to escape—to get away from it all, whatever it was. We enjoyed playing. There'd be four or five or six of us. Jimmy lived across the street from us in a two-story green house. The front door was north of Leschi School.

There were two places where we played—on the field behind Leschi, and on the parking strip by the school driveway. There were two different types of marble games that we played. Our favorite was

potsies—where we'd draw a big circle and we'd put all our marbles in it, and then we'd try to shoot the other guy's marbles out. Then there was another one where we'd dig a hole, and we played that on the parking strip. Then we rolled our marbles in. The one who got the most marbles in took all the marbles. That was the game.

I don't remember Terry playing, but that's not to say he didn't play. We had a pretty serious group of potsie players. Jimmy Williams might have been one of them. Pernell Alexander played every once in a while, but not often.

We had Donald Duck marbles. They were great because they stuck in the pot a lot. They were blue and gold. Donald Duck marbles were hard to come by. Then we had steelies. They looked like ball bearings. Marble games were great fun.

Ralph Hayes

Teacher/Historian

"Teaching is a give-and-take process," says Ralph Hayes, who taught social studies for the Seattle public schools. "To this day I'm still not sure what's teaching and what's learning." Mr. Hayes began his thirty-year teaching career in 1955 at Garfield High School, where Jimmy Hendrix was a student in his United States History class. Mr. Hayes also taught at Franklin High School and Bellevue High School.

As a student in Ralph Hayes' classes for two years, I was profoundly influenced by his philosophy, his dynamic presence, and his determination to bring out the potential in every student. Perhaps the greatest contribution Mr. Hayes made was to instill the idea of independent thinking in his students. He posted THINK signs on the classroom walls. He expected us to come up with answers to things we'd never thought about. Ralph Hayes talked about

heads of state as if they were his neighbors. He would pace back and forth in front of the classroom, choosing his words carefully, and punctuating them with pauses and hand gestures. With his brow furrowed, he would ask questions like, "Why do you think those people did that? How can so-and-so say that?"

Hayes deplored judgmental attitudes. One morning in the school hallway, he overheard a derogatory conversation about a young man we all knew. Hayes stormed into the classroom, "People make me so angry when they think they have everybody pegged," he said. "Anyone who has cubbyholed that guy as a social klutz is wrong. I predict he's going to get the girl you people think he doesn't have a prayer of getting. Just you wait."

According to Parker Cook, a retired Garfield music teacher, "Ralph Hayes once said to me, 'If

anybody gets an A from Ralph Hayes, that person walks like an A, talks like an A, and thinks like an A.'" Ralph Hayes is a nationally recognized authority on Pacific Northwest Black history. The author of *Northwest Black Pioneers*, *Centennial Tribute*, he has an unpublished two-volume history on the same topic. He and his Japanese-American wife, Elaine, live in Seattle. They have three sons and one daughter.

Garfield High School

I have never been any place where there was as much enthusiasm in the student body as at Garfield. It was a most unusual, yet gratifying experience. I had such bright students. I used to tell them, "Some of you could go to the moon, if you'd just *think*. Here in America, we teach our young people to question, to think."

In spite of what went on citywide, even nation-wide, in the fifties, I thought the student body at

Garfield developed a tremendous spirit of unity. For example, I remember one day after school when I was grading some papers on the second floor, on the east side of the building. I heard some noise outside. There were about eight kids out there playing touch football, right outside the school. Two of them were Black. One White kid tackled another White kid, really maliciously. One of the two Black kids stepped between them, and separated them. He said, "No, you're not going to fight. Garfield students don't fight among themselves." I thought that was very interesting—a Black kid stepping between two White kids saying, "Garfield students don't fight among themselves." I never dreamed it would happen. But it did. I saw it. And I found out who they all were, and I called them in. One by one, I talked with them all. I applauded each one, saying "You have the right attitude—the right spirit."

Having Jimmy in Class

As I remember it, Jimmy was in my fifth-period U.S. History class. He was very personable. But he was also a very shy person. I mean very shy. I can't believe that gentleman went on to make the kind of music that he made, because he was so shy. When, sometimes, he was a bit late for class—like a minute or two—he was always apologetic when he'd sit down. I noticed, though, that Jimmy wasn't very interested in class. I wasn't sure whether it was my fault or not.

"Why Don't You Leave Garfield, Get Your Guitar, and Make Music?"

I remember saying to him, "Son, you really aren't interested in this class. Why don't you just leave this place called Garfield High School, get your guitar, and just make music? It's something that you

thoroughly enjoy." I don't say this had anything to do with the young man leaving school, but I was shocked to learn shortly after that he had withdrawn. And that this shy person had volunteered for paratroopers! I just couldn't believe it. From what his father told me, he enjoyed it.

Living Next Door to Jimmy's Uncle

I knew the Hendrixes personally because we moved into the house next door to Frank Hendrix, Jimmy's uncle, after Diane and Bobby and their mom had moved to Spokane. Frank remarried a woman named Mary, and I remember Diane and Bobby used to visit during the summer. Jimmy probably came over then too, but that was before I knew him.

The Pacific Northwest Black Population

Blacks arrived in the Pacific Northwest Territories in

search of a better life, one without prejudice and restriction on their ambition. The state of Washington and the city of Seattle, while not perfect by any means, did offer Blacks opportunities to follow their dreams. Many Blacks opened businesses, pursued professions, reared families and prospered significantly in the growing urban centers of the Puget Sound.

While Blacks were not always significant in number, their contribution to the development of Washington state cannot be ignored. Descendants of the pioneer families still live in Seattle and its environs, and they can feel pride in their freedom-seeking forefathers and the legacy they left behind.

When Washington became a state, in November of 1889, the Black population of Seattle was 408. But, with the next decade and a half, as the railroads were finished, the Black population tripled. Around the turn of the century Seattle's Black population was

about 800. There were about 3,000 in the whole state. It continued to grow and during World War II there was a tremendous increase in the population. By the time the war ended, it had reached a point where Seattle's Black population, in Seattle and King county together, was close to 50,000. That's a tremendous growth. And, of course, this was bound to be reflected in the enrollment in Garfield High School because most of the Blacks tended to live in the Central District. Or—as they call it—the C.D.

Washington is one of the few states of the Union where there are more Black males in the total population than there are females. Nationwide there are two million more Black women in the USA than males, but not in Washington, and not in Seattle. Black males still predominate. This certainly was true when I was at Garfield. I used to talk to students about this, and what this meant for students who

wanted to date now and then. Some of the students baby-sat for us a good deal, and we'd find out a good many things when baby-sitters were around. They'd tell us all kinds of things. And this really made life even more interesting.

Garfield Misrepresented by the Media

I'll tell you something that happened that really hurt the student body. This happened back in the days when drug dealing was almost unheard of, but there were some people out in the community who were in possession of drugs, and they wanted to sell the drugs inside the school to some students. Two young White men overheard these fellows, and went to the principal. The principal and the vice principal met to decide what to do about it. They called one of Seattle's two newspapers and the police department and they organized everything so there would be a completion of the drug deal, and the photographer was supposed to be there to photograph the whole thing—so they could catch the two dealers.

But the newspaper reneged. On the morning it was supposed to take place, the newspaper ran a front-page story about the drug dealing that went on at Garfield High School. The students were just simply floored. "How could they do this to our school?" they asked. "There is no drug dealing in our school! Why would that paper have done that?" The students reacted in such a way that showed that they were just sick, horrified, that a story like that would have been printed when it wasn't true.

Garfield was the most integrated school in the state of Washington. And I observed two things that were outstanding, and probably more true there than at any other high school in Seattle: Garfield students were unified, and the faculty worked together to help students.

Betty Morgan Wallace

Vivacious Betty Jean Morgan Wallace was Jimmy's first love. At 50, Betty looks 35. It's November 12, 1994. Soft autumn light filters through yellow and orange leaves in the picturesque neighborhood where Betty lives with her family. I'm in town for the weekend. She and I are talking in the living room of their comfortable home in Seattle's south end. We've gotten acquainted on the phone, over a period of months. Betty has told me the frustration she feels about not finding the key to the cedar chest where she put the letters Jimmy wrote to her, and some other things he gave her more than thirty years ago. I sense she's also frustrated by questions I have asked that she doesn't have answers for, because the memories have faded with the passage of time. "It's too hard to remember after thirty years," is her answer to most of my questions.

"Ever since we started talking, I've been wanting to open that cedar chest," she says, with a look of determination. "I haven't seen those things in over thirty years. Now that you're here, I'm going to look for that key again. I want to show you those letters and things."

A few minutes later Betty comes back with a grin and a set of keys. "I found it! Now, I'm going to open that cedar chest. I think I have Jimmy's Army dog tags. And I know I have letters and pictures—and a couple of other things." Sure enough. She finds everything intact: letters, a handful of photographs, some newspaper clippings, two Army dog tags, and two silk pillow cases—with handwritten messages from Jimmy. "I knew I saved all of this," she said.

Betty has five photographs of Jimmy that have never been published. Two small shots taken June 25, 1960, in a four-for-a-quarter photo booth, show Jimmy

wearing a plaid shirt and a straw hat. These pictures show the side of Jimmy we knew—the good-natured, fun-loving kid next door. He looks confident and balanced.

The other three were taken in 1961, while Jimmy was in the Army. One captures Jimmy at his guitar in a locker room. It's typical—wherever Jimmy went, his guitar went. Another, taken at the Del Morroco Club, shows Jimmy and two other musicians playing back up for three female vocalists. On the back of the photograph, Jimmy has written "With our singing group the Kasualettes. Love always, Jimmy Hendrix, Del Morroco Club (Nashville, Tennesee). "The third photo, a studio shot, portrays Jimmy in his Army uniform, standing before a tropical scene with palm trees.

Someday Betty may decide to share parts of those letters. Or maybe she won't. Her relationship with

Jimmy broke off, and each moved on with their separate lives. Today Betty is a dedicated mother, grandmother, and wife to her husband Dave. She works with the elderly, and is devoted to her church. Born in Bremerton, Washington, Betty has lived in Seattle since she was six years old. She attended Bailey Gatzert Grade School, Washington Junior High and Garfield High School. She has a son, Eric Daniels, two daughters, Sharmalynn Wallace and Esther Wallace, and two granddaughters, Lanice and Erica.

Memories

I met Jimmy in school, at Garfield. Jimmy was a beautiful person. He was kind and very generous. We'd talk on the phone, and on the weekend he'd come up from 26th and Yesler to my house. I had a close-knit family, so we did things with my family. Sometimes we'd walk over to the lake with my sisters, down through Leschi Park. Back in those days in Seattle we did a lot of things in groups. I remember going to a street dance on Madison, over by the Mardis Gras.

Jimmy and I were engaged to get married, but I was too young. I was still in school, and my mom wanted me to finish school. I don't remember exactly how we broke up. That was more than thirty years ago. It's hard to remember things that long ago. But I sent the rings back.

My mother loved Jimmy. He'd sit on our porch and play the guitar. I was left handed, like Jimmy. I regret never learning to play the guitar.

Caroline Calloway Morgan, Betty's Mother

When my kids were growing up, I opened my home to my kids' friends. I have four daughters and one son. Betty is the oldest daughter. I used to bake cookies and give them Kool Aid. Jimmy was one of my favorites of the kids who came over. He used to sit out on the porch and play his guitar. He was a typical teenager. He had a nice personality. I don't know what happened to his mother. He took to me like I was his mother. I remember Mr. Hendrix. He was a nice man. Jimmy wanted Betty to marry him. He bought her a nice ring. When he went into the service he left his guitar with me. He used to write to me and keep in touch. I didn't save the letters. He wanted Betty to come to where he was in the service, to get married, but I said no. I'm from the old school and I didn't want her to go without an escort. So they didn't get married.

Janet Nosi Terada

Janet Nosi Terada, a 1961 Garfield graduate, had a connection with Jimmy in junior high and high school that was centered around visual arts. Janet has devoted her professional life to technical drafting, electrical drafting, cartography and calligraphy. She lives in Kirkland, Washington, has two sons—Derek and Kelly—and is an active member of the 1961 Garfield class reunion committee.

Jimmy the Artist

When Jimmy and I were friends, back in junior high and high school, we took our art classes together. And what I remember most was how he was always doodling, especially when we should have been doing something else. He loved to draw. And he was good. He was quite an artist.

When Jimmy's first album came out, I said to myself, "This couldn't be the same guy." He was so quiet that I couldn't imagine him on stage singing. But it was the same Jimmy. It's funny, but I remember him shuffling when he walked. It was like his shoes were untied. But that was just Jimmy.

He was basically a real shy person. On a one-to-one basis he was a very talkative person. He and I could talk forever. We used to whisper in the back of the class. I really enjoyed him. He always had a smile on his face. He was so nice.

John Eng

A 1961 Garfield graduate, John Eng was the first Asian to be elected to the House of Representatives in the state of Washington. He served the 37th District for ten years, and in the Peace Corps in Nepal. John and his wife and two children live in Seattle, where he works in real estate development. His friendship with Jimmy Hendrix began in the seventh grade.

Getting Stuffed Under the Desk

Jimmy always had a lot of energy. He loved to talk, and it seemed to me that he always talked fast. He and I became friends in seventh grade at Meany Junior High. I remember there were two guys he was often with—Wallace Coleman and Frank Love. Those three guys were cute together—all small guys, though I was even smaller. Sometimes they would talk in class and be kind of a nuisance. The funniest thing I remember from Meany is that we had an English teacher who used to say, "Hip, hip, one, two, three, the British are coming!" Then she'd march those three guys to the front of the room and make them all get under her desk. She'd sort of stuff them all under there. Then she'd ignore them for the rest of the class period, and we were all supposed to ignore them too.

The Garfield Chess Club

Jimmy enjoyed chess. He and I had a good time playing chess at school. My friend Jay Cook and I were active in the Garfield Chess Club, and Jimmy often showed up to play.

1961 GARFIELD CHESS CLUB OFFICERS AND ADVISOR

James Minor

James Minor graduated from Garfield in 1963. He attended Leschi Grade School and Washington Junior High School. Jimmy taught him to play the guitar.

Straight Blues Player

Jimmy was a straight blues player. He learned the blues right here in Seattle. I know James Thomas taught him a lot about the blues. Jimmy used to like to play "Further On Up the Road," the Bobby Blue Bland piece. He loved "Lucille." And I remember him playing "Wishing Well," "Money," "New Dance," and "Candido." Even back then he was the best guitar player around. We all got started with music and guitars because of Jimmy. He taught me to play guitar. We had fun. I used to listen to him a lot—on his back porch, and at Birdland and Yesler Terrace.

Jimmy was quiet and polite and smart. All he cared about was getting different sounds out of his guitar. He experimented a lot. I remember one time at Yesler Terrace when he played and sang, "In 1814, we took a little trip, down the Mississippi," and everybody started clapping. He was a good guy. All he wanted to do was play music. And that he did.

The Fighting Irish

We played Little League football together, on the Fighting Irish team. He was a good football player. We played at the Army Camp on Martin Luther King Way, and at the Rainier Play Field. When I saw Jimmy in 1969 we were talking about it. He was kidding around, saying, "Your uniform never got dirty." When he was in Seattle for the concert, I went to his house and he gave me free tickets. I was his Number One fan.

Steve Fletcher

Steve Fletcher graduated from Garfield in 1962. He has a degree from the University of Washington, and has worked primarily in corporation management—with the Paris American Corporation, the Union Oil Company, Seattle City Light, and as president of The Paper Company for seven years. He served as a business consultant for Seattle's Best Coffee for more than a decade, and is the author of Practical Techniques for Success. He lives in Edmonds, Washington, with his wife and three children, Janet, Jonathan and Erica.

Jimmy, Garfield and the High Jump

Jimmy and I had a comfortable and easy friendship. I knew him as a quiet person, and, as a lot of fun as an individual. Perhaps it was our mutual boyhood shyness that brought us together. I always felt good when we were together. We had an unspoken understanding of each other and our need for friendship. We enjoyed each other's knack for telling stories. He'd laugh and laugh when I'd tell him a funny story. He had a wonderful laugh that was quiet, but thorough. I remember one Garfield prank largely because of the way Jimmy laughed when I told it to him. Two other guys and I got caught walking down the hallway carrying the door from Mr. Wilson's classroom. The funny part was that Claude Wilson didn't even notice the door was missing. Jimmy thought that story was so funny.

Going to Garfield was the best experience I ever had. The mix of wealth and poverty, the many ethnic backgrounds, the assemblies, the dances, the political environment, Mr. Betz's experimental geometry—all of those things made the experience rich and rewarding. It was an opportunity to have friends from all categories, which is something that has always appealed to me. I enjoy having friends who are not mainstream. Jimmy was someone who was unpretentious and accepting of all people, especially people who were different.

Jimmy and I both did the high jump. Neither one of us was very good. One day we were up at the old Army camp field on what is now Martin Luther King Way, across from the old ROTC place. Jimmy and I kept knocking the bar off. So we consoled each other, and got a friendly competition going. When things got serious, he could always find the light side. He always had a twinkle in his eye.

I have met a few unforgettable people in my lifetime. Once, by chance, I met Elvis face-to-face, and we talked for a couple of minutes. He left a powerful and positive impression. It was a kind of quiet power. Jimmy's presence, for me, created some of the same feelings.

Mike Tagawa

Mike Tagawa graduated from Garfield High School in 1962. He and Jimmy Hendrix were school friends. After serving four years in the Air Force, Mike attended Seattle Community College and the University of Washington. He lives in Seattle where he has a guitar repair business and drives a Metro bus.

Early Years in the Central District

I'm sort of a product of the ghettos, you might say. A proud graduate of the ghettos. Maybe not a graduate, because my heart is still in the Central District. We didn't call it the ghetto back then. It seems to me it was 1967 or '68 when people started calling the Central District the ghetto.

Hanging Out With Hendrix

I never called him Jimmy. I called him Hendrix; he called me Tagawa. I remember him presenting himself as James. At least that's what I recall. Maybe James seemed more dignified and more respectful than Jimmy. But the use of last names back then was common. I first met Hendrix at Washington. He wasn't a close personal friend outside of school, but we were friends at school. At Garfield, Hendrix and I would hang out together between classes and at lunch. We shared a couple of classes and the same lunch hour. We talked about everyday kinds of things. We didn't talk about music probably because I wasn't a musician, and he knew there wasn't a lot I could relate to. Sometimes we'd run down to 22nd and Alder and sit on some steps and smoke.

Hair Conk

Hendrix used to conk his hair. He used to call it do-conk. One time he put too much on, or he let it sit on there too long, and it burned his scalp. So one day he was talking about how to be careful with conk because you could burn yourself. I always thought that was pretty fascinating because I was sort of into hair myself. I had this pompadour, and I used to pile on tons of grease on my own head, although I didn't need to straighten mine with conk.

Football and Basketball

At Washington Hendrix was a member of a football team called the Fighting Irish, a Central District team made up of a pretty good mixture of kids—Blacks, Asians, and Whites. It was a great little team. Some guys who were on the Fighting Irish have told me that he was good at football. But I remember that he was pretty bad at basketball. One time we were down at the playing field at Collins Playfield, which is part of the Buddhist church complex at 14th and Main. We were out there playing basketball and Hendrix stopped to shoot some hoops with us. I remember distinctly that he was pretty terrible. I mean, he was really as bad as me at shooting hoops.

Webb Lofton

Hendrix talked a lot about Webb Lofton, and the group called the Rocking Kings. I got the impression that Hendrix really liked Webb Lofton. He expressed a lot of affection for playing in the Rocking Kings group. He'd tell me how that they were a good group, and that he enjoyed himself. I don't know how much influence that had on Hendrix ultimately, but I know it made a difference to him then. I haven't seen any references to Webb Lofton in the material on Hendrix, although I haven't read all of it. But Webb Lofton's name stands out in my mind because he was one of the only—if not the only—person I heard Hendrix talk about in any extended way.

Hendrix Owed Me a Quarter

Hendrix came from a poor family, and he used to bum cigarettes and borrow money on occasion. One time he borrowed a quarter. You'd think, no big deal.

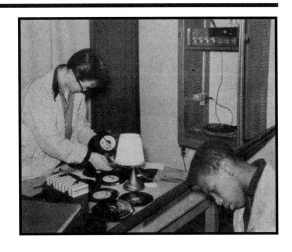

But it actually created a little bit of distance between us because he never did pay it back. And then when we'd go down to the Burger King to eat hamburgers and french fries, he never had the quarter to pay me back. And it was like, man, aren't you going to pay me back the quarter? Well, I never said it like that, but it caused a little bit of discomfort. My family didn't have much money, and I don't think Hendrix's did either. I look back on it now and it's laughable. So Hendrix left Seattle owing me a quarter. To even think about it now seems ridiculous.

Fashion, Myth, and the Holy Ghost at 22nd and Alder

Hendrix was a nice guy, a soft-spoken guy. He always seemed to wear clothes that were a year or two behind in fashion. I remember when Hendrix used to get kind of dressed up, and he'd be wearing things like shirts and pants that were fashionable a year or more back. It was interesting that his clothes were out of fashion, but he also liked to wear his collar turned up. Back then if you wore your collar turned up, you were known as a rink. I can still see in my mind's eye the lasting impression of an outfit that Hendrix wore. He had a striped shirt—a black shirt with white stripes—with the collar turned up, with black peg pants and one of those really skinny, skinny belts. By skinny I mean like a quarter to a half an inch wide. When he was wearing that outfit that was a couple of years old, it was like there he was, looking very rinky. That's the way he was—he was his own person. I liked him. He was nice. He was soft-spoken. He was easy to get along with— easy to talk to. He wasn't a jivey kind of guy. He wasn't—as they say these days—on some sort of trip. He wasn't pretentious. He seemed almost Buddha-like. Very calm and confident.

Contrary to stories I've heard about Hendrix, he may have been poor, but he was always clean. And he always maintained a certain kind of dignity about himself. He didn't have any of this "I'm poor so I'm going to look poor and shabby" attitude. I mention this because I had a conversation with one of my customers who said Hendrix was a filthy guy and he used to stink and go to school shabby and I was astounded. This woman came from Iowa and plays country music, and got the story from some guy who claimed to know Hendrix, a guy who went to high school in Snohomish or Arlington. I was dumbfounded. I said, "That ain't true. I went to Garfield and Washington and I knew Hendrix. There wasn't anything dirty or stinky about Hendrix." She was equally dumbfounded that I said I knew Hendrix. The reaction was really strange. She got very defensive, like how could I possibly have known

WASHINGTON JUNIOR HIGH SCHOOL

Hendrix? She wanted to believe that all the bad stuff was true, and she didn't want to believe that I could have gone to school with Hendrix.

Sometimes when people ask me about Hendrix, they are fascinated and they really want to know what Hendrix was like. Other times I've found people to be disdainful, almost as if they were sneering and leering, and like, that can't be true that you were out there smoking with Hendrix. Some people have put Hendrix on a pedestal, or more—like he was God, or Jesus, or something. Some people can't believe that somebody like me—some old shmuck in central Seattle who drives a Metro bus and repairs guitars—could actually have been smoking cigarettes with Jesus, God, and the Holy Ghost down at 22nd and Alder. It's like they can't believe that I might have touched the hem of his garment. It's interesting to me that people have made Hendrix supernatural and superhuman. I remember

him as just another guy, just like a lot of us at Garfield do. I guess that's what happens when somebody reaches such stature, and becomes a hero to literally millions of people around the world. It's hard for people that didn't see him as a student, doing student kinds of things, like carrying books—or not carrying your books a lot of times in Hendrix's case. Looking at him as somebody ordinary.

Hallway Air Guitar

One day I was walking down the hall, and here was Hendrix coming in the other direction playing air guitar. It wasn't called air guitar. It wasn't called anything. But there he was, playing this invisible guitar. I said something like, "Hey, man, where's your PeeChee, or where's your notebook, or where's your books?" He gave me that nice, warm smile of his and said something like, "I don't need my books. I've got my guitar." I thought that was pretty cool because I

wasn't such a great student myself, and I thought that was really different to be walking down the hall pretending like you're playing a guitar instead of carrying books.

Gym Class

Hendrix and I were in the same gym class and I remember one day we were all filing into the gym to go get suited up, and Bill Diambri, who was the gym coach, and I think maybe Bob Gary, and maybe Mr. Boitano, asked Hendrix not to get suited up and to go get his guitar. While the rest of us guys, the other mortals, got suited up, they had Hendrix bring his guitar into the office, and for the duration of the period Hendrix sat there and played guitar for them. They had heard about how great Hendrix was apparently—it had gone through the grapevine— and that was what he did for that gym class. While we were out there sweating like a bunch of hogs,

161

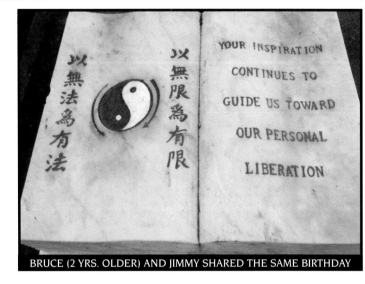

BRUCE (2 YRS. OLDER) AND JIMMY SHARED THE SAME BIRTHDAY

Hendrix was in there sitting on the desk playing for an audience of two. I thought that was pretty funny. They probably wouldn't stand for that today because that would be violating somebody's Civil Rights, or showing preferential treatment. Back then it wasn't any big deal. Talent was recognized and people didn't worry about how things would be interpreted. The gym coaches knew Hendrix could play, and they wanted to hear him. All of us thought it was cool because we knew Hendrix could play. It didn't bother us that he didn't have to suit up.

Bruce Lee in Central Seattle

You know at the same time Hendrix was at Garfield, Bruce Lee started hanging out around the central area. He used to go to Imperial Lanes to hang out and pose, down on Rainier Avenue, and he taught gung fu at a few places. A sidebar here is that back in those days he used to call it gung fu instead of kung

fu. I took a class at a place on Beacon Hill where he was teaching, at the encouragement of Doug Palmer, who also graduated from Garfield in '62 and turned out to be one of Bruce Lee's prize students. I took one lesson from Bruce Lee. It was more like a physical conditioning thing, and it just about killed me and everybody else in the class. So I never went back for another one. But I did see Bruce occasionally around the central area, like during those days when the Chinese New Year would be on. I remember Bruce down there giving a cha-cha demonstration. He used to brag about being the cha-cha king of Hong Kong. Then while he was up there doing his cha-cha, he lost one of his contact lenses and they stopped the whole thing. He was crawling around, along with his dance partner and a bunch of other people on top of this raised platform, looking for his contact lens. Very funny for the Hong Kong

cha-cha king and gung fu champion to be incapacitated by the loss of a contact lens.

Bruce Lee started hanging around Garfield after I left. He was getting involved with a woman named Linda. He'd hang around Garfield to see Linda. Doug Palmer and Roger Kay—Garfield guys—were close to Bruce. Channel 9 made a bunch of videos with the three of tem giving gung fu demonstrations. They were pretty cool.

Air Force Basic Training in Mississippi

The Garfield thing made us more idealistic about what the world out there was like. I went in the service along with Terry Johnson, Ron Jenkins, and probably a half a dozen other people from Garfield. We went into the Air Force together. Some of us went to Greenville, Mississippi, right in the heart of the Delta. Things were different there. When we got to the base, we were told, "If you're going to go into town, then you should be prepared to act like the citizens of Greenville, Mississippi. Don't expect things to be the way they are wherever you're from. Now you're in Mississippi and you should expect to respect the way things are down here." We kind of knew that the South was supposed to be prejudiced and that there was a separation of races, and we saw that. We saw the "Colored Only" and the "White Only" signs in restaurants and in different areas of town. I personally never had any problem. I used to go into town with the Black guys all the time, and I never was treated badly by the Blacks. I was treated just like another guy. And when I would go into town with the Whites, there was no problem there either. I wasn't treated badly by any Whites. I was treated just like another guy. It was interesting. Maybe they just reserved any sort of feelings against me because maybe they didn't see a lot of Japanese down there,

and maybe they didn't know how to fit me into the whole scheme of things. I had a good time in the South. There were no major problems.

Garfield

Back in those days, it was an unconscious sort of thing—all the good feelings about Garfield and how terrific a place it was—it wasn't like a big deal, although talking to kids from other schools at the time made it obvious that we were a little bit different. I remember sometimes referring to Garfield as the United Nations of high schools because we had such a diversity in the mix of people that went there—from all the economic classes and all the different ethnic groups. It was quite an experience. But it was taken for granted that that was the way the world was, and, of course, anytime any of us wandered out from the confines of the Central District or Garfield High School, it became obvious

to us that that was not the way the world was. But for us, growing up in the Central District and going to Central District schools—especially Garfield High School—things were pretty cool. Looking back in retrospect, Garfield was the way society should be. God knows it could certainly be a model for the way society of today could be.

Back in those days at Garfield there was that spirit—the Garfield spirit. It was emphasized in pep assemblies. The thing that I remember from assemblies and sports events is the fact that the Garfield cheerleaders were always the outrageous cheerleaders—the ones who did things differently than the other cheerleaders from other schools. And we had the school band playing "Peter Gunn" at football and basketball games—that da, da, da, da, da, da, da, da. It seemed appropriate for that kind of music to be played at Garfield, rather than the ratty-tatty-tatty kind of stuff that you might expect at more suburban schools. But for an inner city school like Garfield that Peter Gunn theme, that dark kind of rhythm and that heavy sort of beat, made a lot of sense. It was a great time for sports. Garfield at that time was taking state championships in football, basketball, track and everything else. But the feeling at Garfield was the main thing: the camaraderie, the togetherness, the ease with which everybody related to each other—something that seems to be not real common today.

The story about Hendrix being kicked out of Garfield by a white racist art teacher for having a white girlfriend is not true. I'm tired of the lies and unverified accounts of why Hendrix left. There were many interracial relationships at Garfield. The only concern was that children of mixed racial backgrounds might experience difficulty, but this concern came from well-intentioned teachers who weren't as naive as we were about the world beyond Garfield. Authors who refer to racial problems during those years are badly misinformed.

There was a real sense of being a Garfield High School student. And I think it was unique to Garfield. I don't think there was that same sort of pride at other schools, at least not as strong as it was at Garfield. I remember going to parties in West Seattle and it was like, "Wow, you go to Garfield! Do you know how to do the Mashed Potatoes or the Twist? Or the Slow Drag, or the Pony?" It was interesting that Garfield was thought of as being quite a bit different. Kids at other schools used to think going to Garfield was a negative experience too. Because of ignorance. Not stupidity, but ignorance about diversity. Like, if you go to a school with a bunch of Negroes it must be a tough school. There must be a lot of fights there. And I've got to admit that even that idea that Garfield must be a rough or tough school added something to that aura, that charisma of Garfield High School. It was all those things. It was the sports, the roughness and the toughness, it was being in a part of the city that wasn't as economically advantaged as other parts of the city. All those things made you stick your chest out a little more and say, "Yeah, I go to Garfield. And, you know, we're different!" And we were different. Anybody who went to Garfield learned—way before it was popular, or way before it was mandated, or way before it was cool, as they say today—that diversity was really great. Going to Garfield, we had the chance to live the life of cultural diversity. Now corporations and communities are trying to teach their citizens with seminars and lectures and things like that. I think we had a thirty or thirty-five year jump on a lot of people, in that we were fortunate enough to be able to live it and make it work, without any conscious effort to make it work. And that's the real beauty of Garfield. We found out that those kind of differences could make things better. We were able to enrich our lives without having to be told to go to this seminar or go to this class to learn some sensitivity or awareness about the diversity in our work force.

Comfortable with Our Differences

Looking at the yearbooks I have from Garfield, I was amazed at the references there were to race—not in a negative sort of way, but in an innocent way—simply acknowledging that we were different from each other, me from Neil Suckerman and from Hendrix. We were all different, and we could talk easily about it without being concerned about political correctness particularly. I think that we always had a certain sensitivity about not saying

NORTH CASCADES NATIONAL PARK

anything offensive, but it's interesting that what may be offensive today probably wasn't very offensive back in those days. We could talk about racial differences, and joke about it, and even write about it in yearbooks without feeling like "Uh oh, I wonder if this is going to be cool or acceptable?" That whole idea of differences and diversity was on a different level than it is today. Nowadays people get so hung up on saying the right thing that it's harder to

communicate. There's a lack of communication that's come out of that. People are so worried about the right words that they don't use enough words that really mean anything because they're worried about tripping themselves up and looking racist, or any one of the other*ists* that are out there today. Back then we could play with labels in an innocuous way because we knew we were brothers and sisters.

Gordon Shoji

Gordon Shoji is a 1961 Garfield graduate. The son of a Kendo master and a late blooming actress, Shoji has taught Kendo, Gung Fu and womens' self-defense. He sold a food store he owned in Seattle in order to travel and pursue a writing career. Shoji says his strength is fearlessness to do what he believes in and take the consequences. His claim to fame is being a successful single parent; his pride and joy is his relationship with his daughter Noriko, a Garfield and University of Washington graduate. His goal in life is happiness.

Jimmy and I met playing Little League football, on the Fighting Irish. When I think of Hendrix, I see him pointing his finger at me with a look of delight. I think it was our sophomore year of high school football, during a one-on-one tackling drill. First, Jimmy was tackling. Without any fancy footwork, I lowered my head and ran straight ahead. Being "hot stuff" in football, I wasn't surprised when I literally ran over

NORIKO AND GORDON SHOJI

him. Then, Jimmy the "scrub"—the guy who was too mellow to play an aggressive game like football—ran right over me. "Hah! Got you back," Jimmy said. I was flat on my back in disbelief.

I've seen film clips of Jimmy and I understand why young people today are crazy about him. He's perfect for them. There's so much meaning in his music. He's both serious and playful. No matter what the tone is, there's that charisma—and kids feel it. That kind of intensity is rare in performances today.

For years I didn't know much about Jimmy's music. What came to mind was his version of the Star Spangled Banner. Then one day I ran into Leon Hendrix in Seattle. Leon wanted me to stop by and listen to some of Jimmy's music. So I did. I heard Jimmy's blues and some of his lyrical pieces and I began to understand what his music is all about.

JIM BORGEN, GORDON SHOJI, TOM GARRETT

Garfield High School and the Central District

When Jimmy Hendrix attended Garfield, it was a neighborhood school. Boundaries were determined largely by geography—Lake Washington to the east, the downtown area to the west, and the Lake Washington ship canal to the north. Garfield students came from either Meany Junior High or Washington Junior High. The class of 1961, as shown in the yearbook—the 1961 Garfield Arrow*—had 342 students: 124 African-American, 63 Asian-American and Pacific Island-American, and 155 Western or Eastern European-American. The class of 1962 had 448 students: 182 African-American, 69 Asian-American and Pacific Island-American, and 197 Western or Eastern European-American. The labels, however, are misleading and perhaps even inaccurate. Most students were a mixture of different ancestries. Some of the African Americans and European Americans also had Native American heritage. Students at Garfield in the fifties and early sixties used the labels Oriental, Negro or Colored and Caucasian or White.

The following people were at Garfield High School when Jimmy Hendrix was a student there. They have commented on life at Garfield and in the Garfield community in order to preserve the history of the time.

Frank Hanawalt, Garfield principal

Garfield was the most integrated school in the state of Washington when Jimmy Hendrix was there. It was one of the top schools in the state in academics, athletics and the arts. When I was at Garfield I developed a new appreciation for the word respect. Garfield students in a natural way had a genuine respect for each person they associated with. I wish that every student could have the same opportunity to apply this respect to intercultural and interracial groups that Garfield students have done.

Dr. Robert Gary, class of '52, and Garfield coach, teacher and assistant principal

Wherever I go, I find people whose lives have been touched by Garfield. We had an esprit de corps, a sense of unity, that was unique. We had a rich mixture of people with many dimensions who were willing to share. As a school, we were branded as the ghetto school, and I have found that that branding caused us to bond even more. I think of Dr. Jackson's Rainbow Coalition. Garfield had it—people whose backgrounds were from all over the globe. What we had was a family. There were cliques, but there wasn't tension. Everybody was still part of the family. Everybody knew everybody. Most of us knew we

were going to go to Garfield from the time we were in kindergarten. There was a sense of security, of permanence. I had some of the same teachers my older brother and sister had. I think one strong reason why so many Garfield graduates have done so well is due to the sense of community we had. There's no place you can go in Seattle where you don't find someone in power who went to Garfield.

Bob Tate, Garfield coach and teacher

Last Friday I had the 1954 basketball team and their wives over for dinner. I said, "Why can't the world be like you kids?" I still call them kids. The students at Garfield taught me as much or more than I taught them. They all cared for each other. The students and the faculty cared for each other. The prevailing feeling was that we had something more than the other schools because we had each other. Garfield was a beautiful place to be. Last week (10/2/94) I read

in the newspaper that out of thirty-two local National Merit scholars, twenty-seven of them are from Garfield.

Barney Hilliard, class of 1956.

We had such a cosmopolitan student body. It was a melting pot—Blacks, Asians, and Whites of all economic classes. We formed lasting friendships. The people in my class have full reunions every five years.

Judy Calvo Dolnick, class of 1961

Over the years I have spent many hours looking through the 1961 Garfield yearbook, *The Arrow*. A quote by S. Gulshn-i-Raz on page nineteen says a great deal about life and my feelings about Garfield: "Thou thinkest thou art but a small thing whereas in thee is involved the whole universe." Looking at all the beautiful faces in the yearbook, one does see the

universe. If all of society could function as Garfield functioned in 1961, what a terrific world we would be living in today.

Terry Johnson, class of '61

Garfield changed lives. When you live with people of all races, you learn about individualism. You learn you can have best friends and soul mates of other races. We learned about individualism by listening to people's feelings, by watching people cry, and by sharing good times with them. It's hard when you grow up with parents who have stereotypes. Garfield got all of the racial stereotypes out of our systems because we interacted with people of all different backgrounds. We learned that individuals of every race have good qualities and bad qualities. You can find the Fat Guy, the Smart Guy, the Cheap Guy, the Fast Talker, the Slick Guy, the Genuine Guy, the Meek Guy, and the Guy Who Doesn't Have Rhythm

Who's Supposed to Have Rhythm. There's one of those guys in every race.

Around Garfield you'd see three guys walking down the street, and one would be Black, one would be Asian, and one would be White. It was because they had gravitated together as individuals, not because it was forced by anything.

Dick Hutchings, class of '56

If we had to get a hundred of us together in twenty-four hours, it would be no problem.

Jay A. Hurwitz, class of '61, President, Associated Students of Garfield, 1960-61

My father was in Garfield's first graduating class, and my brother and sister attended after me. I remember it as a place where diversity flourished, along with scholastic, athletic, and artistic achievement. Long before the term "multiculturalism" came into vogue,

the best of what is meant by it was thriving at Garfield. Those who never experienced Garfield can scarcely appreciate the extraordinary spirit of the place.

Barbara Heath Evans, class of '61

Garfield was really fun, and not at the expense of education. There was rarely a day that I didn't enjoy going to school. It was an easy place to be. There was a lot of academic competition, but that was fun too. Some of the teachers were inspirational. The music teacher had a marvelous voice. Mr Fitz, the history teacher, made it interesting. Garfield was such a balanced mixture, and it was unplanned. Differences were assumed. You accepted differences and went on. That's the only way to get it right. Now they're trying to reinvent the wheel. Sorry, you can't do that. You can't force people. All the talk about diversity is basically just conversation. They might

show a couple of videos, and then say, "Now, don't you all feel better?" My response is "No, you people just wasted my time." I grew up knowing about accepting differences, and we didn't have to talk about it, we just did it. The diversity talk isn't a bad thing, but it's not changing things the way people would like to think it is. I remember how good it was when we were at Garfield. It was carefree, violence-free, stimulating and fun.

George Griffin, class of '55

I'd gone to segregated schools in New Orleans. When we moved to Seattle, I went to Meany and Garfield. I remember sitting in class my first day at Meany and noticing there was a Chinese guy on my left and a White girl on my right. I looked around and there were kids of all backgrounds. I'd never been in an interracial classroom before. It wasn't long before I had friends who were Jewish, and Japanese, and of all

ROSEMARY WILLIAMSON

other ethnicities. But I'll never forget that first day at Meany. I was marveling at the mixture of people when the teacher started walking around the room at a fast clip and suddenly she said, "Up, up, the Red Coats are coming!" Everybody acted like it was perfectly normal. I remember thinking, "Where am I? Is this crazy?"

Rosemary Williamson Bushnell,
class of '62

Growing up in the projects was a good experience. We had a good clean life there—Saturday movies and church-related activities. At Yesler Terrace we didn't have as much open land as at Holly Park, but I remember a Japanese man who had a beautiful rose garden. All kinds of people lived there—Japanese, Chinese, White, Black, Filipino, and one Mexican family. There were alcoholics and non-alcoholics. The general idea was to get out of the projects, but it

wasn't a hopeless situation living there. It was a set-up that helped many people move on like my husband Ron who went on to Stanford and became a podiatrist. Two of his brothers became ministers.

My family has a connection to Jimmy through Pearl. My stepfather, Henry Brown, went to Spokane to start a barber shop. We were to move there, but he and mother drifted apart. He left my mother to marry Pearl Proctor Hendrix, Jimmy's aunt, after she had divorced Frank Hendrix. I admire Pearl; she is a very calm, accepting person. She was always a positive influence on my brother Gordon Brown. We call him Brownie. He and Henry Brown, Pearl's youngest son, are half brothers—they have the same father. Pearl is a good listener and a very caring person. I've always been impressed by her good-natured attitude.

I met my husband Ron Bushnell at church. Our lives still revolve around the church. We're Seventh-Day Adventist. We have a racially mixed family. I consider myself White, but racial classifications mean nothing to us. Our daughter married a Black man, a physician. Our son is married to a White woman. Garfield was very diverse. There was a camaraderie and a family-like feeling among the students. But I sensed some racism among the teachers at Garfield. One day a home economics teacher called me in and said, "I notice you're walking around with Ron, and he's a nice guy, but if you marry him your children will suffer." We've been married thirty-two years now. I know the teacher meant well, but it doesn't make sense to say children of mixed backgrounds will suffer. Ron has some European ancestry, and he didn't suffer because of it. One of my best friends is a Black woman I met in the projects who married a

30 YEAR REUNION CLASS OF 1961

White man. They're still married and they're grandparents. Our daughter Heather is a counselor at a community college, and she talks well with people of all backgrounds because she's been around all kinds of people—and because Ron and I have interacted with all kinds of people. When we moved to the San Joaquin Valley our kids sometimes said they couldn't believe people here were so culturally deprived. We had lived in the Bay Area for nine years, and it was a complete change. I am very happy being from a diverse family. I love it. It's more colorful. We're open-minded and interested in all cultures.

Betty Lamielle Freedman, class of '61

We were chugging along under the assumption that diversity was good. The Civil Rights movement came along after we graduated. People drew back into their own separate groups. Garfield was a unique place. It's much easier for a group of students to be cohesive than an entire country. It was a great time. We grew up in the era before drugs. We were more naive. I think it was different too because we were in an isolated corner in the North. We evaluated people based on each other's personalities.

Sandra Blanchat Duhon, class of '61

I am sure that just about everyone has used Garfield as an example of peace and harmony among all people. We really did have a unique situation within the walls of our school that I believe carried into our adult lives. It is a shame that the whole world could not have mirrored it.

Sally Grant Wilbon, class of '62

I played flute and saxophone in the Garfield band. I think Jimmy played percussion. There were very few girls in the band—maybe five or six. We had a lot of fun and everyone got along really well. Jimmy was very quiet, but he had a laugh that I'll never forget. It was contagious. Sometimes I'd forget whatever the comment was that made us laugh, and I'd laugh because of Jimmy's great laugh. It was the kind of laugh that reaches from the inside out. One time I nearly fell off my chair because of the way he was laughing.

The musical training we got in the band was rigid. The teacher was very inventive and creative in designing our half-time shows and performances. We looked at the diagrams of our moves on paper first, then we memorized them and practiced them outside in the open space, even in the rain. We were motivated and we worked hard. We earned the money to buy our uniforms. In fact, Garfield's band uniforms today are exactly the same style. So some of the traditions are being carried on. We did a lot of parades, all the games, and a number of concerts. The teacher was an approachable person, easy to talk to. I remember talking to him one time and he said, "You can do anything you put your mind to." I walked away thinking I could do anything by myself, and later I realized all the support we had there.

There was so much talent in that band. There were kids who were writing their own music. I remember how much fun we had riding on the buses together, going to games. We were a rainbow of people, and there were never any racial slurs. We had fun. We laughed and told knock-knock jokes. There was nothing said or done to hurt people's feelings. If somebody didn't catch on to something, we all pitched in to help. It's a shame the whole world isn't the way it was then at Garfield. Garfield is still a good school. In fact, I resent that the media only picks up on the little bad news there is. What

don't they print the good news? There's a lot of good at Garfield still.

I saw Jimmy in Los Angeles some years after our Garfield days. I was manning the phones for a Sickle Cell Anemia Telethon. I had my legs locked in a standing position, a bad habit I've had since I was a kid. Somebody came up behind me and slapped me on the legs. I turned around and it was Jimmy. He said, "Girl, didn't I tell you not to stand that way?" He was there to play for the event. That was the last time I saw him. I still can't believe he's gone. He had so much life, so much to give. He was a very giving, loving, helpful person.

Rosemary E. Sherwood Leiva,
class of '62

My years at Meany and Garfield were some of the most important and significant in my life. I learned valuable lessons in and outside of the classroom

GARFIELD STUDENTS

from excellent teachers and fellow classmates. We truly represented a microcosm of the world. We were a multicultural school long before the term was coined. I learned to value and appreciate our multicultural world first hand at a very early stage of life. In large measure I am who I am today because of having had the privilege of attending Garfield. Many considered us the underdog of our league, but this was to our advantage. This melded us into a unified student body, more so perhaps than any other school in the district. Prominent among the many memories

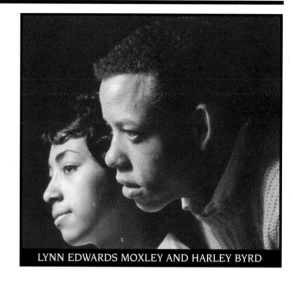

LYNN EDWARDS MOXLEY AND HARLEY BYRD

I treasure are: attending classes with classmates from many cultures and walks of life, the day Martin Luther King spoke to our student body my senior year, the many games I cheered at, the walks and marches we made calling for racial equality and tolerance, and campaigning for J.F.K.

Brigid Truman Stricks, class of '61

Maybe we all feel like outsiders to one degree or another during our school years; I know I did. Yet I look back at the time at Garfield High School in Seattle with surprisingly little pain—in fact, for a person who doesn't thrive in social, institutional settings, I feel a lot of warmth toward that diverse congregation of people in the late 50s and early 60s.

Kids came to Garfield from very rich neighborhoods, middle-class neighborhoods and ghetto neighborhoods; there were Asians, African

Americans and Caucasians. I was middle class and Caucasian, but habitually anti-social—an eccentric, artsy type struggling to appear intellectual. I know there were notable exceptions, but I think Garfield's uniquely varied composition embraced more of us odd-balls than all of the other high schools combined. And, we ranked first academically with the same ease that we enjoyed all that variety! When talking with old Garfieldites, you can notice the swelling of pride we feel about that period of our lives, as we watch diversity turn into a war around us today.

Lynn Edwards Moxley, class of '61

I've always felt that my years at Garfield High School were like a microcosm of the world we would too soon have to face. I'm being presumptuous by using the collective "we," but I know many of the fellow grads feel the same. Our experiences there helped

prepare us for the reality of the ethnically diverse and challenging adult world. We realized we weren't "selling out" by participating and being part of the Garfield experience. We were "buying in" to the possibilities of a better future—a future with hope.

Norman Winton, class of '61

Garfield was a special place during the late 50s to early 60s. It certainly had more influence on me than any other time of my life. I think I learned how to deal with people of all sorts of backgrounds and personalities, which has made career and personal goals much easier to achieve. It has also made dealing in international business a natural for me.

Mark Brenner, class of '61

I met Jimmy Hendrix at Meany. He was a very likable guy. Meany and Garfield were great places. The Central District was just one big, friendly community.

Everybody got along. There were no racial problems. There were a few hoodlums from outside places. We didn't have the problems the rest of the world had. We didn't understand the problems. My awakening came when I went down south to flight training in Pensacola, Florida. I got together with Hartsel Hilliard one evening in Atlanta, Georgia, and we went out with a bunch of guys—back in 1964. I think Hartsel was the first Black pilot with Eastern Airlines. That night in Atlanta we went into a number of different places, and they kept telling us to leave. I'd never seen that before. I was shocked. For me it was completely normal to be with people of different races. I realize now that in central Seattle we grew up in an ideal setting. I remember one time in Florida saying, "What is wrong here? Don't they know that people are all the same?" A guy jumped up and grabbed me by the neck. One fourth of July I went to the beach with a bunch of guys—an integrated

group—and some people got upset because they thought we were trying to integrate the beach. Those were moments of rude awakening.

Maaike Volkersz Del Villar, class of '62

My years at Montlake, Meany and Garfield were not easy, being the daughter of Dutch immigrants. I thought the feelings of not belonging were exclusive, only to me. At age twenty I moved to Mexico, having fallen in love with a Mexican student at the University of Washington who was working on his Master's degree. We have been married for twenty-nine years and have three grown children. After nearly three decades of living in Latin America—Brazil and Mexico—I now fully realize the importance my school years in central Seattle had on me.

Through life and living I've discovered my love for psychology and sociology. I understand how people of many cultures think, act, react and

interact—all of which has made me a much stronger person, raised my self-esteem, and made me unique. All of this, in retrospect, comes thanks to having lived in the international, intercultural, and interracial community at Garfield.

While attending the 25th reunion of my Garfield class, I realized that I really did have "roots" in Seattle, and that somehow I had left my mark with some of my colleagues. I also learned that those high school years were difficult for most everyone. Today I am proud that I am a graduate of the Garfield High School class of '62 because it was the molder of my destiny.

Bette Dennen Luke, class of '61

As a graduate of Meany Junior High School and the Garfield High School class of 1961, I most vividly recall the team spirit and the excitement of cheering the Bulldogs' basketball and football games. I have not been a great sports fan since those days, for sports now seem pale in comparison. My educational knowledge and social skills were enriched by the diverse racial and cultural mix of students. Without regard to race or class, I felt a connection based on different aspects of personality. I enjoyed a sense of humor, and was stimulated by an idea or felt good around someone with a positive outlook. I disliked someone who hurt people's feelings and caused embarrassment. There were certain people I liked to be around and others I avoided. These feelings crossed all color and class lines. Now when I hear people make stereotypical remarks, I challenge them—knowing these remarks are made because of lack of experience and education. I regret they were unable to benefit from experiences similar to mine. In 1968 I married a minority graduate of Lincoln High School and during the late 60s and early 70s I experienced first hand a wide range of both support and discrimination from family and strangers towards a Chinese male and a mixed-race couple. I have been very happily married for 26 years and my life has been greatly enriched by this multicultural relationship and our wide circle of family and friends. *Parker Cook, Garfield music teacher for nearly four decades,* (recipient of the 1964 *Seattle Chamber of Commerce Teacher of the Year Award.* (Interview, Seattle 1991)

Garfield was the best school in town to teach in. It was geographically ideal and had the best ethnic diversity. We had most of the Jewish population, nearly all of the Blacks in town, and many of the Asians. We had successful students from every group—wealthy, middle class, and poor. Garfield's Hall of Fame in music includes Quincy Jones, opera singer Irving Sternoff, Grammy-winning singer Ernestine Anderson, Alvin Alyne, and Jimmy Hendrix. I didn't know Jimmy, but I had Quincy in class. Quincy was writing his own arrangements in tenth grade. There wasn't much I could teach him about orchestration. He was so far beyond everyone else, I told him to ignore my assignments and do his own stuff. I said to him, "Why don't you and your band do the orchestration for the whole Funfest, and accompany the whole show." Quincy said, "Just give us the downbeat, Mr. Cook, and you can step out of the way." When Quincy became so successful, the Garfield auditorium was named the Quincy Jones Auditorium. Then they put up polychromatic busts of Quincy, Jimmy, and me.

The good times changed here after the Watts riots, when organized groups came in from out of Seattle to stir things up at Garfield. Everything changed. It became a bad situation, and almost

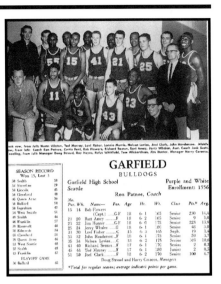

everybody left. The administration wanted to close the school. I decided to stick it out. Frank Fidler and I were the last to stay.

Bill Eisiminger, class of '61,

Student teacher at Garfield in 1965, under Parker Cook

We thought of ourselves as cosmopolitan at Garfield. We thought we could change the world. Music and dance were very important at Garfield. Dances were important to junior high and high school kids all over the city. There were all-city high school dances at the Rainier Field House. Garfield didn't have a good space for dances—with the gym on the second floor—so Garfield students went to dances at the Neighborhood House, Prospect Church, and other places where organizations like the CYO and the FYO (Filipino Youth Association) held dances. Our band, the Stags, played at dances every Friday and Saturday night—KOL and KJR sock hops, school and

CYO dances, and cotillions. I'd go to Birdland with Luther Rabb to pick up ideas from the Dave Lewis Combo. When we heard them play "Louie Louie," we started playing it. "Louie Louie" was new to the Seattle scene then, and everybody loved to dance to it. By 1959 we were playing it a lot. To get people dancing we used to do a dance exhibition to "Pony Time." I'd start by doing the Twist. Then Luther Rabb would do the Pony Walk. Then Terry Johnson would dance. Terry is a fantastic, fluid dancer, and he'd drive the girls crazy. Sometimes we'd get him to do the Watusi. At Garfield there was always music coming from the jukebox in the lunchroom— tunes like "Searchin'."

Gonna find her

I've been searchin'

I've been searchin' every which awaaay, yea yea

Just like a Northwest Mountie

If I have to swim a river

You know I will

And if I have to climb a mountain

You know I will

And if you're hiding up on a corner of Blueberry Hill

Am I gonna find you, child?

You know I will

We had a lot of fun. Garfield was well known for sports and academic achievements, and something else that doesn't get mentioned much—great half-time shows. The drum majors were amazing. Dave and Ron Holden, from the Holden family that's so well known for music, were both drum majors. They wore big tall hats, and did fast-paced, high-kicking, strutting steps. I think that kind of showmanship had a big impact on all of us.

Linda Emery*

BRUCE LEE'S WIFE

BRUCE LEE

Linda Emery Lee Cadwell, class of '63

I first saw my husband-to-be, Bruce Lee, in the hallway of Garfield. He had come to school to give a guest lecture on Chinese philosophy in Mr. Wilson's philosophy class. My Chinese girlfriend, Sue Ann Kay, told me he was her gung fu teacher, and it wasn't long before she took me to one of his classes in Chinatown. That is the kind of experience that could happen everyday at Garfield—exposure to the arts and philosophy of other cultures, firsthand.

The education I received at Garfield and Meany was not available in any book or private school classroom. Some of my best friends were Asian girls and guys. I knew their parents, brothers and sisters. I went to the Japanese Bon Odori festival, and wore a kimono in a dance number in the Funfest. It was as normal as going to Dick's Drive-In for a nineteen cent hamburger.

I doubt I ever would have married Bruce Lee if I hadn't been exposed to the values of different cultures at Garfield. When I met him I didn't think of him as strange or exotic. We went to samurai movies at the Kokusai, he taught me Cantonese words for gung fu moves, and I gained an appreciation for Chinese food. I had learned to look straight across at people, not down on them or up to them, just to accept them for their values and personality. Sometimes the last thing you'd notice about a person was what race he was.

The greatest value of an education is the lessons you take with you. My life's journey has taken many twists and turns, and I believe because of my exposure to the small "world" at Garfield, I have been able to fully appreciate the real thing where rich and poor, Black and White, honesty and guile must co-exist.

Coincidentally, the man I am happily married to today is a Garfield graduate- Bruce Cadwell, Class of '58.

PATRICK MCDONALD, SEATTLE JOURNALIST, AND JIMI

Mary McCarthy, author of nineteen books, and a recipient of the National Medal for Literature

In her biography *How I Grew*, Mary McCarthy tells about performing at Garfield in 1925. Ms. McCarthy moved to Seattle at age thirteen and attended Garfield for one year. She lived in the Leschi district.

"Once upon a time, then, I appeared on the stage at Garfield before a good-sized audience and scored a real success. It was an event designed to bring out the talents of the entering class—something like 'amateur night' in the movie theaters and vaudeville houses of those days, when volunteers mounted to the stage to do solo acts and were judged by the amount of applause they received. If I reconstruct it right, you could sing or yodel or tap-dance or play an instrument such as the banjo or you could recite, but it had to be something light—nothing on the order of 'Lord Ullen's Daughter.'

I had chosen a comic monologue by the Canadian humorist Stephen Leacock: 'I had a little dog and her name was Alice.' It was meant to be delivered in a doleful deadpan voice that would make the recitation all the more hilarious. Well, I brought the house down—a slightly untoward surprise (even though I had aspired to it), as I always thought of my muse as tragic. They clapped and cheered and stamped; if there was a prize, I won it." [pp.48-49]

Letealia Reid-Scott, class of '61

I remember Jimmy in the school halls. He was quiet, polite, smiling, and usually carrying a guitar.

Margaret Bovington Pulliam, class of '60

We were integrated before other peoples' prejudices influenced us. We picked for our close friends not those of our background, but those who shared our interests. We began to realize how fortunate we were

for those conditions when we were visited by Archie Moore. At a Garfield assembly, Archie Moore told us of his high school days under segregation, and said to us, "I wish I could have a garden with as many beautiful colors as I see in front of me." He told us that Garfield was famous throughout the nation for its integrated student body. When I left Garfield, I realized that the equality we experienced at Garfield was the exception, not the rule.

Gordon Shoji, class of '61

Like the majority of students at Garfield who experienced the rare mixture of race, religion, economics, attitude and acceptance, I thought that was the real world. I had the same rude awakening my Garfield friends had when hit with reality after high school. But, unlike most who used the memory of this happy time to cope and to raise the consciousness of those around them, I became disillusioned and bitter, and saw only hypocrisy. It took twenty years for my anger to dissipate, and another ten to redirect my life in spite of setbacks. Finally, at age 52, I have gone full circle. I am once again the happy nice kid I'd forgotten, the kid who was only interested in spreading positive energy, eager and excited to begin productive living.

John Boitano, Garfield teacher and football coach

We knew more about integration than people do today. And we had great guys playing ball, like Charlie Mitchell, who's president of Seattle Community College, and Tim Hansel. We only lost one ball game in four years. In my mind, Bob Gary is Mister Garfield. The only time I ever talked to Jimmy Hendrix was one day at a practice when I told him to take his banjo and leave the ball field. I didn't want him to distract my players.

Beverly Bushnell Johnson, class of '52

We were sheltered in Seattle. I didn't even know prejudice until I left Seattle. And Seattle has so much natural beauty. From the second story of our house on 34th street, up on the hill, we had a view of Lake Washington. The lake is so beautiful.

Vernon Otani, class of '61

At Garfield we had relationships with all ethnic groups. I still think about Garfield. Where I lived was integrated too—Italians on one side, Blacks on the other side, Japanese across the street, and a Jewish family on the corner. There were Blacks and Whites and Asians, just like at Garfield. The exposure to different cultures was part of our every-day lives. We all ran around together.

When I think of Jimmy Hendrix, the first thing I see are the halls at Garfield. We used to run the halls together. We played a lot. I tell people that no matter how famous someone is, there are always people from home who remember that person as a kid. I had a lot of fun with Hendrix at Garfield.

Richard Altaraz, class of '69

I was a student at Garfield in 1968 when Jimmy came to a pep assembly after a concert he gave in Seattle. Garfield made a less-than-successful attempt to honor Jimmy. Apparently he wanted to give a concert there, but the school board nixed the idea. I was on the stage crew, in charge of one of the auditorium doors. I saw a side door open, and Jimmy peeked in. There was a student at Garfield who looked like Jimmy, and at first I thought it was him. Then some girls screamed like groupies, and I knew it was Jimmy. Pat O'Day, a Seattle promoter, walked out and announced there would be no concert. Then Jimmy came out, acting very shy. He said he was real glad to be back, that it was really nice, but strange. He didn't seem to know what to say. He asked if there were any questions. Someone asked why he was wearing a hat. He laughed and said, "If I take off my hat, my head will fall off." Then he added, "It's been nice to be here," and he walked off the stage.

It's unclear why the administration declined to give Jimmy permission to give a concert. Traditionally at Garfield returning celebrities were given a warm welcome with speeches and standing ovations. They were a big deal. In Eye magazine, Michael Thomas ends his article about Jimmy's appearance at Garfield with this question: "Who needs a diploma from Garfield High School? Who needs the keys to Seattle?" To that I say: Who indeed? Jimmy Hendrix, the shy genius who is always referred to as a "high school dropout," and never got the recognition from his home town that he deserved. A solid anchor from home would have helped to counter the worshipful

PAT O'DAY, SEATTLE PROMOTER, AND HENDRIX

reverence for Jimi the Myth. But things had changed at Garfield. It didn't happen.

Recognition is being given now by the Seattle community—too late for Jimmy Hendrix to benefit from it in his lifetime, but in time for fans to realize that Hendrix's Seattle history is real. He didn't explode out of nowhere.

Robert Iverson, teacher, Garfield and West Seattle High Schools

When I tell my students at West Seattle High School what it was like at Garfield when Jimmy Hendrix was there, they don't believe me.

Meany Junior High Scrapbook

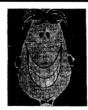

JIMMY HENDRIX: SIXTH ROW,
FOURTH STUDENT FROM THE LEFT

MARCH 28, 1958   NUMBER 3

Meany's Annual Talent Show Huge Success

by Nancy Nelson

This year's talent show was based on the theme "Around The World."

Miss Lickens has done another outstanding job in supervising the talent show.

The acts were based on the different countries of the world. The different countries were Canada, Russia, Holland, Switzerland, Scotland, England, Germany, Bagdad, Egypt, Japan, Hawaii, Mexico, Ireland, Paris, Alaska, and Brazil.

We all want to thank the art and music departments, the stage crew, and last but not least the performers and their sponsors for the time and effort put forth to help make the show the great success it was.

The acts were as follows:
Opening Number — "Around The World"
  French Canada — "Alouette" —bouncy lumberjacks
  Russia—folk dance solo
  Russia—spacemen
  Holland — "Tip-toe Through The Tulips"
  Switzerland—tap dance
  Switzerland—tumbling
  Scotland—sailor's hornpipe
  England—florescent clothing—ghostly effects
  Germany—German Band—hilarious faculty act
  Germany—ballet solo
  Bagdad—harem girls
  Egypt—dancing mummies
  Japan—wonderful costumes
  Hawaii—Hula
  Mexico—bullfight
  Ireland—Irish Washerwoman" —tap dance
  P.T.A.—phone call
  Paris—"Autumn Leaves" and Modern Dancing
  Alaska — penguins, snowmen, and Eskimos
  West — "Tumbleweeds" and square dance
  Combo—dancers
  Brazil—South American Dances
  Finale—"One World"

All in all the Talent Show this year was a great success. The acts were all great.

DECEMBER 19, 1957

T.V. POLL

By Norm Redding

During the month of December, the following TV programs were listed as favorites:
1. American Bandstand
2. The Real McCoys
3. Zorro
4. Cheyenne
5. Steve Allen
6. Maverick
7. Sugarfoot
8. Silent Service
9. Men of Annapolis
10. Wagon Train
11. Wyatt Earp
12. Ozzie and Harriet
13. Father Knows Best
14. Mickey Rooney
15. Lassie
16. Susie
17. Whirlybirds
18. Californians
19. Broken Arrow
20. Mickey Mouse

JUNE, 1958   PAGE TWO   MEANY NEWS & VIEWS

Meany News and Views

Editor .... Ruby Willis
Assistant Editor .... Alice Kihara
Copy Editor .... Arnold Bender
Assistant Copy Editor .... Brenda Hampton
Feature Editor .... Brigid Truman
Business Manager .... Carol Wold
Assistant Business Manager ...... Jim Fletcher
Boys' Sports Editor .... Henry Del Rosario
Girls' Sports Editor .... Gwenieth Downie
Feature Writers ... Stephen Weinstein, Toni Nelson, Midge Olswang, Wendy Soth, Janet Nosi
Reporters ..... Judy Warshal, Jean Nishio, Alice Crawford, Ann Miller, Arnold Bender, Vicki Honman, John Carithers, Bruce Culver, Charlotte Jacobson
Circulation Manager .... Lee Levy
Assistant Circulation Manager .... Barbara Ringold
Head Typist .... Nancy Nelson
Typists ... Judy Warshal, Nancy Simon, Carla Reiter, Annette LaLime

"THE BEATITUDES OF BUDDHA"

Blessed are they who know, and whose knowledge is free from delusion and superstition.

Blessed are they who speak what they know in a kindly, open and truthful manner.

Blessed are they whose conduct is peaceful, honest and pure.

Blessed are they who earn their livelihood in a way that brings no hurt or danger to no living thing.

Blessed are the tranquil, who cast out ill will, pride, selfrighteousness, and put in their place love, pity and sympathy.

Blessed are ye when ye direct your best efforts to self-training and self-control.

Blessed beyond measure, when ye are by this means unwrapped from the limitations of selfhood.

And blessed, finally, are they who find rapture in contemplating what is deeply and really true about this world and our life in it.

—The Reader's Digest, July, 1955

5 - 4 - 3 - 2 - 1
ZERO !

SOME DO !

CHOW
AND
BOP

GO TEAM !

YEARBOOK

EDITOR - Brigid Truman

PLANNING COMMITTEE - Alice Kihara, Ann Miller, Betty Ruth Brandt.

BANQUET

ARRANGEMENTS & DECORATIONS - Ric Wilson, Bill Stull, Roger Buss, Jerry Whalen.
SEATING & SERVING - Carla Ritter, Steve Wharshall, Ken Wheeler, Ann Stephens.
DISTRIBUTION - Judy Calvo, Barry Davidson.
PROGRAM & DANCE - Bonny Barret, John Dailey.
TICKETS & GIFTS - Ann Herm, John Nelson, Alma Massey, Richard Semon.
GYM DECORATIONS - Gary Robison, Nancy Himeho, Alice Hess, Jimmie James.
COURTESY - Steve Singer, Tia Niewenhius.

NO. 3 and NO. 4
TALK TO ME - LITTLE WILLIE
DREAM - EBERLY BROTHERS

NO. 5 and NO. 6
YOU MEAN EVERYTHING TO ME - SHADES
EVERY NIGHT - CHANTELS

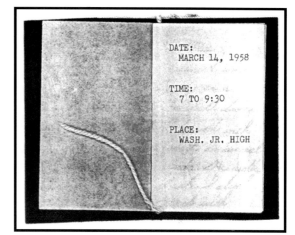

DATE:
MARCH 14, 1958

TIME:
7 TO 9:30

PLACE:
WASH. JR. HIGH

The Washington Surveyor

May, 1958   Washington Junior High School

Cape Washington

Around the World in 80 Minutes

VARIETY SHOW

Around the World in 80 Minutes is the theme of our Variety Show.

The idea is that two boys are taking a trip around the world. They stop in quite a few different places like France and Arabia. The background music is "Around the World".

The scenery is one big background of the world. When each country shows its act, it adds a little scenery to make it look more like the country the boys are visiting. The idea of the show is to show off the boys and girls talent. The boys and girls have to make their own costumes. More boys are participating in the show this year.

Some of the acts are:

From Jamaica, a calypso.
From Arabia, an Arabian scene and an Arabian dance.
From Japan, a Japanese umbrella dance.
From Italy, a barber will be singing while he's shaving the boys.
From America there is going to be rock'n roll singers, music, girl's trio, and a combo dance. All this is going to be done in a night club.
From Russia, a gypsy dance.
From Mexico, a dance "Tequilla"
From India, a ballerina and a sari.
From England, a trombone trio.
From France a night club dance.
(Con't next page)

AROUND THE WORLD IN 80 MINUTES

This year, as the title explains, the show is going to be about 80 minutes long. In this show, Augustine Stills and Nelson Leviar will open the show, and talk between the acts. During these 80 minutes, we will visit many places in the world. In Spain we will see a gypsy dance. In Africa we will witness an African dance with tom-toms in the background. In Germany there will be a German band, and with it there will be a unique act. Also, Leonard Smith, David Madayag, Terry Johnson, Barbara Heath Lynn Edwards and Pat Jackson, will sing a song in German. From the southern part of the United States there will be a gunny-sack dance, but don't think times are getting hard.

....Kenny Kudo
Josephine Parker

TAP DANCE - Barbara Hollingsworth
PETER GUNN - Connie Nakao, Margie Suko, & Nancy Yamada
VIENNESE & LATIN DANCE - Donna Eldefonso & Mike Eldefonso
CHARLIE BROWN - James Hendrix, Roosevelt Hubbard, Melvin Jackson,
       Preston Traxler, & Eddie Wells
DIXIELAND BAND - Fred Hirota, Donald Moore, Toshi Moriguchi, Irene Nagai, Stanley
       Neft, Rita Pulido, James Smith, Ted Tomita & Tommy Yook
CHARLESTON - Eunice Nakao, Linda Nitta, Beverly Obayashi, Judy Okada,
       Lillian Omori, Rita Pulido

DANCE PROGRAM

1. Do You Want to Dance? . . . . . . Bop
2. Talk to Me . . . . .Two Step
3. Falling Star . . . . .Two Step
4. High Blood Pressure . . . . . . .Bop
5. Dream . . . . .Chalypso
6. Been So Long . . . . .Two Step
7. For Your Love . . . . .Two Step
8. Don't You just Know it. . . . . .Bop
9. There Goes My Heart . . . . . . .Two Step
10. Claudette . . . . .Bop
11. Come To Me. . . . . .Two Step
12. Skinny Minnie . . . . .Bop
13. Twilight Time . . . . .Two Step
14. In the Still of the Nite. . . . .Two Step
15. Summertime. . . . . .Chalypso
16. You Send Me . . . . .Two Step
17. La De Da . . . . .Chalypso
18. All the Time. . . . . .Two Step

Selections by the Shalamars and the Boptones

Hirst, John-att. honor roll
Holmes, Charales-hall squad, at honor roll
Huguley, Joyce-Simplicity style show
Hunter, James-Roll Prexy, basketball, baseball,
    Lt. Patrols
Ingraham, William
Ishida, Mitzi-Citz and att. honor roll
Ishino, Kinuko-Citz. honor roll
Isomura, Rikio
Jackson, Asia
Jackson, Doris-Att. honor roll
Jackson, Pat-G.C. rep., Shalamars
James, Willie
Jinka, Joyce-Little "W", Sch. & Att honor roll
Johnson, Bobby-Lunchroom, B.C. rep
Johnson, Lula Mae
Johnson, Marvin-Track team
Johnson, Terry-Concert band, dance band, Boptones
Jones, Lorenzo-Lunchroom
Kano, Julie-Little "W", Glee Club, Sch & Att. honor
    roll, Hall squad
Kawaguchi, Sukiko-Little "W" Att. honor roll
Kimura, Ellen-9th grade class pres. hall squad,
    Little "W" pres. Att. honor roll
Kirksey, Vera-citz. honor roll
Kondo, Ray-B.C. rep., Citz and att. honor roll
Kunkel, Sheila-Citz. honor roll
LaBelle, Kenneth-Hall squad
Lake, Tyrone-Hall squad
Lamielle, Betty-Sch. & citz. honor roll, MC
    Style show
Levias, Nelson-roll pres. football, basketball,
    Concert band, Dance band, Track team,
    Baseball, M.C. Variety Show.
Lew, Quock Eng-Hall squad, Citz honor roll
Lewis, Mattie
Locke, Virjeanne-office, hall squad, Little "W",
    Att. honor roll
Lofton, Web
Lord, Roberta-Septet, Glee Club, Sch & and Citz
    honor roll

Stereo Follies of 1959

A C K N O W L E D G E M E N T S

DANCE BAND

Anthony Atherton
Jimmy Kamada
Terry Kato
Frank Kikuchi
Dick Meyers
Donald Moore
James Morris
Rose Nakagaki
Terry Nakano
Rita Pulido
John Shigaki
Gene Shimada
James Smith
Don Taniguchi
Arthur Taylor
Ted Tomita
Ken Yabusaki
Tommy Yook
Roger Young

PAGES & ASSISTANTS

Janice Israel
Janet Mizuki
Sharon Flores
Kristine Hamasaki
Pauline Yoshida

PUBLICITY

Erica Tatsumi
Linda Nitta
Dawn Watanabe
Owen Hirai
David Yoshino
David Shimono
Mike Tagawa
Mary Phillips
Lillian Omori
Martha Rice
Earl Freeman
Jacqueline Williams
Rodney Katayama
All Art classes

BOYS' GLEE CLUB:

Grant Allsion, Richard Blank, Ronald
Bushnell, Albert Cohen, Allan Cohen,
Fred Dangerfield, Gerald Deutsch,
Gaines Dodson, Jerry Fukuhara, Gilbert
Imori, Terry Johnson, Douglas Jue,
Ray Kondo, Reed Lockwood, Webb Lofton,
David Madayag, Barry Mar, Ronelle
McGraw, Edward Minato, Lloyd Mulkins,
Timothy Miyahara, Jimmy Nagai, Bryon
Nakagawa, James Ofrancia, Ronald
Patterson, Charles Richardson, Ronnie
Rideout, Donald Shimono, Ronald Shimono,
Gordon Shoji, Glenn Tamura, Joseph
Walls, George Williams, Norman Winton,
Mike Wong, Harold Young

Garfield High School Scrapbook

'LOADED' PRINCIPAL: Frank Hanawalt, left, principal of Garfield High School, was loaded down this morning with trophies won by Bulldog athletic teams this school year. Handing Hanawalt more trophies were Bob Gary, left, track coach; Jay Hurwitz, student-body president, and John Boitano, baseball coach. The huge bauble in Boitano's right hand was the All-Sports Trophy. Garfield earned 21 All-Sports points, most ever scored by a Seattle high school. In Boitano's left hand was the Ardis Hunter Memorial Trophy, presented to the school's top two-sport athlete, Girard Stone, not shown, won it this year, the first time it has been given.

ORCHESTRA NOTES

—Cut by Bettie Luke

Garfield Band Presents Half-time Entertainment

Garfield's band will present "Calypso Holiday" for half-time entertainment at the Garfield-Cleveland game tomorrow.

"The band takes the audience on an imaginary voyage to Calypsoland," explained Mr. Waldo King, director.

Formations will be a top hat and cane, a sombrero, two maracas, and both school letters. The songsters will also present a routine with real maracas.

"Different schools are designated as home, and the home team provides entertainment. Visiting teams provide the color guard," said Mr. King.

Friday, October 23, 1959

What Do You Think?

Have you come to the point where you think Garfield is lacking in many things? If you are at that point, then you've come to the right place. Here are a few items that Garfieldites would like to see in the classified section of the Messenger. (If there were one!)

Wanted: Life guard for fourth floor swimming pool. Must have first, second, third, fourth, fifth, and sixth periods free.
Wanted: Policeman to direct traffic outside of study hall. Must have accident insurance.
Wanted: Juke box in every room. Must be in good condition and be able to play without money
For sale: Bamboo cane in good condition. If interested, see R. Hayes.
Wanted: More food for fifth lunch.
Wanted: Beatnik painting for front hall.
Wanted: Red carpets on the stairways.
Wanted: Padded ,reclining seats in the auditorium.

Friday, November 4, 1960

Pre-game Practices Of Bulldog Players

by BOB FLOWERS

Steve Green: "I go to the Buddhist Temple and pray to Alla."
Norm Winton: "I wear the same pair of socks to every game and never wash them."
Hartsel Hilliard: "I go by O'Leary's before every game."
Jim Takeuchi: "I go to Temple De Hirsch before the game and pray."
Jack David: "I eat a furburger at about five o'clock."
Leroy Falles: "I wear the same purple and white jersey under my shoulder pads."
Gordon Shoji: "I clap my hands twice, turn around, stomp my foot, and bow to the east."
Leroy Hartwell: "I shine my shoes. If they are not shined things will not go right for the game."

REPLY TO BETSY

Dear Editor:

In the September 30 issue of the **Messenger,** we noticed the letter written by Betsy Crookes on how disturbing the juke box in the lunchroom is to some people. However, since the majority of other students find it more pleasant to eat in this kind of atmosphere, we think another place, other than the lunchroom should be found for those who dislike this music with their lunch. Although we do not agree with her point of view, we can sympathize with it, and think every effort should be made to find another eating place for those who enjoy quieter surroundings so that lunch can be made a pleasant and relaxing time for all.

Sincerely,
BIRGIT POVLSON and LINDA EMERY

Hey, Cats! Red Running Hood

By MARCIA LEVINSON

Hey, cats! This is a story of Little Red Running Hood (an innocent chick) and a big bad Beatnik. The scene opens as Little Red Running Hood is walking through the woods and is encountered by the Beatnik.

Beatnik: Like what scene are you digging, Chick?
Little Red Running Hood: I'm going to my grandmother's house.
Beatnik: Cool, man, like where's the old lady's pad?
Little Red Running Hood: Are you a Beatnik?
Beatnik: You're on my wave length, baby, now like tell me where your grandma lives.
Little Red Running Hood: But, why do you want to know where my grandmother lives, Mr. Beatnik?
Beatnik: Baby, don't make with the questions, like you're making me flip already. Man, this question bit is off my track, like it's from the other end of town—Squaresville.
Little Red Running Hood: Mr. Beatnik, you know perfectly well I won't tell you where my grandmother lives so why don't you leave me alone?
Beatnik: Baby, like you're bugging me. If you won't tell me about grandma, then come up to my pad and we'll listen to a little Modern Jazz Quartet.
Little Red Running Hood: Crazy, man, like that's what I was waitin for. Let's split this scene. Take me to Endsville.
Well, cats, this may not have ended exactly the way you maybe like had planned it to, but as we split the scene, Little Red Running Hood and the Beatnik are strolling hand in hand. Man, like this is getting too far out for me.

THE GARFIELD PEN

王顏菓

THE GARFIELD PEN: Published each semester by the students of Garfield High School. Distributed to activity card holders without charge; cash subscriptions 50 cents.

GARFIELD HIGH SCHOOL
SEATTLE, WASHINGTON

Jade Apple

My jade apple is my karma, or so it seems to me. I build my karma with each passing day; it is what I am each day — inconsistent.

The core of my apple was already formed when I awakened into this world. The core is my many past lives mentally placed together by me.

The fruit of my apple is the nun within me; the seeds of my apple the imperfections within me.

The skin of my apple is jade — my inheritance, an inheritance of wisdom and superstition.

My jade apple is my conscience — I may hold it or it may hold me.

JOYCE JINKA, Junior

The One I Love

The beating of my heart is like thunder when you're near.
I want to reach out and touch you, but I am petrified with fear;
Fear that you might shun me and pass me right on by.
So I stand off from the rest of them and only give a sigh.
But you pass them by and come to me, and you smile and take my hand,
And together we walk side by side through love's enchanted land.

LYNN EDWARDS, Junior

Desire

Write of the stars and
Of the moon, and you write of
Man's innermost dreams.

LYNN EDWARDS, Senior

Revelation

I go to the sea
as if pulled by the force of a magnet.
I stand in peaceful solitude on the towering cliff
overcome with emotions.
I meditate . . .
To be filled with the overwhelming sense
Of power, and greatness
of the vastness of the ocean beyond,
To sense my infinite smallness
as I gaze into the craggy depths below,
I know, as I look at the beyond,
the revelation I am perceiving
Is truly that I am one with the world.

MARY WILLIX, Junior

Man

I am man.
I am a creature created by God to glorify,
to tend His earth.
I am man.
Not a pleasant creature with which to dwell,
difficult to understand.
I am man.
Inconsistent in consistencies,
lying in my truths.
I am man.
A searching adult,
an inquisitive child.
I am man.
For what do I search?
Where shall I find it?

JEAN HARRIS, Junior

Car of the Week

Friday, November 4, 1960 — Page Seven

By MARK BRENNER

This week's featured car is a good looking, sleek, 1957, blue and white Pontiac belonging to Garfield senior Vernon Otani.

Vernon's car, believed by some to be one of the fastest cars at Garfield, features a 1957 Pontiac frill that was completely balanced with a C and T stroker balance kit. This means all parts of the engine are in complete balance with one another. The car also has a racer brown roller tappet cam.

The heads are ported, polished, and milled to .030. The ignition has Mallory dual points and a blue streak coil. The car's engine is 387 cu. in.

The car also has a B.N.M. beefed up Hydramatic transmission, and a positraction rear end. The gear ratio in the rear end is 4:30.

Vernon's future plans are to install custom upholstery, repaint the car, lower the front end two to three inches and lower the rear one to two inches. He also plans to completely customize the exterior.

During the year's time that Vernon has owned the car, he has entered five drag races at some of the local drag strips. Out of these five, he has won four trophies in the C/gas automatic transmission classification. Vernon is also an active member of the Deacons Car Club of Seattle.

Mature Girl, Boy Desire Fair Trial

One quality of a mature, well-adjusted person is his desire to seek the truth and to judge others fairly.

There are many occasions when people get together. Sometimes their conversation may focus on a certain individual (naturally, not present) and his faults or behavior.

This type of gossip has been referred to as "tearing him up". It is unfair and petty. The helpless subject is never present to defend himself, and has no chance to right any wrongs that may be said concerning him.

Constructive criticism, if presented in a tactful manner, will, in most cases, be helpful and well received. This differs from gossip because gossip has no constructive purpose and serves only as a small, petty, and unkind topic of conversation.

Persons with interesting things to talk about do not have time to indulge in gossip. These people are able to divert a group engaged in gossip to some other topic.

If you find yourself gossiping or being gossiped about, it is your duty to find out why, and to be grown-up enough to handle the situation in the way you know right.

Garfield Messenger

"A Paper with a Purpose"

Published every Friday in the school year, except on holidays, vacations or examination weeks, by the students of Garfield High School, 23rd Avenue and East Jefferson Street, Seattle 22, Washington. Printed by the Ballard News, 5410 Ballard Avenue, Seattle, Washington.

What A Life!

Garfield has celebrities too . . . **Mason Mitchell**, fearless football player, and Coach **John Boitano** appeared on television after the Sealth football game . . . **Judy Kind**, petite junior, is sitting on folded blankets in order to drive her huge Oldsmobile Dynamic "G-8" . . . **Bruce Culver** has a new addition to his car. A large white toy dog with a bee on its nose, sits proudly on the back window ledge . . . **Molly Haun** went to the car races and then visited Mt. Rainier last weekend . . . **Janice Johnson** celebrated her "Sweet Sixteen" birthday Oct. 16, and now she is anxiously waiting to get her license! . . . **Mike Stozhiese** sprained his ankle recently while doing flips on a trampoline . . . **Bill Stull** played at a dance and met a saxophone player who played in the Fats Domino band . . . **Richard (Sebo) Vaughn** was seen skin-diving at Vashon Island over the weekend . . . **Roger Vining** recently attended the car races over the weekend . . . **Rufus Whitfield** wants to go out for the football squad now that he has received "scholarship eligibility" . . . **Charles Tillman**, commenting on the touching-the-floor tests, replied, "If only my fingers were two inches longer!" . . . It looks as if **Jim Rose** is going to be a Spanish professor now that he has met three Spanish girls from Forest Ridge at a dance! . . . Congratulations to **Carolyn Daye** on being appointed to the Girls' Advisory Board . . . **Carol Doolittle** just got back from a three-week vacation in New York with her family . . . **Leon Bedford** won $175 in a baseball pool where he works (Jr. Boot Shop). He picked No. 12 and was lucky! . . . Are the girls taking over the boys' shirts again? . . . Two pals are seen wearing those dark green corduroy shirts with white blouses underneath . . . But the boys have their own fad now . . . **Tom Mathers** and **Donnie Howell** proudly wear their green sweat-shirts and tan levis . . . **Mary Willix** is helping to continue the Garfield tradition of "a party after every game", even though she didn't know she was having one! . . .

A Look at Yourself!

Page Two — Friday, October 14, 1960

Now that the gruelling ordeal of five-week tests is past, it is a good time for all students to take a good inward look at themselves, and decide just what their goals are for this and coming school years, and how they must set their standards to attain these goals.

Most students came back to school, after a fun-filled summer, determine to settle down and "crack the books" in order to make this year a successful one academically. As in the past, such ambitions have perhaps been dulled by the busy social and extracurricular programs which such student devotes so much of his high school time.

It is important, therefore, that every so often, each student re-evaluates his standards and revises them to fit his changing goals.

The goal of excellence in scholarship is the highest that can be attained by a high school pupil. To achieve this goal a student must set his standards high, and pursue them relentlessly. This "stick-to-it-ivity" is what makes the difference between a person who will meet such success and one who is defeated before he begins.

A thought to the future will prove that some of the foundations which are being molded in high school are based on unsound attitudes.

Take a good look at your standards.

Take a good look at your goals.

Are they leading to the best possible future?

What Boys Like In Girls

Friday, October 14, 1960 — Page Five

In a poll recently conducted among a number of Garfield students, the following answers were given to the question: **What do you not like about girls?"**

James Williams — "I don't like the big social type and I hate girls who smoke. Girls just shouldn't smoke. The aggressive girls bother me quite a lot too."

Bob Lattimar — "I don't like it when they start laughing, silly when they start chewing their gum like a horse I really back off. It's terrible!"

Sebo Vaughn — "I don't have anything bad to say. I like them any way they come."

Irv Pass — "I don't like conceited girls who think they are everything. Girls are always keeping boys guessing. This is okay though, because it gives us something to think about. Girls should smoke only occasionally, and girls should let the boys be the aggressive ones instead of trying to take away our part of the fun."

John Jacobs — "I don't like the door-huggers. When I go out on a date I want to have some fun. Of course, that's only when I've known the girl for a long time."

Weldon Lee — "I don't like girls who wear a lot of junk, who are gossipers, chew gum, and think they know everything. A girl should have a good sense of humor."

Bob Cozzetti — "If you are a football player, they just like you because they can go around and 'pose' in the halls. Another thing that I don't like about girls is long hair. If you ask me, they just hang around so that they can steal all of your money."

What Girls Dislike

Now the girls tell what they dislike about boys. Here are some opinions:

Marietta Van Eck — They just talk too much . . . about people they don't know . . . every place they go.

Mildred Suko — The way some of them gossip and spread false stories.

Saki Kawaguchi — I don't like some of their ungentlemanly manners!

Mae Carter — I dislike them when they're too immature to discuss problems without giggling and making absurd remarks.

Mary Willix — I don't like boys who tell the same joke more than twice.

Judy Nelson — I hate to be specific, but I don't like boys who aren't intelligent, cute, good dancers, and considerate.

Lynn Adams — I dislike boys who are conceited, loud-mouthed, and who are always trying to be the big wheel of everything.

Ann Miller — I dislike boys who are always telling everyone how great they are.

Wendy Soth — I dislike the big, conceited, " oh-boy-am-I-neat" type.

Jan Blanchet — I dislike their attitude towards themselves.

Ruth Fairclough — I dislike boys who are always talking about football.

Suzie Thieme — I dislike simple boys who think they are COOL!

Jennie Maxwell — The way their heads swell when you compliment them.

Mary Langdon — The way they "strut" down the halls.

Marjo Olswang — When they look at other girls (blonds especially).

Spring Comes to Garfield

Ah . . . . beautiful Spring has finally arrived at James A. Garfield.

The warm rays of the sun have begun to peek through the windows of classrooms, to awaken students from hibernation.

Boys and girls have begun to eat their lunch on the lawn, and some classes are conducted out doors.

Girls hang their flower weighted heads to one side, as they attempt to maneuver their full skirts through doorways and in between desks.

Boys seem to show an added interest in the girls who crowd among their thoughts of baseball, track, golf, fishing, and cars.

Studies, however, are beginning to pile up. Students sigh as they think of term papers and finals ahead.

Outdoor activities are reaching their height.

Parades of students can be seen walking home from school, while others shout greetings as they pass by in convertibles.

Friendship among everyone prevails in Spring. Problems of winter and its chilly mornings are over.

Spring is here! The season that is God's gift to youth.

The Garfield Messenger

Volume 39   GARFIELD HIGH SCHOOL, FRIDAY, APRIL 17, 1959   No. 2

ANNOUNCING THAT....

The Bellami Y-Teens are sponsoring a Japanese movie at the Seattle Buddhist Church, February 25. There will be English subtitles and the movie is to be in Technicolor.

* * *

Garfield Messenger

This is the finest "MESS" ever.

Vol. 42   GARFIELD HIGH SCHOOL, SEATTLE, WASHINGTON, FRIDAY, DECEMBER 9, 1960   No. 9

Boys' Club Chooses 'Santa's Stomp' As Dance Theme

"Santa's Stomp" has been chosen as the theme of the Boys' Club dance to be held at Temple De Hirsch on December 17, from 8:30 p.m. to 11:30 p.m., announced Denny Rosencrantz, dance chairman.

Tickets will go on sale next Monday at 50 cents per person. They will be sold all three lunches in the front hall.

Local Band Provides Music

Music will be provided by the Stags, a local band which includes two Garfield students, Bill Eisiminger and Terry Johnson.

Garfield Messenger

The finest "MESS" ever.

Vol. 42   GARFIELD HIGH SCHOOL, SEATTLE, WASHINGTON, FRIDAY, SEPTEMBER 30, 1960   Number 2

Mary Willix, Arrow Editor, And Staff Are Working Hard

Mary Willix, editor of this year's Arrow, says she is very pleased with her staff of 20, and is now acquainting them with their positions.

The artists, Eugene Graham, Missy Kaylor, and Brigid Truman, are now creating under the direction of Mr. Iverson, the adviser.

Virjeanne Locke, typist, will be typing copy as quickly as Joyce Kihara and Sue Umphrey write their stories. Robin Ackerley and Ann Herm will be compiling the sections of Productions and Organizations.

The layouts for the Sports Section will be prepared by Bart Amey, Bob Seaton, and Wendy Soth. Working as photographers on the staff this year are Charles Caplan, Jennie Maxwell, Ron Patterson, and John Shoemaker.

Personnel will be assembled by Doralee Schaefer and Marjie Suko. The final product will depend upon the skilled work of the layout technicians, Alan Hoshino and Dave Sandberg.

About the only thing that'll give you more for your money now than ten years ago is the penny

The Boys' Club color guard snaps to attention at each assembly. The new members are, from left to right: John Numoto, Jim Dowell, Lee Wyatt, Barry Mar, Steve Weinstein. — Photo by Charles Caplan.

Garfield Must Have Double Assemblies In Near Future

"Garfield serious assemblies will soon be scheduled as double assemblies because of our inadequate seating accommodations," announced Mr. Bruce Wilson, activity co-ordinator.

The change will be made in order to give every student equal opportunity to see assemblies. Majority of pep assemblies will be held before school.

"With these new adjustments we hope to vacate our balconies; then our speakers will all be heard," commented Mr. Wilson.

Previously Garfield was faced with similar problems but enrollment has increased, intensifying seating problems.

This year to relieve the seating problem a temporary arrangement was organized by Steve Singer, representative council president. He assigned four fewer seats to each roll than there are students. He also expressed the hope that four students in each roll would like to attend study period in room 208 during the assembly.

A.S.G. Announces New Roll Officers For This Semester

"New Roll officers for this semester were elected last week," announced Jay Hurwitz, A.S.G. President.

The duties of these newly elected representatives, as in the past years, will be to carry out school functions, take roll, and to increase the percentage of students that bank.

The new roll presidents are as follows:

103—Annie Watson; 104—Carla Reiter; 105—Irene Nagai; 106—Martin Oiye; 114—Ed Lowinger; 115—Sakiko Kawaguchi; 117—Isabelle Leaks; 201—Mason Mitchell; 202—Norm Winton; 203—Bonnie Yamamoto; 204—Richard Samon; 205—Doug Palmer.

206 — Helen Johnson; 208 — Cheryl Yusutaki; 209—Leigh Davidson; 210—Linda Burnett; 211—Renee Washington; 213—Patricia Jefferson; 214 — Eileen Nakatani; 215—Hartsel Hilliard; 216—Diane Okada; 219—Jacob Collins; 221—JoAnne Brokke; 223 — Sandra James; 225—Brian Storie.

226—Leroy Hartwell; 227—Jennie Maxwell; 228—David Walls; 229—Mary Rhodes; 230 — Leah Miyahara; 231a — Bill Nicholai; 231b—Carrie Hirano; 301 — Jim Hunter; 302—Jim Dowell; 304 — Robin Ackerley; 305—Mike Bell; 306—Jacquire Kay; 307 — Alice Byrd; 308—Eveyln Rubens; 309—Carolyn Daye; 310—Jean Nishio; 312—Cecilia Raine.

313—Mike Fuson; 314 — Julie Pauline; 315—Levi Fisher; 316—Charles Horn; 318—Margo Goslin;

Life at Garfield

Nobody could have dreamed up the Garfield Experience. Yet it happened almost as if it were destined. Let's imagine a master planner saying, "I want a racially and economically diverse community in a secluded and spectacular corner of America. I'll put them on the western shore of Lake Washington, west of the Cascade Range and north of Mt. Rainier, where Native Americans claim the Great Spirit lives. This community has open-minded, strong-willed pioneer types who love the land. Their children will receive a solid, multifaceted education. Their high school will bear the name Garfield. There, music and artistic expression will be an assumed part of their lives. The children will learn that the land is sacred and that what they have in common is more important than their differences. They will bond freely, and their understanding will spread like a ripple in a pond."

Central Seattle in the fifties and early sixties could be recorded as a community equal to the one in Toledo, Spain, during the time of Alfonso el Sabio, the Wise, when Arabs who practiced the Muslim religion, Catholics, and Jews all lived and worked peacefully together. In the Garfield district students were Catholic, Buddhist, Greek Orthodox, Protestant and Jewish. There were Protestants of all varieties. The Jews were Reform and Orthodox. Some were Southern European Sephardic Jews whose parents and grandparents spoke Ladino at home. There were students whose ancestry had biological ties to Europe, Africa, the Americas, and Asia. The Asian Americans were almost exclusively Japanese and Chinese, mostly second and third generation. Many of the African Americans had European or Native American ancestry, or a mixture of the two. The Pacific Islanders were mostly Filipinos. There were Scandinavians, Italians, Irish, English, French, German, Scottish, Dutch, and Eastern Europeans.

There were mixed heritages of all kinds. We all considered ourselves American.

There were probably some like me who thought their ancestry was something that it was not. My dad considered himself Scottish and Irish. "Willix," he said, "is a purely Scottish name." So I did Scottish and Irish dances all over town. But Willix, it turns out, is a made-up name—probably one of those Ellis Island deals. On top of that, Dad never knew his grandfather was French Canadian, not Scottish. When his grandfather died, his grandmother married a man named Willix who adopted her children and gave them his name.

Garfield was a visionary school and a place of celebration. Even during nationally tense times, we had exciting events to plan. As an integrated, neighborhood school that won top honors in all areas, Garfield back then embodied all that multicultural experts are trying to define, create, and make happen in the nineties. Call it cultural diversity, multiculturalism, pluralism, or whatever "ism" you prefer, at Garfield it happened. It was a state of being, and what we were doing was the result of an attitude. We walked the walk. We didn't even know how to talk the talk. When I met people from the all-White schools at city-wide events, they often asked, "Why doesn't Garfield let other schools win any games?" Since I have never understood competition, and never liked the "winners and losers" paradigm inherent in competitive sports, I was at a loss to answer that one. I've never subscribed to the "good guys vs. bad guys" duality either. I prefer "on the path vs. off the path," which offers a more relaxed possibility for those who are on track to reach out a helping hand to the ones who are derailed.

The next question they'd ask was usually, "Aren't you afraid going to Garfield?" My mind would search wildly to find a time when I felt threatened or scared. All I'd see was a sea of familiar faces and I'd hear laughter and music, and I'd be more at ease with the scene in my mind than with people whose questions reflected limited information and experience. Innocently I'd ask, "What would I be afraid of?" Eyes would roll. "Aren't there a lot of fights and thefts?" In my six years at Meany and Garfield I'd seen only two fights, and both lasted about four seconds. At Garfield I often left school after dark and rode the city buses with no fear. In those six years, the only theft I experienced was the loss of the pennies from some penny loafers I'd left in a gym locker. The truth was I felt completely safe at school and outside of school. I simply didn't know how to respond to the fear students from all-White areas had about life in

an integrated district. Negative stereotyping creates fear in those who are unwilling to accept individuals as individuals.

If you believe in stereotypes, and you visited Garfield on any given day in the late fifties, you could have found the kind of cultural assimilations that result from cultures in contact. You might have said, "Oh, man, this is all mixed up. These people are getting all blended up." We weren't worried about any loss of personal identity. We could blend, and in the blending individual uniqueness was not lost, it was enhanced. We learned we could play many roles and every time we tried on a new hat, we experienced how someone else felt. Each time we stood in someone else's shoes, new opportunities for growth opened up. Garfield at its best was a whole crew of nonconformists ignited for performance in the theater of life.

When I was seventeen, I left Seattle to attend Washington State University, in the southeastern corner of the state of Washington. I was in shock for weeks. Never in my life had I seen so many White people. It did not feel natural or normal. It certainly didn't feel like home. I felt as if I'd been dropped into a field of single-colored tulips after growing up in a colorful mountain meadow. I'd always breathe a sigh of relief when I'd run into Nelson Levias on campus, an African American from Garfield. I'd say to myself, "Thank you, God, for bringing Nelson into the tulips."

Garfield was rather like an Aleph—one of the points in space that contains all other spaces, according to Jorge Luis Borges, the Argentine writer. In his story titled "The Aleph" there is a tiny sphere, no more than one inch in diameter, on the back of the nineteenth step of the basement stairs in the home of a poet, which is an opening to the entire universe. But can anyone see it? "Truth," says the poet, "cannot penetrate a closed mind." For the Garfield student with an open mind, and I dare say that most of them were open-minded, a new part of the universe could be explored every day. Unlike the aleph in the poet's cellar, the Garfield kaleidoscope was real. I cannot imagine that anyone there was ever bored. We appreciated the myriad variety of people even more because we understood that what we had in common, what connected us, was more important than our differences.

No one I've talked to believes the stories about Jimmy being asked to leave Garfield. All versions of the story are contrary to the Garfield spirit. In the largest sense, the Garfield experience meant accepting each person as an individual, with all of his or her feelings and potential to become. We engaged in what I think of as the adolescent dance—letting down the guard, and putting it back up. Now it's down, now it's up. In and out of each other's spaces. When we listened to each other with appreciation and no judgment, when we allowed bonding to take place and trust to be the norm, genuine open communication took place. When I was willing to surrender to the moment, a kind of blending occurred in which racial, economic, and all other labels vanished, and a spiritual awakening took place. At those moments I understood the meaning of "I and my brother are one." There was no separation. Society tends to separate us from each other. At Garfield these lines of separation didn't matter when we were trusting and open. Being open to another person means giving something of yourself and taking in a little bit of that person. It doesn't mean losing your own true self, but it can create an identity crisis for the ego. And when ego gets in the way, magic ceases to happen.

191

My parents supported the Garfield experience—sometimes in unexpected ways. One Sunday afternoon I looked out our living room window and saw Eugene Graham, an African-American artist on our yearbook staff, out in the bushes with my dad. Eugene had a wooden statue in his hand. I had no idea they were acquainted. They were an unlikely pair—my dad, the wordsmith who had never tried the visual arts, and Eugene, the brilliant visual artist who did not find it easy to express himself with words. Dad had decided to bring art into our little yard, and he had commissioned Eugene to make several pieces. One piece sits in my living room, a treasured item. It not only reminds me of the relationship Dad struck up out of the blue with a Garfield artist, but brings back the day I walked out the back door and discovered Dad painting an enormous, brightly colored, abstract design on the side of the garage. His first attempt at art was truly outrageous—and undoubtedly inspired by Eugene.

Garfield was a place where even those of us who didn't belong to certain subsets still belonged to the whole. I was not a "sosh"—though many "soshes" liked me and accepted me. "Soshes" (from the word "social") could be White, Black or Asian; soshes went to the right parties, hung out with popular people, said the right things, and wore the right clothes. As a teenager I hated the economic disparities. We had classmates from some of the richest families in Seattle. I disliked feeling less valued because I lived in a very average house and wore month-end-clearance clothes. I was relieved on days when all of the girls at Garfield wore "middies"—even our rich classmates from Madison Park and Broadmoor. Sometimes I'd stand by the lagoon in the Arboretum and look at the back gate of Broadmoor, a wealthy gated neighborhood where many of my classmates lived, and feel baffled. Were they trying to keep people out, or keep people in? Why did they want to be separate? Yet, even economic separations disappeared with the realization that money did not equate with happiness. At Garfield we learned that rich kids and poor kids can share pain, joy, concerns, dreams, sadness and aspirations. We all have the same emotions. It has been said that when a person listens deeply to another person's pain, there is no room for hatred.

For the person who was aware, Garfield was a place where a transformation could take place. For me, Garfield meant not only an academic, cultural and social education—it was a spiritual experience. I believe Jimmy Hendrix possessed qualities that he inherited from Garfield—musical affinities, acceptance, sensitivity, multicultural influences in

music expression, optimism, and a desire to succeed.
Garfield history is a key to better understanding the
boy behind the myth. Jimmy Williams has said
that Jimmy Hendrix was the most compassionate
person he's ever known. Life is a process of gaining
levels of awareness. None of us can go beyond the
level of our own understanding. As we learn many
lessons from one another, there are times when we
don't understand, or don't feel understood. At those
moments, compassion is the best tool. It is one of
the highest forms of unconditional love. Jimmy
Hendrix understood it well.

GARFIELD HIGH SCHOOL

p.s.

In the months after finding you larger-than-life on Jason's wall, I was forced to face the grief I had felt about your death. Simply put, Jason had moved you into our house and I could no longer block out my feeling of loss. As I let the pain in, your friendship comforted me. I began to feel your spiritual presence pushing me along the path toward this project.

One afternoon about ten years ago, while walking through a shopping mall, I heard some Ray Charles music coming from a music store. Ray Charles' upbeat tunes instantly put me into an open-hearted, playful mood. So I said to myself, "Time out to play a game. Where would you like to go right now?" With no hesitation, my intuition found the closest bookstore. Once inside, it led me to David Henderson's 'Scuse Me While I Kiss the Sky. I chuckled. Apparently it was time to dig in.

My journey into the land of Hendrix history was underway. I read nearly everything that had been written about you. A lot had been said, but so much was missing. There were inaccuracies and misrepresentations. There was almost nothing of value about your years in Seattle.

I felt that you were nudging me to check on your dad and put a book together. Our "conversation" went something like this:

"Whoa. I'd be happy to check on your dad, Jimmy, but a book? You've got to be kidding?"

"No, I'm not."

"Why me?"

"Because you went to Garfield, and you're someone from that scene who cares more about me as a childhood friend than as a mythical rock star."

"True. And?"

"It would be a fresh angle. Not contaminated. You know what I'm saying?"

"Keep talking."

"It would be the Seattle story—the music scene back then, what Garfield meant, growing up in central Seattle—like a Hendrix-Seattle News report, like a spin-off from your dad's Seattle city news column."

"Oh, man. I can't write like my dad."

"Maybe you write better than you think you do."

"Maybe. But I've got these three part-time jobs, and the boys, and a husband. How could I do it?"

"Three part-time jobs doesn't sound good. Call my dad. Call a few Garfield people. This is important."

"Okay, I'll call your dad. But how do I find him?"

Intuition kicked in. I called my old friend Kathy Kanazawa Hutchings—though I didn't even know if she knew you. But she did. She said, "Why don't you

call Ellen? She lives right behind Jimmy's dad." I called Ellen and she looked out her window. "Mr. Hendrix is out mowing the lawn. I'll give him your number." Twenty-four hours later, your dad called me. The book idea was set in motion.

I remembered a dream I'd had about fifteen years earlier of walking out of the front door of Garfield High School and seeing a guitar player sitting on the roof. It was you. Maybe it meant something.

You and I had talked about life after death back in junior high school. We wondered if people in the spirit world know about what's going on down here. Are they connected to us? Like my Aunt Helen, who died after she got hit in the head with a basketball. When I first started shooting hoops, I told God I didn't want to be paralyzed with fear knowing how she had died.

In the fall of 1984 I started reminiscing about you the way I used to about Aunt Helen. Jason was about to undergo major surgery because his deformed chest wall had displaced his heart, and I needed reassurance. Jason and his doctor were confident, and yet I was still nervous. Jason's dad had no patience with my anxiety, so I turned it over to spirit. I talked to God. And because Jason felt connected to you through your music, I also found it easy to find support by remembering you.

I felt you reassuring me that everything was going to be okay. It was. Jason's five-hour surgery was enormously successful. It transformed his life. "Talking" to you during that traumatic time linked me back to my childhood, and deepened my connection to spirit, erasing the limitations of linear time. I always feel more whole when I'm suspended in the eternal moment.

A few years ago my boys and I went to church in your old neighborhood with Terry Johnson and his family. During the service, some children sang a song they had written called "God Has a Plan." I believe He does. But if we don't pay attention, we miss it. God had a plan for you. Not only that, he gave you a special talent to reach out to people to fulfill that plan. Back in the 1950s and early 1960s, some of us recognized your inner beauty, but none of us knew the depth of your creativity, your determination to succeed, and your initiative. Paramahansa Yogananda wrote a paragraph on the creative power of initiative that makes me think of you.

What is initiative? It is a creative faculty within you, a spark of the Infinite Creator. It may give you the power to create something no one else has ever created. It urges you to do things in new ways. The accomplishments of a person of initiative may appear as spectacular as a shooting star.

Apparently creating something from seemingly nothing, he demonstrates that the seemingly impossible may be possible by one's employment of the great inventive power of the Spirit.

In central Seattle we all grew up knowing that magic happens on stages. We had an unconscious awareness that when performers are genuine, and the audience is appreciative, an electric current beams out from the performers to the audience and circles back to the performers, connecting and transforming everyone who feels the surge of energy. Playing your guitar, you connected and transformed people with ease and flair. Millions of people appreciate your gift of music and poetry. It is my prayer that your legacy will be returned to your family while your dad is still alive.

As the years go by, my desire to reach out and thank you for many things keeps growing. I am thankful for your spiritual presence, your example of

warmth and acceptance, your ability to create bridges between people, to make them laugh, and help them grow. A passage from A Way of Being, by Carl Rogers, reminds me of your keen ability to listen and appreciate others.

"Some of my experiences in communicating with others have made me feel expanded, larger, enriched, and have accelerated my growth. Very often in these experiences I have felt that the other person has had similar reactions and that he too has been enriched, that his development and his functioning have moved forward. Then there have been other occasions in which the growth or development of each of us has been diminished or even reversed.

When I can really hear someone, it puts me in touch with him; it enriches my life. It is through hearing people that I have learned all I know about individuals, about personality, about interpersonal relationships. There is another particular satisfaction in really hearing someone: It is like listening to the

music of the spheres, because beyond the immediate message of the person, no matter what that might be, there is the universal.

When I am not prized and appreciated, I do not only feel very much diminished, but my behavior is actually affected by my feelings. When I am prized, I blossom and expand; I am an interesting individual. In a hostile or unappreciated group, I am just not much of anything."

Young people need to be heard and feel prized. We, the passing generation, need to give them the tools to overcome depression and other obstacles, to recover a sense of trust and purpose, and to move beyond all labels and ideas that inhibit them. Suicide is never a solution. Every person is an artist with free will and the ability to create beauty in their lives. We can choose, on an hourly basis, to align with the vital life force, and keep our inner banks filled with life-giving energy. Fate may give us our circumstances, but our attitude can set us free. It is said that healing must first take place in the mind of the healer. The healers of tomorrow may very well be those who are hurting today.

The seed for this project was pain, but a thread of healing weaves its way throughout. As I look at your circumstances and your pain, at the feelings I have about the exploitation and loss of a friend, and at the world that needs to be healed, I am inspired by our collective roots and what our community represented and achieved. Yours is a story of pain, tragedy, suffering, joy, creativity, playfulness, and bonding all mixed together. Out of this comes a wave of optimism. When the healing takes place, the good remains and the pain loses its power. My son Jason is grown, Jimmy, and a poster of you is now on my bedroom wall.

Quotes for Life

I had a visionary experience about healing. The message was that every cell in the body has a note, and each organ makes its own chord. When you become perfected in Spirit, and someone comes into your presence with an illness, you will be able to sense the dissonance that comes from a lack of harmony in the body, and you will know the correct note or chords to sing, play or sound to reconstruct damaged cells. Light and color are also part of the healing process. It said, "Listen to Jimi Hendrix and read the Book of Corinthians." Then I woke up. Soon after that I received as a gift "The Essential Jimi Hendrix," two albums in one packet. I read on the album cover that Jimi knew that music can be healing. He had been studying ancient music and believed that music—in its ancient form—could filter through the body like rays of light, and ultimately heal.

The vision I had completely changed me. I understand the power of sound in a new way.

SYLVIA ST. JAMES, singer, songwriter, artist, and coordinator for the Gospel Brunch at the Los Angeles House of Blues

---

Establishing a purpose for living is crucial to maintaining the will to live.

EDITH R. STAUFFER, PH.D, author of *Unconditional Love and Forgiveness*

It is necessary to be noble, and yet take humility as a basis. It is necessary to be exalted, and yet take modesty as a foundation.

LAO TZU, *Tao Te Ching*

You've no doubt heard, "And you shall know the truth and the truth shall make you free." The interesting thing about this statement is that it does not say the truth shall make you free. Knowing the truth makes you free.

REVEREND HARRY MORGAN MOSES, New Thought Center of Religious Science, San Diego, CA, and author of *It's So Easy When You Know How*

The love that brings peace goes beyond Webster's definition of love as "a feeling of warm personal attachment or deep affection." A feeling of love must be transformed into "actions of love" that begin with acts of kindness towards ourselves, and are balanced with unselfish actions of true concern for another's best interests.

CHRIS COTE, wife of Greenpeace cofounder Paul

Cote, and 1989/90 winner of the California Mother/ Daughter Pageant with her daughter Cheryl Bingham

Once upon a time, somewhere, anywhere in the world, there was a man (or a woman) sitting on a mountain top, quietly observing nature. He became so inspired by the movements of the world around him that he began to dance, imitating all the elements he could easily identify. He opened himself completely to the forces of nature. He became the forces: sky, earth, fire, water, trees, flowers, wind, cloud, birds, fishes and butterflies. His dance became ecstatic, completely transforming and transcendent. So happy with himself, he then poetically named each movement motif: Bubble of the Cosmos, Yin/Yang Harmonic Loop, White Cranes Flashing Wings, Cloud-Waving Hands, Golden Birds Balancing on One Leg, Embrace Tiger Return to Mountain.

He or she was the creator of the Tai Ji dance. His movement could have happened thousands of years ago or could have happened right now, somewhere, anywhere in the world. This person could be you. You are the potential Tai Ji creator. You are the dancer and the dance.

CHUNLIANG AL HUANG, President of the Living Tao Foundation, Tai Ji teacher, and author of many books, including *Embrace Tiger, Return to Mountain*, *Tao: The Watercourse Way* (with Alan Watts), *Quantum Soup*, and *Tai Ji*

Attitude is everything. It effects the way we talk, the way we walk, and the way we eat our toast.

MAURA WIEGAND, Host of Talk Show—*North County Live*, San Diego, CA, former mayor of Encinitas, CA, and author of *San Dieguito Heritage*

Four elements are needed to break up blockages and release the past: willingness, forgiveness, compassion and release.

Forgiveness is the willingness to give up blame, with the understanding that the only thing there ever is to blame is ignorance—someone not knowing, not understanding. Willingness should not be confused with willfulness. Willingness is being available, allowing, letting what is happening cosmically happen on a local level, where you are. So you're not going to make anything happen. Simply allow the presence of God to move through you. With the willingness to forgive, you move into compassion.

Compasssion is the highest form of love because it is the understanding of a lack of understanding. When you are forgiving, and when you give up blame, you come into the consciousness of understanding your own or someone else's lack of understanding. Release is the willingness to let go of limiting thoughts and old habit patterns.

REVEREND MICHAEL BECKWITH, Agape International Center of Truth, Santa Monica, California

---

Being an artist requires more enthusiasm than discipline. Enthusiasm is not an emotional state. It is a spiritual commitment, a loving surrender to the creative process, a loving recognition of all the creativity around us. Enthusiasm (from the Greek, "filled with God") is an ongoing energy supply tapped into the flow of life itself. Enthusiasm is grounded in play, not work. Far from being a brain-numbed soldier, our artist is actually our child within, our inner playmate. As with all playmates, it is joy not duty that makes for a lasting bond. . . .

JULIA CAMERON, *The Artist's Way, A Spiritual Pathway to Higher Creativity*

Mere technical knowledge of gung fu is not enough to make a man really its master; he ought to have delved deeply into the inner spirit of it. The spirit is grasped only when his mind is in complete harmony with the principle of life itself, that is when he attains a certain state in Taoism known as "no-mindedness." No-mindedness consists in preserving absolute fluidity of the mind by keeping it free from intellectual deliberations and effective disturbances of any kind at all.

BRUCE LEE, as quoted in *The Bruce Lee Story*, by Linda Emery Lee (Cadwell), Garfield class of '63

Visualizing is having a mental image that you consciously make happen. Visioning is becoming still and staying still long enough to capture the grand vision that God has in store for us. When you begin to capture that vision, ask yourself three questions: What must I let go of to be a large enough place for this vision to happen? What must I embrace for this vision to unfold? How does this vision serve my local, national, and global communities? Everything we do comes back to the two fundamental questions of life: Who am I, and what am I here for? The answers to these questions remind us of our greater identity—our essential being—which is unlimited, multidimensional, timeless, and unbound by circumstances or situations. Who am I? I am the radiant expression of the divine, God made manifest in form. What am I here for? To glow for God, to glorify the awesome scope of God, to radiate the magnificence of God at play with itself, dancing on the lightbeams of creation.

NIRVANA REGINALD MORGAN GAYLE, Modern-day Griot, Director of Education, Agape International Center of Truth, Santa Monica, Administrator for the Los Angeles County Department of Childrens' and Family Services, and author of *God Sings My Soul*

You must believe in the possibility of what you are praying for. Most persons become self-satisfied about what they have read of truth, without ever having experienced it. In India we do not seek spiritual guidance from someone just because he has a theological degree, nor do we seek out those who have studied the scriptures without experiencing their truths.

PARAMAHANSA YOGANANDA, founder of the Self-Realization Fellowship, author of *Man's Eternal Quest, The Autobiography of a Yogi*, and other books

"Movement is my medicine. Rhythm is our universal mother tongue. It's the language of the soul. But it's a forgotten language because we live mostly cut off from our source, the source of real personal power. We live in our heads. We live some idea of who we are. We think that all we are is our personality. But a body without a soul has no rhythm. A person without moves is a walking stiff."

"In my vision everyone is a dancer. Everybody has a shaman inside. Waiting for a wake-up call. Ready for dancing on the edge."

GABRIELLE ROTH, WITH JOHN LOUDON, *Maps to Ecstasy*

When you were born your ancestors gathered around you like good fairies for a princess. They gave you their hands, their eyes, their voices, their ears and their minds. But what is in your heart is up to you. You decide how you will use their gifts. With them, you could be a great scientist or a carpenter, a dancer or a teacher, a father or a mother. With those gifts, you can truly be anything.

TONI THOMAS, Editor, *Voices from Home*

MT. RAINIER, SEATTLE

Epilogue... Strange Beautiful

From a Journal.

"Soon enough," Jimi sings, "time will tell. About the surface of the wishing well . . . ." I drive my Jeep up the psychedelic rocks above Flaming Gorge, Utah. Park on a peak—edge of the world. His voice sails from the speakers, catches updrafts and tilts toward heaven with the eerie cry of a redtail hawk; black diamond sparkles on ravenwings. Visions of Jimi in my head: hunched over the notebook, writing those words as the dark jet carries him over the black sea, to England, to his fate. What will become of him? Will anyone hear his music? Everyone around him is asleep, and he sighs, and he writes: "Loneliness is such a drag." Can you see his eyes as they close? Dream on, Jimi. Dream on.

I drive down into Flaming Gorge still listening. Fossils all around me in the brightly hued cliffs, and Jimi's music now a fossil itself. All of Jimi's heart and terror and rage and hope burned through his guitar, and the feedback doubled back and took him away. Jimi's gone on the wings of a dragonfly. Other substances have seeped into his songs now. All our myths and legends and prejudice and need, and they have filled the spaces between the notes and hardened there and turned the music into a gem. These facets reflect ourselves to ourselves. "Third Stone from the Sun" still trying to show me the world where I move so blindly: Jimi's soaring, melting, burning, storming guitar is the exact portrait of this landscape: black spaceship clouds crawl on lightning legs across screaming stone.

I had a dream: a small store around the corner. In a glass cabinet, three small flames bright on small white stones. "These," the owner said, "are the last flames left from Monterey. He burned his guitar at Monterey." I bought one flame, carried it out in a jade box. . . . Somewhere in the desert I put the flame to my tongue, lay back and waited. He came to me. Walking through the stars. *The story of life*, he said, *is quicker than the wink of an eye. It wasn't long ago*, he said. *But it seems like years ago since I felt the warm hello of the sun.* And he sang, I *feel the ocean swaying me . . . . Washing away all my pains. See where I used to be wounded— Remember the scar? Now you can't see a thing. And I don't feel no pain.*

I awake to a morning—golden rose. Wherever I go, I know he's gone there too. In midnight terror, his fear has been there too. His loneliness, laughter, dreamtime, and sorrow. He's far before me, walking too. Jesus, he told me, *went all across the desert, and in the middle, he found a rose.*

I throw a rock full of fossils in the back of the Jeep. The map is wet: *still raining . . . still dreaming.* How can you love a soul through a few electric notes?

I drive down the crimson gorge. *Dear Jimi,* I think, *the wind really does cry* Mary.

LUIS ALBERTO URREA, winner of the 1994 Western States Book Award for *The Fever of Being.* His other works include *Across the Wire, In Search of Snow,* and *Dalton's Luck,* and numerous magazine and newspaper articles.

Lyrical Excerpts

"Little Wing"

Well, she's walking through the clouds,

With a circus mind that's running wild.

Butterflies and Zebras,

And Moonbeams and fairy tales.

That's all she ever thinks about.

Riding with the wind.

"Are You Experienced?"

If you can just get your mind together

Then come across to me

We'll hold hands and then we'll watch the sunrise

From the bottom of the sea

"Angel"

Angel came down from heaven yesterday

She stayed with me just long enough to rescue me

And she told me a story yesterday

About the sweet love between the moon and the deep blue sea

And then she spread her wings high over me

She said she's gonna come back tomorrow.

Sure enough this woman came home to me

Silver wings silhouetted against a child's sunrise

And my angel, she said unto me

Today is the day for you to rise

Take my hand

You're gonna be my man

You're gonna rise

And then she took me high over yonder, Lord

Fly on my sweet angel

Forever I will be by your side.

"May This Be Love"

Waterfall, nothing can harm me at all

My worries seem so very small

With my waterfall

I can see my rainbow calling me

Through the misty breeze of my waterfall

Some people say daydreaming's for the lazy-minded fool

With nothing else to do

So let them laugh, laugh at me

Just as long as I have you to see me through

I have nothing to lose.

"Bold As Love"

Blue are the life giving waters taken for granted, they quietly understand.

"Power to Love"

With the power of soul anything's possible.

"Message of Love"

I said find yourself first

And then your talent,

Work hard in your mind for it to come alive,

. . . in the eyes of God we're all children to him.

"Up from the Skies"

If my daddy could see me now.

"Spanish Castle Magic"

We mustn't be late for the show,

Neptune champion games to an aqua world
so very dear,

"Right this way," smiles a mermaid, I can hear
Atlantis is full of cheer.

"Moon, turn the Tides . . . Gently, Gently Away"

Your people I do not understand.

"Third Stone From the Sun"

But it's all in your mind

Don't think your time

On bad things

"One Rainy Wish"

It's only a dream, but I'd love to tell somebody
about this dream

The sky was filled with a thousand stars

While the sun kissed the mountains blue

And eleven moons played across the rainbows
above me and you

Gold and rose, the color of the velvet walls that
surround us.

"Night Bird Flyin'"

Please take me through your dreams,

Inside your world I want to be.

Until tomorrow no tears will be shed

Hold on till the sun gets out of bed.

Photography Credits

p.v Ron Raffaelli, courtesy of Michael Ochs Archives; pp.vi-vii Mary Willix Collection, Robin Landholm, Terry Johnson Collection, Hendrix: Dave Sygall; p.ix Ira Spring; p.x upper left: Ulvis Alberts, bottom left: Peter Riches, right: Joseph Sia; p.2 Peter Riches; p.3 Ryan Farmer; p.4 Chris Whitney; p.5 Hendrix: Jill Gibson, birds: Chris Whitney; p.6 Maura Wiegand; p.9 Robin Landholm; pp.10-11 Terry Johnson Collection; p.12 Ken Matesich; p.13 Bette Luke; pp.14-15 Marsha Burns; pp.16-17 Terry Johnson Collection, band photo: Garfield Arrow; pp.18,19 and 23 Marsha Burns; p.25 Terry: Ken Matesich; Florence: Mary Willix; p. 26 Marsha Burns; p.27 Ken Matesich; p.28 Mary Willix; p.29 Mary Willix Collection; p.31 Garfield Arrow; p.33 Jill Gibson; p.35 Mary Willix Collection; p.37 Ken Matesich; p.39 Marsha Burns; p.41 Mary Willix Collection; p.43 Dave Sygall; pp.44-45 George Griffin Collection, Barney Hilliard Collection; p.47 Mary Willix; p.48 Peter Riches; p.49 Dave Sygall; p.50 Mary Willix; ppp.53-54 Peter Riches; p.55 Marsha Burns; p.57 Dave Sygall; pp. 58, 59, 61, 62, 63 and 64 Marsha Burns, p.65 Meany Junior High School Year Book; p.67 Luther Rabb Collection; p.68 Bill Eisiminger Collection; p.70 Luther Rabb

Collection; p.72 Mary Willix, Lester Exkano Collection; p.73 Marsha Burns; p.74 Mary Willix Collection; p.75 Ken Matesich; p.76 Eugene Tagawa Collection; p.78 Al Hendrix Collection; p.81 Marsha Burns; pp.82-83 Mary Willix Collection; p.84 Ken Matesich; pp.85-86 Mary Willix Collection; pp. 88-89 Marsha Burns; p.90 Garfield Arrow; p.92 Al Hendrix Collection; p.93 Ken Matesich; p.95 Garfield Arrow; p.96 Bill Eisiminger Collection; p.98 Don Williams Collection; p.100 Garfield Arrow; p.102 Dave Sygall; p.103 Manual Stanton Collection; p.104 On Site Photo Graphics; p.105 Band: Garfield Arrow, Hendrix: Peter Riches; p.106 Peter Riches; p.107 Hendrix: Peter Riches, bands: Al Hendrix Collection; p.108 Pearl Hendrix Brown Collection; pp.109-110 Al Hendrix Collection; pp.111-112 Pearl Hendrix Brown Collection; p.113 Marsha Burns; p.114 Mary Willix; p.115 Ken Matesich; p.116 Marsha Burns; p.117 Al Hendrix Collection; p.118 Peter Riches; pp.119-122 Pearl Hendrix Brown Collection; p.122 house: Ken Matesich; p.123 Pearl Hendrix Brown Collection; pp.124-126 Diane & Ed Colley Collection; p.127 Peter Riches; p.128 Mary Willix; p.129 Ken Matesich; p.130 Ulvis Alberts; p.132 Peter Riches; p.133 Mary Willix;

p.135 Al Hendrix Collection; p.136 Peter Riches; p.137 Ken Matesich; p.139 Seattle-King County News Bureau; pp.140-141 and143-144 Peter Riches; p.145 Mary Willix; p.146 Maura Wiegand; p.147 Dave Sygall; p.148-151 Marsha Burns; pp.152-153 Betty Wallace Collection, photo of Betty: Mary Willix; p.154 Marsha Burns p.155 Garfield Arrow; p157 Garfield Arrow; p.159 Alan Corral, Mike Tagawa Collection; p.160-161 Washington Junior High Year Book; p.162 Ulvis Alberts; p.165 Ira Spring; p.166 Gordon Shoji Collection and Garfield Arrow; p.168 Mary Willix; p.170 Rosemary Leiva Collection and Garfield Arrow; p.171 On Site Photo Graphics; pp.172-174, Joseph Marshall, courtesy of Ralph Hayes; p.176 Fred and Eli Stahlhut Collection; p.177 Linda Emery Lee Caldwell Collection; p.178 and 181 Peter Riches; Scrapbook collections (182-188): Jay Hurwitz, Lynn Edwards Moxley, Carla Reiter Greenwald; Nancy Yamada Jang; p.189 Mary Willix Collection; p.193 Joseph Marshall, courtesy of Ralph Hayes; p.195 Marsha Burns; p.197 David Muench, Tony Stone Images; pp.198-199, 201 Mary Willix; p.202 Seattle-King County News Bureau; p.203 Mary Willix; p.207 Maura Wiegand; p.208 Art Wolfe, Tony Stone Images,

Mountain Top Home

Jimmy wanted a place called home. He wanted it to be on a mountain. When you grow up around mountains, you dream about living in the mountains. Jimmy not only wanted to live in the mountains, he wanted to live on top of the mountain—so he could be closer to the sky, closer to the maker, and closer to the sphere that surrounded the maker. He also wanted a family. Sometimes he'd say he wanted seven kids. Love and family were very important to Jimmy.

JOEY DAVIS SUTHERN, ex rock promoter and friend

Love always

Jimmy Hendrix

Creative Forces Publishing, P.O. Box 22536, San Diego, CA 92192-2536. 619-457-7875